CLASSICAL LANDSCAPE
WITH FIGURES

Osbert Lancaster's Other Works

Pocket Cartoons

CLASSICAL LANDSCAPE WITH FIGURES

BY

OSBERT LANCASTER

Illustrated by the Author

LONDON

JOHN MURRAY, ALBEMARLE STREET, W1

To
PRU

First published 1947
Fourth impression 1962
Reprinted with an addition to Introduction 1975

© Addition to Introduction, Osbert Lancaster, 1975

Printed in Great Britain by
REDWOOD BURN LIMITED
Trowbridge & Esher
Cased 0 7195 0789 8
Paperback 0 7195 3234 5

CONTENTS

ILLUSTRATIONS

ACKNOWLEDGEMENTS

My thanks are due to my friend George Seferis, from the French edition of whose poems the lines printed on page 125 are quoted; to Professor Hon. Steven Runciman, to whose article on S. Luke the Stiriot published in Athens I am indebted for much of the information embodied in Chapter VI; to Professor Xingopoulos of the University of Salonika, in whose informative company I visited the principal Byzantine monuments in that city; to Major Ogilvie-Grant, without whose fluent knowledge of modern Greek the conversation, so vividly recorded on page 124, could never have taken place; and finally to T.E. Sir Reginald and Lady Leeper, on whose indulged staff and in whose delightful company I enjoyed my first acquaintance with the Greek landscape. Extracts from the chapter 'Athens' are reproduced by kind permission of the Editor of the *Architectural Review*, and certain drawings in the same chapter by kind permission of the Editor of the *Cornhill Magazine*.

INTRODUCTION

FEW branches of literature have been so diligently cultivated in the last few years as that dealing with foreign countries and, as intense activity invariably results in change of form, the old-fashioned travel book has become a thing of the past. Gone are those fat green volumes with wide margins, thinly spaced type and, by way of frontispiece, a sepia photograph, slightly out of focus, of the authoress on her favourite mule contemplating through bewildered pince-nez the ruins of Baalbek. The Wanderers and the Ramblers with their Watman sketching-pads and HB pencils and limited but genuine culture have been replaced by the socially conscious reporter and the witty introvert. This being the case, it is only honest to point out by way of warning to the resolutely contemporary that, lacking both the self-confidence and keen social conscience necessary for inclusion in the latter school, I approximate spiritually more to the mule-riding female water-colourist, and that the present work is likely to be considered closer in feeling to *Little walks in leafy Umbria* (now unfortunately out of print) than to *Storm in the Caucasus* or *Wings over Olympus*. Having issued this warning I can freely point out that my aim has been slightly different from those of any of the above and considerably more old-fashioned. This is not a ramble, nor a travel book, nor yet a guide, but a *description* in the eighteenth-century meaning of the term.

It may well be pointed out that the need for an informative work of this kind dealing with Greece has long since been satisfied and that the author's energies would have been better employed in describing the Gran Chaco or even the lesser explored regions of West Kensington. But such an objection, I submit, is not so easily sustained as might be imagined for, owing to the unique position that Greece occupies in world-history, speciali-zation has from the first been encouraged at the expense of the general view. As a result, in modern times, anyhow since the days of the ever-admirable Colonel Leake, the literary travellers who pass across the Greek landscape tend to divide themselves into tight little groups of varying size closely following certain well-defined routes. Looming large in the foreground is a long subfusc procession of sixth-form masters and dons (the figure of the great Mahaffey leading the adolescent Oscar by the hand well to the fore) gripping tight their Pausanias and resolutely turning their backs on any-thing post-dating the battle of Chaeronea. Beyond are to be observed a few angry and aggressive little figures, quarrelling violently among them-selves and on the worst possible terms with the classical party down below, following the dynamic form of Robert Byron bearing a banner with a strange device on which is inscribed the single word 'Byzantium'. More recently a new contingent has arrived, easily to be distinguished from the others by the erratic and seemingly purposeless nature of their course and by the fact that they are entirely unencumbered by guide-books or intellectual impedimenta of any sort ; these display no interest in either the landscape or the ruins and close observation will show that their dartings back and forth are occasioned by the necessity under which they labour of having to put in long-distance calls to Fleet Street or New York at regular intervals.

The object of the present work, therefore, is to provide some general account of the present appearance and condition of Greece that may perhaps prove of use to that small minority who are likely in future to receive the necessary passports, visas, priorities, travel-permits and foreign exchange enabling them to leave these shores, to awaken a not-too-painful nostalgia in those who have visited the country in the past, and to provide some slight entertainment and instruction to the vast majority who lack the memories of the latter and entertain no hopes of immediate inclusion in the narrow ranks of the former. (Needless to say, this avowed intention, like so many purposes boldly proclaimed on title-pages, was, of course, only formulated when the book was nearing completion and will be taken by the wise as being in the nature of the official declaration at the customs which leaves a quantity of less disinterested and more personal motives tucked away undeclared at the bottom of the suitcase.) Having made this avowal, however, it would be both rash and improper not at once to qualify it.

The landscape which I have attempted to unroll in the following pages, though entirely Greek, is by no means the whole of Greece. Lacking the creative imagination of certain writers that enables them vividly to describe scenes and monuments which they have only beheld with the eye of faith, I have been forced to confine myself to things seen. Thus, whatever completeness was intended, the result is at once observed to be marred by a number of large blanks, many occurring in irritatingly important parts of the canvas, and not even the dim lines of a preliminary sketch are visible in the places which should properly be occupied by Macedonia, Thrace, most of Thessaly, the Cyclades and the south-western corner of the Peloponnese. Less important but still sufficiently annoying in a landscape that is avowedly topographical, are further sections which should by rights be richly detailed but which have in fact been lightly indicated in an unavoidably impressionist technique. To these faults of omission must be added others that arise from undue emphasis : the lighting will be found to be sadly uneven in its distribution, frequently illuminating the architecture with a distracting brilliance while leaving the flora and fauna in almost impenetrable gloom and imparting a chiaroscuro from which the Byzantine cupola emerges more frequently than the classical colonnade.

These grave inadequacies I readily acknowledge and regret, but to a further criticism which may well be levelled I have a reply. It may be contended that in a work intended to give a picture of the Greek scene as it presents itself to-day so obvious a preoccupation with the past is entirely misplaced ; or conversely, that in a landscape which at the present time can only be regarded as historic such contemporary elements as intrude are as uncalled for and as irritating as the little boy in the cloth cap who invariably slips into the foreground of what would otherwise have been an exquisite camera study of the ruins of Sunium or the bay of Salamis. But the present and the past are always and everywhere inseparable ; scratch is a position from which one can never start, and history a meaningless fantasy if not interpreted in the light of present-day experience. In Greece, where a more determined effort to disregard it has been made than almost anywhere else on earth, this truth is more than usually inescapable. Here, where it is still too often assumed that nothing of importance ever happened between the death of Alexander and the arrival of Byron and that, as a result of this long interregnum, all threads connecting antiquity with the present day had long since perished or been broken, every other mile affords vivid demonstration of an intimate inter-penetration of epochs. The pillars of the Ionic temple are found built into the fabric of the Byzantine monastery, the Cyclopean masonry of the Mycenean strong point has been re-erected to protect an Axis gun-site and the mortar batteries of ELAS have left scars on the Acropolis that are already indistinguishable from those caused by Turkish gunners. In the realm of ideas this persistence of the past is no less real, though perhaps less immediately apparent ; disquieting memories of the wide empire of Justinian are said occasionally to have troubled the realistic mind of Venizelos and remain uncomfortably but excitingly vivid for many of his compatriots to this day ; Papandreou denounces Marshal Tito with the same lack of restraint and much of the eloquence of Demosthenes anathematizing Philip of Macedon ; and the Centaurs still haunt the imagination and frighten the children of the peasants of Pelion.

But by what right, it may be argued, does a landscapist concern himself with humanity at all ? The presence of a picturesque peasant tastefully disposed on a broken column in the middle distance is perhaps allowable, but why is the whole foreground cluttered up with a heterogeneous collection of human oddities whose generally unromantic aspect fits them only for appearance in a news-reel ? The answer is that in Greece the inhabitants are part of the landscape and that were they omitted the picture would take on an unreal lunar bareness carrying no conviction to those acquainted with the reality. For as the physical features of a country everywhere condition the character and development of the inhabitants, so in Greece the latter react in some mysterious and not easily definable way upon their surroundings, and although one may remain at a loss for a reasonable explanation one knows quite certainly that without their presence these coasts and mountains would remain as boring and as unsustaining as the Riviera or the Bernese Oberland. It is largely, of course, a matter of scale ; in the high Alps or on the vast plains of eastern Europe man is reduced to complete unimportance and neither his presence nor his absence can possibly affect in the smallest degree the scene's significance, but here all the natural features seem to have been deliberately conceived in relation to our human stature. Unpeopled, these plains and valleys, headlands and coves would be as incomplete and purposeless as brilliantly illuminated settings on an empty stage. That the earliest religion of the people of this countryside should have been anthropomorphic was as inevitable as that the Egyptians should have bowed down to vultures and jackals, and the birth of humanism could only have occurred in a setting where man's proportion was so exquisitely adjusted to his environment. In the north his vision was clouded by mists and twilight and oppressed by the immensity of ocean and mountain, while in the south the featureless desert and tractable Nile exaggerated his stature and induced profitless illusions of megalomaniac grandeur.

Having thus justified my inclusion of the human element, I must straightway reveal the limited nature of my qualifications as a figure-painter. The total period of my residence in the country did not exceed eighteen months ; I never succeeded in acquiring a knowledge of the language that enabled me to do more than reveal, in exceptionally favourable circumstances, the simplest of human needs ; and my contacts were almost entirely confined to Athenian politicians and officials. Moreover, I am constantly humiliated by the painfully acquired knowledge that I am singularly lacking in that gift, which, to judge from their writings, is widely distributed among my contemporaries, of straightway establishing the most intimate and cordial relations with the common man of every nationality. Fortunately in Greece, where a proper degree of social consciousness remains to be enforced, this disgraceful failing is of less importance than elsewhere, for it is the common man who here at once takes the initiative and whose exquisite courtesy and insatiable curiosity easily enable him to surmount all barriers of race and language save that which, in certain rare cases, has been erected by an orthodox Marxian training.

Not only am I thus palpably ill equipped for the task I have attempted, but I have consciously added to my offence by deliberately flouting the best traditional advice. No warning is so frequently voiced to those about to write of foreign peoples as the injunction to avoid at all costs judging one's subjects by British standards. My reaction to this hoary maxim is to ask by what conceivable standard is one then to judge them. Their own? Then a lifetime spent in the country were surely insufficient to achieve the necessary qualifications. By those which it is hoped will prevail in the ideal supra-national world state of to-morrow? In that case I am too sadly out of tune with the cosmic consciousness to utter a word. Rejecting all such foolishness, in-so-far as I employ the comparative method, my criteria, political, architectural and scenic, remain firmly Anglo-Saxon, and the standards of judgment are always those of an Anglican graduate of Oxford with a taste for architecture, turned cartoonist, approaching middle age and living in Kensington.

Such are the standards I have unashamedly adopted; their application it will soon be discovered is almost exclusively visual. No analysis of deep underlying causes has been attempted, and no effort has been made to display an acute pyschological insight. For one reason I lack both the temperament and knowledge necessary for such an enterprise; for another, I have a very shrewd suspicion that in Greece there are no deep underlying causes and that the facts which meet the eye are all-important. The Greeks are of all people the least inhibited (it is significant that the only two professional psychoanalysts practising in Athens have large private incomes) and their passions, both amorous and political, are seldom indulged under a bushel. But whereas elsewhere politics may do little to enrich the landscape, here they find visible expression in a variety of ways all of which lend character to the scene and which to omit would be to falsify the whole. Among these the red and blue slogans that form such significant patterns on the walls of every town, the banner-waving processions that every Sunday troop off to the Stadium or Syntagma are the most immediately apparent and least violent. But on occasions politics provide a more macabre emphasis to the view and indeed the first Greek figure on whom I set eyes was a bearded warrior rolling in agony in the foreground of the long perspective of an empty Kolonaki street, closed in the distance by the dramatic silhouette of Lycabettus, who had, so subsequent investigation revealed, just been slugged through the stomach by a political opponent concealed behind some shuttered second-empire façade away in the wings.

Having thus made my formal declaration at the *douane* there remain two unavowed motives which, safely across the frontier, I can now perhaps without danger confess. First, the presumptuous idea that as a great deal of nonsense, most of it ill-informed and much of it wilfully prejudiced, has recently been written about Greece, a fresh attempt to provide a picture, even one so personal and specialised as this, of a country with which, as the latest development of American foreign policy has forcefully demonstrated, our own future is so intimately bound up, might not be untimely.   Second, the memory of the intense pleasure which I experienced in Greece, the significance which for me its monuments and landscape will always possess and my deep appreciation of the kindness, sympathy and spirit of the inhabitants have all combined to encourage me to some open acknowledgement.

Warning To Readers (1975)

In the thirty years that have passed since this book was written Greece has undergone many changes and the author, whose knowledge of the country is rather more extensive than it was then, is himself, for better or worse, not quite what he was. For one less indolent, the urge to revise would, therefore, have been overwhelming; that it was successfully resisted was largely due to the fact that inertia was reinforced by a prolonged absence. After the advent of the Colonels, Greece became for him a cherished memory unrevived by personal acquaintance.

> The mike behind the architrave
> Consolidates Athene's loss
> And Agamemnon's mask must save
> The face of Cononel Pattakos.
>
> Of no avail to ask just now
> The barman at the Grande Bretagne
> For news of friends, or why and how. . . .
> His lips are sealed, and so are mine.
>
> The Pythian rocks are slogan-scrawled,
> "The army's backing Greece and so
> Must you!" The guides are too enthralled
> To hear the Sibyl answer "No!"
>
> ΧΡΙΣΤΟΣ ΛΝΕΣΤΗ! But I would not care
> To greet My Lord in Constitution Square,*

It is, therefore, a keen source of satisfaction that the appearance of this edition should follow so swiftly on the downfall of that sordid little junta whose dictatorial regime was unredeemed either by the comic panache of General Pangalos or the undoubted efficiency of General Metaxas.

---

* 'On not going to Greece, Easter, 1968', printed in *The Sunday Times*, 14.iv.61.

Of the many changes that were already visible seven years ago, the majority are, as elsewhere, deplorable. Almost all the charming old Othonian houses in Kolonaki have been replaced by vast apartment blocks in which the mediocrity of the design is imperfectly concealed by marble facing; Plaka is become a noisier Montmartre with a bar or a bazouki on every step; in Thessaloniki the old Turkish quarter has been progressively eroded by development. On the credit side, however, must be counted the new motorways, well designed and usually well maintained; for those in a hurry, who are indifferent to wayside advertising, they are a boon; for those who are not they perform the welcome service of siphoning off most of the heavy traffic from the older and far more interesting routes they have replaced. Thus the prestigious new Corniche to Sunion has halved the number of cars on the old road via Lavrion, which runs through the loveliest and least spoilt part of Attica and, on long stretches of the former trunk road to the north, horses and mules outnumber minis, and the Vlachs still pursue their seasonal migrations undisturbed by long-distance buses. Also to be welcomed is the network of small comfortable hotels, well designed and tactfully sited (but not at Delphi), which has replaced the handful of flea-bitten caravanserais in which, thirty years ago, the unvariable courtesy of the proprietors could not always compensate for a total lack of those amenities which modern travellers have come to expect.

What has not changed, save in the immediate vicinity of Athens and on the bay of Salamis, is the landscape. The mountains still look on Marathon, Delos remains inviolate, and the Vale of Argos seen from Mycenae is much as Lear recorded it over a century ago. Likewise the national character which, as recent events have so happily demonstrated, armoured divisions, international finance and the C.I.A. were unable permanently to modify. Today we are confronted by a free and united Greece where all, I have no doubt, are eagerly looking forward to a resumption of that enjoyable political chaos, the suppression of which during the last seven years is likely to have been among the most resented deprivations imposed by the mercifully defunct regime.

O.L.

ALBANIA   MACEDONIA

THESSALONIKI

SAMOTHRAKI

METSOVO   METEORA

JANNINA   EPIRUS   TRIKKALA

CORFU

PAXOS   ARTA   LARISSAO

LIMNOS

THE IONIAN ISLANDS

LEVKAS   THESSALY

ITHAKA   oLAMIA   EUBOEA   THE SPORADES   MYTILENE

AETOLIA PHOCIS   SKYROS

CEPHALONIA   AGRINION

MISSOLONGHI   DELPHI   CHALCHIS   THE AEGEAN ISLANDS

NAVPAKTOS

ZANTE   PATRAS   LIVADIA   CHIOS   NEA MONI

PYRGOS   ANDRAVIDA   ACHAEA   BOEOTIA   THEBES

GASTOUNI   AEGOSTHENA   ATTICA

OLYMPIA   NEMEA   MYCENAE   CORINTH   MEGARA   ELEVSIS

ELIS   MEGALOPOLIS   ARGOS   SALAMIS   ATHENS

KYRAITINA   TIRYNS   EPIDAURUS   PIRAEUS   SAMOS

TRIPOLIS   NAUPLIA   AEGINA   MAKRONISI   ANDROS

ARCADIA   ASINE   POROS   SUNIUM   TENOS   IKARIA

BASSAE   MISTRA   HYDRA   KEOS

SPARTA   KYTHNOS   SYRA

THE PELOPONNESE   LACONIA   MYKONOS

MESSENIA   SERIPHOS

MANI   GYTHION   THE CYCLADES   PAROS

SIPHNOS

N   MONEMVASIA   KIMOLOS   NAXOS

W   E   IOS   AMORGOS

S   CYTHERA   MELOS

SANTORIN

ANAPHE

CRETE

CANEA

RETHIMO

HERAKLION

KNOSSOS

One very ingenious person terms them the ' natural allies of English-
men' ; another, no less ingenious, will not allow them to be the allies of
anybody, and denies their very descent from the ancients ; a third, more
ingenious than either, builds a Greek empire on a Russian foundation,
and realizes (on paper) all the chimeras of Catherine II. As to the
question of their descent, what can it import whether the Mainotes are
the lineal Laconians or not or the present Athenians as indigenous as
the bees of Hymettus, or as the grasshoppers, to which they once likened
themselves ? What Englishman cares if he be of a Danish, Saxon,
Norman, or Trojan blood or who, except a Welshman, is afflicted
with a desire of being descended from Caractacus ?

                                                    LORD BYRON

THAT the inhabitants of Greece are of very mixed stock is a fact so
obvious after five minutes in an Athenian crowd that one tends
to forget how frequently, and with what unfortunate results, it
is overlooked by those who have never enjoyed that experience. On the
one hand, there are the optimists who, like the nineteenth-century English
Philhellenes, people the country in their imagination with a god-like race
of Phidian profile universally inspired by the ideals current in fifth-century
Athens (or rather with what are held in the sixth-forms of our public-schools
to be the ideals of fifth-century Athens) ; on the other are those who,
accepting unreservedly the dubious ethnology of Professor Fallmerayer,
assume that not one drop of ancient Greek blood flows in veins of the
present-day inhabitants of Hellas, who are just a Balkan race *comme une*
autre. It is hard to say which school of thought is doomed to the bitterer
disappointment.

At the beginning of history, after the dust raised by the passage of vast
hordes of beaker-folk and battle-axe folk, of long-barrow men and megalith-
builders, of bracicephalics and dolicocephalics wandering round Europe
and dropping an untidy trail of arrow-heads and potsherds behind them,
has temporarily subsided, the islands of the Aegean are seen to be inhabited
by a people whose origins cannot by the strictest standards of racialism be
adjudged wholly pure. The majority appears to have belonged to the long-
headed, dark, Mediterranean type, fine specimens of which are still to be

15

observed on any bathing-beach of the southern European littoral and which gained a notable, though temporary, ascendancy in Hollywood in the early

'twenties, but there was also present, and one can almost hear the sob in the anthropologist's voice as he admits it, a distinct Armenoid strain. However, dubious as this people's ancestry may have been, their character, thanks to the abundant remains of their civilization uncovered in Crete, is tolerably well defined. Their art reveals them to us as sophisticated, realistic and pleasure-loving ; their architecture as peaceable and fussier about plumbing than any race in history before the Americans. Of these traits it is only the two last of which it is difficult to find any trace among their descendants to-day. Their empire at its height was confined to the Aegean islands and a few settlements on the mainland chiefly on or near the coastal fringe. The interior of the country save for Thessaly, always old-fashioned, where a stone-age culture still belatedly flourished, was inhabited by bracicephalic Alpines who were probably not, as the name invariably suggests, exclusively a race of bullet-headed yodellers, but one much resembling in appearance the majority of the inhabitants of western Europe to-day. Round about 1200 B.C. there occurred another *Völkerwanderung*, when the vast semi-permanent racial traffic-block to the northeast suddenly disentangled itself, releasing a stream of newcomers to the south and west, and the Cretan Empire disappears almost overnight. The period of the incursions was, however, prolonged and the first arrivals were themselves in due course pushed in the wake of the Minoan refugees to find themselves new homes on the seaboard of Asia Minor. The invaders, Achaens, Ionians, Aeolians, Dorians and all, do not seem to have come from very far afield and were racially akin to the broad-headed Alpines whom they enslaved or dispersed.

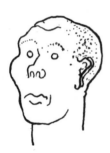

That the Dorians were an advance guard of the northern *Herrenvolk* is a theory for which little or no evidence exists, and despite the undoubtedly unpleasant character of their most prominent clan, the Spartans, there is no reason to saddle them with a Teutonic origin. It was not until much later that the long-headed Blond Bore makes any contribution, and then much modified, to the racial hotch-potch of Greece.

The bond which united these various tribes among themselves and marked them off from the earlier inhabitants far more rigidly than race was that of language. The Cretans had spoken a tongue of which we know nothing save that it was not Aryan ; what the Pelasgians [1] spoke remains a matter for eager dispute among philologists ; but the invaders were one and all Aryan-speaking. Thanks in no more small measure to this common language, the Greeks had by the beginning of the eighth century achieved as high a degree of unity as they were ever to enjoy. That is to say, that the various tribes, cities and political factions into which this nation is for ever divided were as capable then as now of a high measure of co-operation—for a strictly limited period—in the face of a threat from an alien race. Indeed, the comparison between the national reaction to the Persian peril in the sixth century B.C. and to the German menace in the twentieth A.D. is so striking that it once more raises the old question as to how far the modern Greeks can claim to be, if not ethnically then spiritually the heirs of the heroes of antiquity. Up till quite recently the reaction from the Byronic disappointment at finding Capodistrias living so much less sympathetic than Pericles dead has encouraged the belief that if the modern Greek was to be described as the descendant of the classical, then the term demanded the prefix ' degenerate ', but for one who first read Thucydides' account of the rebellion at Corcyra in an Athens base-ment in December 1944 it is impossible unquestioningly to accept what seems in the face of the evidence a hasty over-simplification. If you take the view that Pericles, Demosthenes and Themistocles were, despite the unavoidable disadvantage of a non-denominational education, made much in the image of Dr. Arnold, then it is indeed difficult to prove that they have anything in common with Messrs. Papandreou, Tsaldaris and Plastiras ; but if, on the other hand, you take a less Rugbeian view of these great men, then the differences separating them from their modern counterparts appear at least no greater than those existing between, say, St. Thomas à Becket and Mr. Ernest Bevin.

[1] The amateur archaeologist in Greece will find this name of the greatest use. It may be used of any site or piece of masonry of undoubtedly immense antiquity but unspecified authorship and serves to give a very classy tone to the conversation. As it has never been unanimously decided who exactly the Pelasgians were or even if they ever really existed it may safely be employed by the merest tyro. It is in fact almost the exact archaeological equivalent of that good old medical stand-by ' pyrexia of unknown origin '.

Racially, however, the Greek nation has un-doubtedly been subjected to considerable modifica-tions in the intervening millennia, and even during the classical period itself was being continuously if very gradually transformed, for the economy of ancient Greece rested on slave labour largely recruited from non-Greek territories (the Athens police, for instance, were all Scythians, a people of dubious antecedents inhabiting the northern shores of the Black Sea), and it would be idle to suppose that the Greeks were any more likely then than now to allow social or racial prejudice to stand in the way of venery. The Romans during the period of their domination do not appear to have mixed much of their blood with that of the native population, contenting themselves with planting

'*J'ai sauvé la Grèce*'

colonies of veterans in certain cities such as Corinth and Patras, but with the decline of their power Greece, along with the rest of the Empire, was increasingly subject to the inroads of tribes from beyond the frontiers. Somewhere away in central Asia another great traffic-block was dispersing and wave after wave of barbarians were released southward and westward, each, if we are to believe contemporary accounts, more ferocious in their behaviour and brutish in appearance than the last. At first these in-cursions in so far as they involved Greece were transitory in character and impermanent in their effects, but at last when Goths and Vandals and Huns had run their course across the face of Europe there appeared a race, the Avars, so un-bridled in their ferocious greed for territory and slaughter, that they did what none of their predecessors, however savage, had accomplished, and penetrated into the vast and dreary Pripet marshes, expelling the Slavs who hitherto had been the only people stupid enough to live there. The immediate result of this intemperate action was to let loose a swarm of flat-faced morons who overwhelmed the lands of south-eastern Europe, not so much in a wave but rather in the manner of sewage

'*Populist*'

18

seeping into the water supply through the cracks in a faulty drain, until they had at last penetrated to the extreme south of the Peloponnese, where the sea, an element with which they were quite unacquainted, barred their further passage. This inundation is frequently cited by those who hold that the modern Greeks have nothing but their name and their language in common with their classical forerunners, and it would be idle to deny that a very large number of the population, particularly of the Peloponnese, have a considerable dose of Slav blood, but it in fact constitutes the most striking possible testimony to the national vitality and power of absorption. To-day, all that remains to tell of their passage, even in districts which we know the Slavs totally engulfed, are a few place-names and a tendency for cheek-bones to be worn high.

'The Black Horseman'

Both the Latins and the Turks were cut off from the people they ruled by differences of religion which successfully prevented intermarriage on any wide scale, but it would be wrong to suppose that the long period of the latter's domination was without effect on the national character. The cooking, the beads with the twiddling of which so many Greek gentlemen beguile their leisure, and the hubble-bubble, banned by the late General Metaxas as un-Greek, all represent the superficial effects of long contact with the Turk ; evidence of the deeper, psychological result is provided by the prevailing attitude to women and that sudden surprising suspension of will-power, doubly strange in so tireless a race, which not infrequently causes such distress to British and American advisers zealous for national reconstruction. Even after independence had been finally achieved, Turkish influence was still indirectly felt, for it is too often forgotten that until 1912 Greece was cut off from the rest of the continent by a strip of Turkish territory stretching from the Black Sea to the Adriatic. The feeling of isolation which this engendered has not yet wholly vanished, and many a well-educated Greek contemplating a visit to Paris or Geneva will to this day quite naturally speak of 'going to Europe'.

Another isolated effect of Turkish misrule is

19

'His Beatitude'

represented by the Albanian communities in Attica and elsewhere, the most extraordinary minority in Europe. When maladministration had reduced the population of whole tracts of southern Greece almost to vanishing-point, colonists from Albania were forcibly installed by the Turks. These have kept their identity and language to the present day, and in many a village not twenty miles from Athens the whole population will prove to be Albanian-speaking. Nevertheless, these people in their political outlook are wholly and firmly Greek. In the War of Independence many of them played prominent rôles, and to-day, paradoxically enough, they form the most reliable and solid bloc of voters supporting the parties of the extreme right, one of whose most popular rallying cries is ' Down with Albania '.

In our own times one further element has been added to the racial admixture of modern Greece. After the 1922 disaster a million and a half refugees were transferred to their fatherland from Asia Minor. The majority of these came from territories which had first been colonized by Greeks in the eighth century B.C. and represented a stock in which national consciousness had from the first been kept lively by the presence all around of alien races, and latterly reinforced by religious faith, with the result that their blood had, in the course of centuries, become far less diluted than that of their fellow-countrymen on the mainland. To-day, if one meets a dark, Mediterranean type, with, perhaps, that disturbing Armenoid strain, conforming closely to the conception of the typical Greek made popular by American cartoonists, it is ten to one he is an Asia Minor refugee.

It is, perhaps, hardly surprising that, in view of the many strains and stocks from which the modern Greeks derive, one of the first of the many differences which distinguish them from other nations of which the foreign visitor becomes aware is their striking nonconformity to type. Elsewhere, particularly in Anglo-Saxon countries, a fearful and increasing uniformity is the rule, which is discernible not only in the great mass of the population, where one might perhaps look for it, but also in those walks of life where one would be justified in expecting to find some outstanding signs of character and individuality. In England, the Labour Government has held power for over a year, yet few save the experts can tell the Under-Secretaries apart, while in the United States none save those who have devoted a lifetime to the subject can possibly memorize the features of any individual politician for more than five minutes. How different are things in Greece ! Here, where politicians are in proportion to the population so much more numerous, no possibility of

' *L'homme de la Gauche, l'homme civilisé* '

mistaken identity exists ; their faces, figures and deportment are as individual and readily distinguishable to the naked eye of the man in the street as their thumb-prints would be under the microscope of Monsieur Bertillon. Consider his Beatitude the Archbishop, six foot six in height, weighing seventeen stone, with cheekbones as rugged and prominent as the Pindus ; M. Mavro-michaelis, rosy and monocled, as fine a specimen of the bracicephalic White's Club type as you could find in Pall Mall ; Comrade Siantos, a cross between King Zog and Mr. Emlyn Williams in a Welsh character part ; General Plastiras, thin as string, fiercely moustachioed with eyes like Kalamata olives ; M. Papandreou, so nobly Thespian in the old Lyceum manner that one automatically expects to be addressed as 'laddie'. These and half a hundred others lend infinite colour and variety to the Greek political scene and (*experto crede*) render

' *The Admiral* '

21

'_G. O. M._'

enviably easy the lot of the Athenian carica-
turist.

It is not without design that the above
examples have all been chosen from the political
world, although the rule holds good in every
strata of Greek society, for nothing is likely to
strike the foreigner so forcibly as the magnitude
of the rôle which politics plays in the life of
every Greek, of whatever age, sex or employment. What, however, is not so immediately
obvious, is that the Greek conception of politics
is no longer ours—a fact the failure to realize
which on the part of so many earnest and
otherwise well-informed Anglo-Saxon commentators has led to an infinity of trouble and
misunderstanding in the past. In Greece one
is back in the world of the Duke of Bedford
and the Rockingham Whigs, where personalities
count for more than principles and a pro-
gramme forms no part of the equipment of a party ; a world in which the
Memoirs of Saint-Simon are likely to prove a more useful guide than the
pamphlets of the P. E. P. or the leaders in the _Economist_. Keen students
of such well-informed but slightly inhuman publications as these last may
well be constantly appalled at the rumour of some harmless little 'job'
which would not have caused Horace Walpole to
blink an eyelid, and will certainly be grievously dis-
appointed at the failure of the magic word 'Planning'
to awaken the customary eager response in any Greek
politician. Quite at a loss to understand the old-
fashioned idea, still widespread in Greece, that the
state exists for the benefit of the individual, not the
individual for the state, they may easily be reduced
to a condition of despair in which they are prepared
unquestioningly to proclaim the rosy glow of dialectical
materialism visible across the northern frontiers as the
dawn of a better day.

For those, however, who are prepared to accept the
fact that in a country where everyone from the shoeshine
boy in Ommonia to the cotton millionaire in Kolonaki
regards himself, quite rightly, as uncommon and unique,

'_Ancien Régime_'

22

the coming of the century of the common man is likely to be indefinitely postponed, Greek politics provide a profitable subject of study and an inexhaustible source of entertainment. They are in a very literal sense, and in a way unparalleled elsewhere in the modern world, power-politics; that is to say, that power is the prize for which every politician strives, and his pursuit of it is all the more vigorous for the fact that he is quite unencumbered with any preconceived ideas of how or for what purpose it is to be applied when attained. In such conditions where economic and social factors count for very little and personal relationships assume enormous importance, ideologies are only proclaimed in order subsequently to be abandoned, party loyalty is purely a matter of temporary convenience and the floor of the house is frequently impassable for the number of members crossing it. For those accustomed to the more-orderly and less dramatic functioning of British parliamentary government the scene is not uncommonly distressing, and if, in addition, they have acquired no understanding of the Greek conception of the *politikos kosmos*, invariably incomprehensible.

Among the Greeks this institution, for which the term 'political world' provides an entirely inadequate translation, fulfils a rôle for which it is quite impossible to find a parallel in our own country. Its members enjoy a regard which may once, if Sir Max Beerbohm is to be believed, have been accorded to Victorian elder statesman but can to-day be claimed solely by the more popular American film-stars. Their form is assessed and their performance judged with a passionate interest which among us is only displayed in the case of racehorses and greyhounds, and a change of party arouses as widespread an excitement as is here occasioned by the transfer of a professional footballer from one club to another. While the entire population feel themselves as directly concerned in the activities of the *politikos kosmos* as do subscribers to a pool in the fortunes of League Football, it remains, nevertheless, an exclusive and to some extent a closed world. The hereditary principle is strong, and well over half the membership is derived from the various political dynasties, the Tsaldaris, Mavromichaelis, Dragoumis, Venezelos, etc., and their clients. Of the remainder, some have gained entrance by way of local politics (the great Venezelos himself, for instance, and the veteran M. Sofoulis who first came into prominence as the leader of a successful revolt against that least known of European potentates, the Hereditary Prince of Samos, in the 'seventies of the last century), others by way of the law-courts, journalism or, very occasionally, the trade unions. Where, however, the whole system differs most noticeably from that which prevails in our own country is in the presence of the *ex-officio* members. With us, the line dividing the civil servant from the politician is rigid indeed;

in Greece it does not exist. The more important officials in the Treasury, the Foreign Office and, above all, the Service departments are by virtue of their office active participants in the political strife, to the fortunes of which they in most cases owe their appointment.

While civil servants have their allotted place in the established hierarchy of the *politikos kosmos* it is well below that reserved for the leaders of the armed forces, for without the active participation of the latter it would soon prove quite impossible to play the game according to the rules. In Greece, as with us, hard though it may be for some of Western democrats to credit it, governments are dependent on popular support; and the principle difference lies in the manner in which that support is expressed or withdrawn. There, when a government has exhausted the patience of the country, it is as often as not removed from office not by the ballot-box but the *coup d'état*, and for many years the technique has remained unchanged. One morning a band of Colonels and Major-Generals, judging the state of public opinion to warrant such an enterprise, marches across Constitution Square, firing a ritual volley down University Street *en route*, takes possession of the Ministries of War and the Interior and arrests the Cabinet. Next morning a new government is installed, the leaders of the old one have been condemned to death and the Colonels and Major-Generals are gazetted Lieutenant-Generals and full Generals. A few days later the sentences on the defeated politicians are commuted to life imprisonment, subsequently to be reduced to banishment to the islands where most of them have already provided themselves with comfortable villas against just such an emergency. A few months pass, a general amnesty is proclaimed, and everything goes on as before. In these circumstances the *coup d'état* becomes an accepted constitutional device

and is usually attended with far less bloodshed than a general election, but its success depends on the strict observance of the rules by both sides. On the two occasions in recent years when the rules have been infringed, wounds were inflicted to the aftereffects of which the present melancholy state of the country can in no small measure be attributed. After the Asia Minor disaster, Colonels Plastiras and Gonatas went so far as to carry out the death sentence on six of the Royalist leaders, a gross infringement of the accepted code, which, whether or not there existed legal justification, left a legacy of bitterness which even Venizelos himself was never effectually able to surmount and which was active for harm up to the outbreak of the last war.

In 1935 General Metaxas, having seized power in the accepted fashion, so far forgot himself as to keep his political opponents in the exile to which they had been traditionally banished for an indefinite period, and by so doing prevented the normal functioning of the *politikos kosmos* from then onwards. It was for this far more than for those totalitarian gestures which so excited the wrath of foreign anti-fascists that he earned the cordial dislike of his fellow-countrymen; while supplying an unaccustomed quantity of bread in the form of improved social services he was forced, in order to maintain himself in power, to close down the principal circus.

While the actual manœuvring and strategy is confined to a compara-

25

tively small team, it should not be supposed that the spectators are doomed to a passive rôle or that their opportunities for political self-expression are few or unsatisfying. Quite apart from the organized rallies and demonstrations which provide the regular Sunday amusement of every self-respecting citizen, political enthusiasm manifests itself in every department of everyday life in a manner which, to us, who are accustomed save at election time to keep politics confined to the decent obscurity of the university discussion-group and the National Liberal Club, is apt to appear almost excessive. Thus, seldom has a man been more distressed than a young English musician invited to conduct a concert of modern Greek music when, at the first rehearsal, the composer of the work in progress having informed the orchestra that the next twenty-five bars of his tone-poem represented the triumph of democracy over Fascism, all the strings got up and cheered and the brass [1] and percussion walked out in a rage. Similarly, few of the English present are likely to forget a memorable first-night of *The Merchant of Venice* when his political opponents in the stalls opened up on Shylock with a tommy-gun, inflicting a nasty flesh-wound on Bassanio and killing Lancelot Gobbo.

Overwhelming as is the prevailing enthusiasm for politics, it is likely that the visitor to Athens will be struck more immediately by the Greek passion for noise. There are some who hold that this extraordinary trait in the national character springs rather from insensitiveness or indifference than from any positive liking ; but this is a theory which I consider has been rendered untenable by my chance discovery, in a car-park in the Piraeus, of a motor-bicycle fitted with two exhausts, each provided not with a silencer but an amplifier. The means whereby this passion is given expression are manifold and ingenious and there is no department of life in which it is not fully satisfied. Political demonstrations, in addition to the high-powered stream of oratory and the rhythmical chanting of slogans, are invariably enlivened by the presence of one, if not two brass bands, while sessions of Parliament, thanks to the high pitch of development to which the slamming of desk-lids and banging of despatch-boxes has here attained, frequently astound even French observers brought up in the hard school of the Chambre des Députés. In everyday life the polite commonplaces of social intercourse are normally exchanged in the ringing tones of Demosthenes sharing his candid opinion of Philip of Macedon with a crowd of several thousands in the open air, and in summer the traveller approaching the coast of Attica across the waters of

---

[1] In Greece the woodwinds are almost always Liberals and, in this instance, by remaining quietly on the fence and doing nothing they were loyally following the example of their venerable leader M. Sophoulis.

the Saronic Gulf is frequently puzzled by the continuous buzzing that first becomes audible soon after passing the point of Aegina, increasing in intensity as he draws nearer the shore which, he is startled finally to discover, proceeds from the casual conversation being sustained on the bathing-beaches of Phaleron. Nor is it only the human figures in the landscape who are subject to this weakness, for in Athens, and nowhere else so far as

I know, the cocks are accustomed to greet the dawn at all hours of the day and night : as almost all Athenians, even flat-dwellers, are enthusiastic keepers of poultry, this contribution to the general din is not to be despised. Needless to say, while there is every reason for supposing that this passion is deep seated and of long standing, the modern Greeks with their great powers of rapid assimilation have availed themselves of all the discoveries of modern science to such good purpose that they have far surpassed the best which their great ancestors could achieve. The radio, the gramophone and the internal-combustion engine are all employed to the fullest advantage, but it is noticeable that in-so-far as modern research has tended towards the elimination of sound its results have been firmly rejected ; thus the majority of the Athenian trams are of the oldest and noisiest vintage, and such few comparatively new models as appear on the streets have all, by skilful handling and a few minor adjustments, been rendered in this respect almost as good as old.

Nowhere is this carefully cultivated talent for noise more vigorously, or to the Anglican ear more surprisingly, employed than in the service of

religion. Here the very church bells call with an insistent, imperative clang which to those accustomed to the gentle summons from the steeple of St. Fridiswede's sounding softly across the sunset fields of Birckett Forster, would seem more suited to the tocsin than to evensong. (Owing to the rugged nature of Greek political life it must be admitted that they are, in fact, almost as frequently employed for the former task as for the latter.) In many of the monasteries, however, the monks still cling to the older fashion of calling the faithful, traditional in the Orthodox Church, beating on a suspended wooden beam with a hammer, holding that this instrument, while possibly inferior to the bell in carrying power, is even more insistent at close quarters. In some cases a long iron bar has been substituted for the beam, and the results thus attained are said to be even more satisfactory. But these are

merely the everyday routine practices and it is only on the great festivals that one is able to appreciate the real pre-eminence of the Church in this field.

Easter, in the Orthodox Church, far surpasses in importance all other feasts, and in Greece it is celebrated by the whole nation, including even those who for the rest of the year are notoriously indifferent in such matters, with a fervour and intensity considerably greater than that which we are accustomed to display at Christmas. The fast of Lent has been observed in progressive stages, culminating, in Holy Week, for the devout in almost total abstinence and in an absence of meat even on the mondaine dinner-tables of Kolonaki. All Good Friday the bells have tolled ceaselessly from every belfry in Athens, and after dark the Bier has been carried in procession round the confines of every parish. Holy Saturday is a *dies non* ; for the only time in the whole year the cafés are empty and even the terrace at Yennaki's is deserted except for a handful of foreigners, while in the church all is dark save for one solitary candle on the altar. Towards midnight the space opposite the great west doors of the Metropolis, and of every church throughout the land, is gradually filled by an immense crowd in whom the fasting of the previous week and the unaccustomed gloom of the day, so foreign to the nature of a people not markedly austere, have induced a nervous condition bordering on hysteria. The wooden platform erected on a line with the high altar is now occupied by members of the government and representatives of the diplomatic corps, the latter holding their candles in the slightly embarrassed manner of grown-ups participating in a game of oranges and lemons, while from the open doors the sound of the chanting which has been going on within the darkened cathedral for many hours takes on a more urgent note. A few minutes before midnight the Archbishop emerges attended by two deacons, one carrying a lighted candle from the altar, and mounting the platform begins the reading of the Gospel. By now a deathly hush, or what passes in Greece for a deathly hush, that is to say an absence of sound that compares not unfavourably with the noise of the small mammal-house on a quiet afternoon, has fallen on the vast crowd, which is maintained unbroken until, on the stroke of midnight, the Bishop pronounces the words ' Xristos anesté ', ' Christ is risen '. At this the night is rent by a wave of sound in comparison with which all the noises to which one has grown accustomed on other days of the year are as tinkling cymbals. A massed choir and two brass bands burst into powerful, though different, songs of praise ; the guard of honour presents arms with a crash unrivalled even in the Wellington Barracks ; every bell in the city, ably assisted by air-raid syrens and factory whistles, clangs out the good news, while the cheering crowds greet their Risen Lord with a barrage of rockets, squibs, Roman candles, Chinese crackers, and volley after volley of small-arms fire discharged by such of the devout, a not inconsiderable proportion, as have come to the ceremony armed.

It is not, perhaps, strange that those whose sole experience of Greek religion is gained at a ceremony such as that described above, or who have witnessed the frequency with which the secular power successfully intervenes in the business of the Holy Synod should incline to dismiss the national form of Christianity as being encrusted with superstition and hamstrung by Erastianism. And it must be admitted that the Greek Church does suffer in some degree from both these faults, but it nevertheless enjoys certain compensating advantages which are too frequently ignored by Roman Catholic commentators with a smug loftiness more irritating because less justified than that which they habitually reserve for the institutions of Protestant sects.[1]

To the Papist the close connection of Church and State in Orthodox lands has been a long-standing source of irritation, and the ebullience which characterizes the co-operation of the Greek laity in the celebration of the sacred rites seems undignified in itself and likely to detract from the respect properly due to holy orders ; while the Protestant is pained to discover how little apparent effect belief exercises on conduct and is hard put to it to discover signs of the existence of any idea of personal communion between

the believer and his Maker. Both, therefore, tend to overlook one great virtue which the Greek Orthodox Church has retained and which both their own sects, anyhow in their English manifestations, have undoubtedly lost, and that is the attitude of straightforward acceptance with which the church is regarded by the vast mass of the population. The village *pappas* may be, and not infrequently is, regarded as a joke by his parishioners, but as a man not as a priest ; he is accepted as one of the familiar features of everyday life along with the horse-dealer, the rural guard and the driver of the local bus, as equally liable to human weaknesses [2] and seldom their superior in education. The village priest, however, being drawn from the ranks of the secular clergy, who are permitted to marry but on doing so forfeit all chance of preferment, while enjoying an indulgent familiarity which is not displayed toward the more exalted members of the Orthodox hierarchy, is equally debarred from the undoubted respect with which, in most cases, they are generally regarded. Apart from the considerable influence which a bishop enjoys in his diocese by virtue of his position and which he is usually sufficiently well-educated

[1] For an extreme expression of this attitude see Mr. Edward Hutton's *A Little Tour in Greece.*

[2] Colonel Leake informs us that in his day in the Mani country the participation of priests in blood-feuds was governed by certain well-defined laws. Thus while Holy Orders were not in themselves regarded as sufficient to remove him from the category of fair game, the Man of God could not be potted while actually officiating behind the *ikonostasis*. On the other hand, he was obliged to remove whatever firearms he carried concealed beneath his cope before approaching the altar. While this was a century ago in a district notoriously the most violent in Greece, the Greeks seem still to be unvisited by any revulsion of feeling at the idea of blood being shed by a priest, and during the occupation many of them played an active rôle in the Resistance, and in the island of Chios the most successful guerrilla band was actually organized and led by a priest.

profitably to exercise, the old belief that whoever is rude to a bishop will not survive the next Good Friday, still widespread, both serves to protect his prestige and testifies to the exalted character which attaches to his rank in the popular estimation.[1] This position is one which, so one is constantly being informed, is never compromised by political activities; but despite the manifest sincerity with which this disavowal is invariably offered, it has sometimes proved difficult in recent years unhesitatingly to accept it at its face-value. The close connection of Archbishop Chrysanthos with the inner council of the Populist party on the one hand and the well-publicized activities of the 'Red' Bishop of Kozani on the other may both be considered open to some question.

That many of the beliefs and practices of Greek Christianity possess a superstitious rather than a doctrinal sanction is undoubtedly true. Greece, considering its geographical position, was a comparative latecomer into the Christian fold (certain districts in the southern Peloponnese remaining pagan until almost the end of the eighth century), and it is hardly surprising that many of the old classical myths should have proved exceptionally hardy growths in the land which gave them birth. The policy of the Church when

confronted with these apparently ineradicable survivals from the heathen past was, wisely enough, one of absorption rather than suppression, and the shrines, anniversaries and, on occasion, even the statues, of the old Olympian and local deities were simply apportioned out among the innumerable available saints and martyrs, with the result that to-day all over Greece the inquiring visitor to many a country chapel will find that 'new Demetrius is but old Demeter writ large'.[2]

However, while much which passes for religious

[1] For some strange reason this does not hold good in the islands, where the local episcopate is generally credited by public opinion with the most extraordinary eccentricities.

[2] For a full discussion of this interesting topic, see that fascinating volume, *Modern Greek Folklore and Ancient Greek Religion*, by Lawson.

fervour has little enough to do with Christianity, while many of the lower clergy are ignorant and the higher preoccupied with secular ambitions, and while a regularity in outward observance seems too seldom to be reflected in conduct,[1] the Greek Church has one distinction of which most foreigners are ignorant but which no Greek is ever likely to forget. It is in a very large measure due to the Church that Greece exists as a nation to-day ; during the long centuries of the Turkish domination she it was who preserved the language, kept alive the spark of nationalism, and finally provided the rallying-point for resistance.

One reason, however, for the vast crowds which throng the churches at Easter has little enough to do with religion. The Greeks are, of all nations, the most gregarious, and any occasion which provides an opportunity for them to congregate in masses, be it religious, political, or sporting, is sincerely welcomed. To the quality of the entertainment offered they appear quite indifferent, holding the pleasure of standing for two or three hours wedged among some thirty thousand or so of their fellow human beings in itself sufficient recompense. Nor are they dependent for the satisfaction of this particular whim on fixed celebrations previously announced, but will spontaneously gather in droves on the most trivial pretexts ; a squabble between two cigarette-boys, a broken-down motor-bus, a performing bear will in any Greek town draw crowds which in England only popular film-stars arriving at a Command Performance can attract. This powerful instinct, of course, renders them unrivalled blockers-up-of-gangways, and when it is allied to an unfailing ability to select at a glance the narrowest strip of pavement, the sharpest corner of the stairs, slows up the tempo of every-day life to a pace which those not similarly gifted occasionally find distress-ingly slow. This passion for crowds is accompanied, logically enough, by a dislike of solitude correspondingly intense. Thus in the height of the summer one never finds a beach, no matter how convenient or delightful, in the possession of half a dozen bathers ; it is either completely empty or occupied by upwards of fifteen hundred people. Similarly a wealthy Greek, building himself a country villa, will reject any secluded spot, even if not inconven-iently remote, in favour of a site in a suburb already overcrowded by his friends and relations. Nor, even if he is as rich as Croesus, will he buy sufficient land or plant trees in order to ensure what we should regard as a minimum degree of privacy, arguing that it is practically impossible to escape

[1] A well-known Communist trade-union boss, guilty without question of at least half a dozen singularly brutal murders, on one occasion pleaded absence from a conference, perfectly genuinely, on the grounds that he had to make his Easter Communion, much to the shocked embarrassment of the stolid Yorkshire chairman.

being overlooked by the neighbours without at the same time depriving one-self of the pleasure of overlooking them.

Allied to this formidable passion for company is a trait which in the author as a small boy was invariably dubbed vulgar curiosity but which a maiden aunt used convincingly to justify in herself as ' taking a healthy interest in one's fellow beings '. Needless to say, in this matter the Greeks are entirely of the aunt's way of thinking. One's health, one's income, one's children, one's sex-life are all matters in which they are prepared to take a burning and perfectly genuine interest and on which deliberately to withhold information would be considered churlish. Fortunately any suggestion of offensiveness in this string of personal questions posed, as often as not, within a few moments of first meeting, is entirely banished by that most endearing of all their national virtues—their unfailing and exquisite courtesy.

This virtue is all the more delightful for being unexpected ; for the Greeks are a formidably intelligent people and among us, in the days when we could still as a nation lay some claim to it, politeness was seldom found allied to intellectual eminence and to-day can hardly be described as con-spicuous among the logical and quick-witted French. In Greece, where both stupidity and rudeness are exceptional, they are usually discovered in firm alliance, and when a Greek is stupid he is very, very stupid indeed. In this connection it should perhaps be pointed out that the majority of rude Greeks seem always to gravitate towards the service of foreigners, a phenomenon which, while it undoubtedly testifies to the judgement and shrewdness of the average Greek employer, has an unfortunate effect on the national prestige.

In order to avoid subsequent disappointment it would be as well per-haps, at this point, to attempt some analysis of the nature of Greek intelli-gence and to define its limitations. Its principal characteristic is the speed with which it works which renders the Greek peculiarly formidable in all matters requiring rapid decision while leaving him more vulnerable when long-term issues are at stake. Thus time and again an apparently insoluble political crisis which seemed destined to plunge the whole country into chaos, has by some brilliant feat of *legerdemain* been solved at the eleventh hour ; but the deep underlying causes, political or economic, which have really occasioned the deadlock invariably remain unheeded and unresolved. In a humbler sphere it renders the Greek the best mechanic in the world when it comes to doing roadside repairs and the worst when it involves main-taining a car in good running order over a period of time. This being so, it is not surprising that he should have most profitably exploited this remarkable gift in the field of international commerce operating under the principles of *laissez-faire* economics. Here his quick wits have from time immemorial enabled him to out-distance almost all rivals, save perhaps the Armenian who, together with an equally rapid brain, combines the dogged persistence of the Scot with a more than Jewish willingness to sacrifice personal dignity in the interests of business.

The ability to amass wealth is of course no more equitably diffused among the Greeks themselves than among other nations ; on the contrary, to them that hath shall be given in Greece even more abundantly than elsewhere. Nevertheless, despite a fantastic disparity in incomes there is little or no resentment of great riches on the part of the have-nots, and all the desperate

efforts of the Communists to wage the class-war have as yet met with little or no success. This is to be explained both on psychological and economic grounds ; the moneymaking gift is generally held in such high esteem among them that its successful exploitation on the grandest scale is a matter for respect and emulation but not for envy. Economically, the fact that the majority of rich Greeks have from time immemorial amassed their fortunes by grinding the faces of other peoples' poor, exploiting the workers of Alexandria, Bombay, Manchester or Cardiff, but seldom their own, has successfully prevented the formation within Greece of an industrial proletariat. Thus the poorest peasant in the land, unless he happens to be in the employ of one of the big tobacco magnates, is unable in his extremely logical mind to trace any connection between his own miserable condition and the usually far from discreet display of riches in the millionaires' quarter of Kolonaki.[1]

Furthermore, this state of affairs is rendered difficult to upset by the almost total absence of class-distinctions. Save for the existence of a few old Phanariot families, Greece is a country almost completely without an

[1] The civil war of 1944-45 was a struggle for power, not a social revolution. Each side enjoyed the support of certain sections of both the haves and the have-nots. Thus certain wealthy industrialists afforded ELAS discreet but considerable assistance, while the Government could rely on the passive aid of the vast majority of the peasantry. On a cash basis ELAS was in a better position, and to this day the Communists remain the wealthiest political party in the country.

hereditary aristocracy ; and where few of the most prominent citizens are more than a couple of generations from the soil, many of the richest started life in the gutters of Smyrna or Constantinople, and where education is free and compulsory it is no simple matter to establish the social rule of privilege.

This is not altogether for want of trying. In Athens there exists a small and immensely wealthy set who strive desperately but with indifferent success to emulate the dubious achievements of the more sophisticated *café society* of other capitals. As it draws its strength almost entirely from the Alexandrian and Constantinopolitan millionaires, assisted by the representatives of certain Corfiot families who cling with a pathetic and, to the majority of Greeks, ridiculous obstinacy to their old Italian titles, it entirely lacks the traditions which give to certain Hydriot and Peloponnesian clans an established position in the social scheme. Unfortunately, owing to the skill with which they have managed to preserve their fortunes intact and the not altogether disinterested hospitality which they lavish on our countrymen, they have recently achieved a prominence out of all proportion to their importance. This is particularly disastrous, as in the eyes of the majority of Greeks this minute section of the community is almost as heavily tainted with collaborationism as certain elements on the extreme left. The completely unjustified result has been that the whole Greek upper class is now not infrequently condemned by the less responsible type of journalist and politician for the sins of a small clique whose pretensions they have never recognized and whose way of life they condemn.

For the Englishman it is not always easy to bear in mind the fact that even among those families whose prominence dates from the War of Independence, so brilliantly assimilative is the Greek genius, a perfect Western European polish is in most cases but recently acquired. For among no race do the educated classes approximate so closely in appearance and manners to our own, and time and again one realizes with a shock of surprise that the courteous Guardee with his old Etonian tie and neatly clipped moustache, whose English would only be remarkable at the bar in White's for its grammatical accuracy, is in fact at no more than two removes from the whiskered old Hydra magnate with his pistols and his fez, whose forbidding features look woodenly down from the naïve canvas above the Louis-Seize fireplace : and that that old ruffian lived in a society which, as far as social conditions are concerned, finds its closest historical parallel among the Highland lairds before the '45. If this fact were more closely borne in mind by English diplomats, advisers and commentators, much unnecessary disappointment would undoubtedly be avoided.

Fortunately for the national character the Greek's ability to make money is only equalled by his genius for spending it, and on inquiry it will usually be discovered that the millionaire whose name is a household word for opulence is halfway through his third fortune. This light-hearted expenditure particularly excites the contempt of the Jews, who tend to despise the Greeks as being far too talkative and woefully irresponsible. The Greeks for their part entertain no envy or hard feelings for the Jews (in no country did the Germans have less success with their anti-Semitic campaign, which aroused the openly expressed horror of the whole nation), knowing full well that they have in Greece to work a twenty-four hour day simply in order to keep their heads above water. Indeed, the Greeks are singularly free from that distressing and to-day almost universal complaint, xenophobia. It is, of course, true that few can be found who are willing freely to admit that Bulgarians are human beings, a large proportion holding the view that they cannot, strictly speaking, even be classed as mammals, but in general they regard foreigners with an amused and kindly tolerance, and in certain cases with a degree of admiration as considerable as they could reasonably be expected to manifest for any beings labouring under the appalling disadvantage of not being Greek.

The position which our own nation occupies in the affections of the Greeks is exalted but rather less secure than we are apt lightheartedly to imagine. On the credit side there remains Byron and 'all that', for so historically minded are even the most ignorant Greeks that to-day the English traveller can still cash cheques on the goodwill accumulated by our fellow-countrymen in the War of Independence. Against this must be set the fact that for a large and influential section of the population, the Asia Minor refugees, our national genius is typified not by the figure of the Pilgrim of Eternity dying for liberty in 1824 but by that of Mr. Lloyd George selling Greece up the river in 1922. Similarly in recent times our record in the late conflict enormously increased our prestige, which was further strengthened in the eyes of the vast majority by our intervention in 1944. But on the other hand, a small but excessively vocal minority will not soon forgive us the latter action, while our popularity with all parties has undoubtedly decreased as a result of our failure to support sufficiently vehemently Greek national claims at the Paris Peace Conference. Moreover, there remain certain sections of the population in whom the traditional anglophilism has always been more than offset by education or interest. Thus the intellectuals tended, before the late war, to look to Paris, and the professional and military classes to Berlin, rather than to London, while the considerable, though frequently exaggerated, influence of the Greek community in the United States is, at the time of writing, deeply tinged with anglophobia.

Nevertheless, it seems probable, unless we are more than usually maladroit in our foreign policy, that we shall continue to enjoy the benefits of an emotional most-favoured-nation clause for some time to come. This optimistic assertion is based not so much on the memory of past sufferings shared as on the undoubted existence of certain traits in the Greek national character which find their parallels in our own, and which are not markedly conspicuous among the other nations of Europe. For instance, the average Greek is naturally lazy, without any belief in all that nonsense about the dignity of labour or work for work's sake, and in Greece the English traveller is seldom afflicted by those vague feelings of guilt to which in France and Italy the depressing spectacle of the toiling peasantry too frequently gives  rise. Then both nations are afflicted by an extraordinary inability to comprehend the ways of other peoples, which in our case finds expression in a pained incredulity that foreigners can be so stupid as to doubt the purity of British motives and in the Greeks in a righteous and clamorous indignation at the base ingratitude of those who refuse to honour the enormous debts which all nations, at some time or other, either individually or collectively, are held to have contracted to the founders of Western civilization. Both of us in fact like to be liked and neither has yet lost, despite innumerable bitter disappointments, the ability to register pain and surprise when it is unmistakably demonstrated that we are not. More important, perhaps, than all else, we both cling pathetically to the old world idea that the integrity of the individual is something to be respected. To us, admittedly, the sturdy individualism of the Greek appears on occasion excessive and the fantastic ritualism attaching to the national conception of ' philotomo ' almost incomprehensible (though one cannot be long in Greece without gaining some familiarity with an idea for which the Oriental term ' face ' provides the best, although inadequate, rendering and which underlies the whole conduct of social life in every class of the community). Nevertheless, it is an ideal for which we and the Greeks, alone among all the United Nations, actually went to war, as opposed to being pushed in, and if it is again endangered we shall, I fancy, once more find ourselves on the same, perhaps unfashionable, side of the fence.

The Englishman should, however, always be on his guard against pushing these comforting analogies too far ; even qualities which both nations can with some assurance be said to have in common find, beyond a certain point, different modes of expression. Thus both English and Greeks can justly be considered kind-hearted, but with the latter kindness does not inevitably, any more than with the Austrians or the Irish, neutralize a strain of cruelty. For the Greeks can on occasion be ferociously cruel, and one has only to read the history of either the Peloponnesian or Independence Wars to realize that this deplorable failing is deep rooted and not, as many sincere and patriotic Greeks, appalled by the atrocities which rendered the Athens rising of 1944 one of the bloodiest and most ghastly chapters in the whole depressing history of civil strife, so desperately maintain, just a bad habit acquired in the subhuman conditions of the German occupation. In mitigation it should, however, be emphasized that it is almost always a hot-blooded, unpremeditated cruelty fulfilling itself in sudden massacres and passionate reprisals, not in Belsens or Buchenwalds. It is, therefore, very different in degree and kind from the savage insensibility of the Slav or the calculated sadism of the Teuton, and while no Greek would think twice about dropping an atomic bomb on Sofia, one would search in vain, I think, even among the most ferocious and vocal Bulgarophobes for those capable of initiating or carrying out a scientific and remorseless extermination of the whole race. In the final analysis it is a trait which history and ethnology teach us almost invariably goes hand in hand with exceptional physical courage at a certain stage in a people's development, and in this case is closely connected with the prevailing attitude to death. In Greece human life is held as cheap as human personality is held dear, a fact for which abundant evidence is provided not only by the high homicide rate but also by the everyday performance of chauffeurs and pilots. The spectacle of

38

death arouses no feelings of pious horror and sensitive foreigners are frequently distressed by the sight of the dear departed being conveyed to his last resting place insecurely strapped to the luggage grid of the family car, or, if he has been the victim of political enthusiasm, and it is thought that capital can be made of his martyrdom, hoisted aloft on a pole at the head of an indignant procession. Curiously enough, once the corpse is below ground this realistic attitude immediately gives way to one of irrational horror. No Greek will live near a graveyard or even go through one if he can possibly avoid it, and a highly intelligent acquaintance once confessed that the first months of his time at Oxford had been rendered miserable by the Great Western Railway's practice of halting all trains for a probationary period alongside the local cemetery before allowing them into the station.[1]

However, if among the Greeks kindness of heart does not invariably prove an altogether effective antidote to an indifference to death and suffering, it never, as is so often the case with us, degenerates into a vague ineffective benevolence, nor is its expression characterized by any trace of sentimentality. Of this unamiable and depressing failing which mars so much of our art and literature, wrecks our foreign policy, renders ridiculous our religion and is responsible in our social life for as much unhappiness as downright cruelty, the Greeks are entirely free.

Of all the qualities which the Greeks display in a marked degree this almost terrifying realism which successfully renders impossible the harbouring of any illusions, sentimental or otherwise, and which characterizes their personal relationships, their art and their conduct of business, is perhaps their most distinctive attribute ; and one which, in a punch-drunk world muzzy with ideologies and doped with false ideals, may well prove of the greatest value both to themselves and the rest of us. How far the successful cultivation of this virtue is due to the climate must be determined by those who have made a study of the effect of environment on character, but certainly it is difficult even for those born and bred in the damp Celtic twilight of the West or the green Wagnerian gloom of the North to retain their romantic illusions in the fabulous clarity of this extraordinary atmosphere. Here supernatural sanction for political ambitions is not easily assumed, and unaided goodwill no longer appears as an adequate remedy for the world's ills ; prosperity is not just around these angular and all-too-

---

[1] No single action on the part of British troops in Greece caused such general resentment as the establishment of the British Military cemetery in the heart of the residential district of Phaleron. Regarded by all as the height of bad taste, the neighbouring landlords were particularly furious as the value of their property was thus reduced to next-to-nothing overnight.

well-defined corners, and the doctrine of original sin gains a new validity. The foreigner soon discovers that the injunction inscribed on the Temple of Apollo at Delphi is less easily disregarded in the land of Apollo's birth, and that personal motives cannot so casually be concealed beneath a top-dressing of disinterest. Fear does not convincingly masquerade as prudence nor can pride get by beneath the trappings of justifiable self-respect. And while it is hard to deceive oneself into elevating lust to the rank of love it is impossible to write off love as lust.

Thus in the final event the figures remain inseparable from the landscape and must be considered not through a telescope but with the naked eye. The spectator himself then becomes a figure in the foreground, as subject to the prophylactic quality of the air as those he regards, and, however romantic his approach, the scene of which he is now a part remains firmly classical. No matter how he cherishes them, his romantic illusions wither and die ; and none is likely to perish quicker or respond less readily to his efforts at preservation than any which he may have acquired about the Greeks.

However, I am at least quit of Athens, with its stupid classic Acropolis and smashed pillars.

BERNARD SHAW TO ELLEN TERRY

At Constantinople I visited the Mosques, plains, and grandees of that place, which, in my opinion, cannot be compared with Athens and its neighbourhood ; indeed I know of no Turkish scenery to equal this, which would be civilized and Celtic enough with a little alteration in situation and inhabitants.

LORD BYRON

FEW cities of the western world are so unrewarding to those with a highly developed sense of the past as Athens. The principal monuments of antiquity, isolated in space and time, are linked to the present by no thread of continuous tradition and, with one exception, have long since ceased to fulfil any functional purpose. Elsewhere, in Rome, Florence or even London, any escape from history is blocked at every street corner by the existence of palaces, churches, counting-houses, all serving, however inadequately, the purposes for which they were originally built ; in Athens the Olympeion or the Temple of the Winds have far, far less connection with the life going on around them than has Stonehenge with the unchanging, agricultural rhythm of the Wiltshire downs. This is not to say that these tremendous relics of a vanished age have lost all meaning, but simply to point out that a sense of history is better nourished by continuity than by association. It is, indeed, possible that the heart of many a sixth-form master or rural dean, fresh from the stimulating atmosphere of an Hellenic cruise, has beat the faster when gazing on the Ilissos for the reflection that here Socrates went paddling, but in those of us of less-specialized powers of imagination the sight of this stone-embanked, rubbish-blocked little gully is unlikely to awaken any very powerful emotion.

Fortunately for my purpose, which is to write of Athens as it is rather

41

than as it was, the classical remains are few in number, conveniently segregated, and have been exhaustively described by those highly competent to do so. The principal of them has also inspired almost every travelled European writer of the last two centuries to favour us with a description of the sentiments which the first sight of it aroused in his breast, of which Chateaubriand's is perhaps the most demonstrative, Arnold Bennett's certainly the most banal; nevertheless, even in writing of modern Athens one cannot possibly ignore the Acropolis, for it dominates every prospect of the city and, on occasion, reverts to its original function and controls its life.

This function, which tends to become obscured by the beauty and interest of the temples, was in the first instance defensive, and of all the cities of Europe which I have seen the Acropolis finds its closest visual parallel in Edinburgh, where the Castle rock plays just such a similar rôle in the local history and landscape. This point is perhaps one which it is not difficult in normal times to overlook, but the circumstances in which I myself first climbed this celebrated crag were such as to render it inescapable.

For more than a week a handful of British paratroops had held the summit against repeated attacks and only the day before had they been able, as the result of the arrival of reinforcements, to advance their perimeter to the edge of the Agora. Above us the skies were those one finds more frequently in the Derbyshire landscapes of Mr. Piper than in the posters extolling the beauties of the eastern Mediterranean; below, the whole overgrown city sprawled across the plain of Attica to the foothills of Parnes and Penteli. The usual deafening hubbub of Athenian life—the clanging of trams, the shrieks of the street-vendors, the crowing of backyard fowls—which in normal times is here audible as though detached from its background and existing, as it were, in a void, was stilled and the prevailing quietness was emphasized rather than broken by the continuous machine-gun fire in the streets immediately below, the detonations from the direction of Patissia (where the proletariat were blowing up houses to form street barricades) and that peculiar sound, half-whistle, half-rending calico, which shells make as they pass immediately overhead. Somewhere beyond Ommonia Square a group of buildings was on fire, probably a petrol dump, as the tall column of smoke was oily black against the snow of the distant mountains ; behind the Theseon mortar shells fell with monotonous regularity on a corner house by the tram-stop, sending up yellowish-white clouds that hung in the air, round and compact, for a full five minutes before dispersing. On the Acropolis itself a group of trigger-happy gendarmerie lounged with an assumed nonchalance by the lower entrance ; alongside the Themistoclean wall a pile of cartridge cases indicated where until very recently a machine-gun had been emplaced ; in the empty museum a few grubby plaster casts surveyed an accumulation of military debris. Over all towered the Parthenon, its clear unequivocal statement in no way blurred by the barricades hastily erected from fragments of its pillars and caissons, its own internal rhythm uninterrupted by mortar fire or rockets.

For once the eternal underlying significance of the Acropolis was immediately apparent, unmasked either by troops of tourists and their attendant guides, touts and post-card sellers, or, as it must have been from the fourth century onward, by a Wembley-like accumulation of statues and temples, memorials and votive offerings, and all the gaudy monuments to the personal grandeur of visiting firemen from Rome and Asia Minor. So must it have appeared to the Greeks returned after Salamis, and the very reasons which to-day had led General Scobie to maintain its garrison were those that had seemed cogent to generations of Minyans and Achaeans and Dorians, of Romans and Franks and Catalans, of Venetians and Turks and Germans. Above all the Acropolis is a symbol of power.

It is, I fancy, the acceptance and expression of this primary fact which renders the Propylaea so impressive.

Here, quite apart from the exceptionally difficult nature of the site, the architects were faced with a far from simple task ; they were to provide a fitting entrance for an enclosure which was to be at one and the same time a shrine and a fortress. Maybe the use of both the Doric and Ionic orders represents a conscious attempt to symbolize the dual nature of their task. At all events their triumph was complete ; the Propylaea remains the most impressive entrance with which any man-made structure has ever been provided. Compared to this the great Gothic porches with their concentric rings of saints and their sculptured tympana appear confused, the rusticated heraldry-laden gateways of the High Renaissance bombastic. But not only is the Propylaea perfect in itself, but in addition it provides the ideal frame through which to catch one's first sight of the Parthenon. And this is no trifling matter but one that is worthy of some careful consideration.

In the Romantic Age, when the rule of taste was as yet unchallenged, conscientious travellers went to immense pains to insure that the vista or monument to which they were making pilgrimage should burst upon their properly conditioned gaze at precisely the right angle, in exactly the correct light. A first visit to a really important sight—the Colosseum, the Rhine Falls or Lincoln Cathedral—required a previous preparation and a carefully worked out plan of approach, and in time certain prospects became obligatory. Thus Rome must be surveyed from the Pinzio, Oxford from Headington Hill, Florence from Fiesole. To-day we have long since abandoned this ' première communion ' attitude to sight-seeing much, I fancy, to our impoverishment, for if a thing is worth seeing it is worth seeing well, and one's whole attitude towards, and appreciation of, any monument such as the Parthenon can be as successfully warped and affected by an unfortunate first encounter as can one's sex-life, or so we are credibly informed by the psychologists, by a fortuitous sight of the housemaid undressing gained at an unduly impressionable age. In the case of the Parthenon such a disaster is all too easily sustained. Thanks to General Metaxas, whose errors of policy have frequently been condemned with a warmth that would more appropriately have been reserved for his errors of taste, the Acropolis is now formally approached by a neatly macadamised by-pass bordered with newly planted groves of pine and fir. The atmosphere thus happily created is nostalgically Bournemouth and it is with genuine surprise that, having completed the ascent, the English visitor finds himself faced, not with Branksome Chine, but the Propylaea.

The tourist of sensibility should be in no hurry to gain his first view of the Acropolis at close quarters, for more perhaps than any other architec-

44

tural achievement of a similar order this gains from being seen frequently
at a distance. As to which distant prospect is the finest everyone will have
his own opinion : I myself favour the view gained from the back road to
Vougliameni whence the Parthenon, unexpectedly small, suddenly, but as
it were casually, rises above the intervening hills, isolated and remote against
the great wall of Parnes with all Athens and its sprawling suburbs lost
behind the folds of Hymettus. This is an early morning approach ; later
in the day few prospects can compare with that to be obtained on the descent
from Kaisariani with the great rock floating above the heat-hazed town, its
temples and colonnades lit from behind and silhouetted against a burnished
sea. In the evening there are just two minutes, if the sky is clear and the
traditional transformation scene is going according to plan, when the last
rays of the sun having already abandoned the town itself still rest on the
Acropolis, and Hymettus forms a rose-red backdrop, richer and more daring
in effect than anything conceived by Bakst. This is the hour when Socrates
is said to have drained the hemlock. However, to witness the spectacle
at its best one must see it from the road coming down from Daphni and this
involves one sooner or later in a controversy which still wrecks the peace
of senior common-rooms and shatters the harmony (never, be it admitted,
very profound) that occasionally prevails in schools of archaeology. For
here we are brought face to face with the reconstructed north colonnade
of the Parthenon, a feat of archaeological rehabilitation to which many
have never become reconciled. Lacking personal knowledge of its former
condition it is hard to offer an opinion, but at the risk of appearing a
sentimental old ruin-fancier one may perhaps express the hope that the
process will not be carried any further as it can only logically end in total
reconstruction. Before we know where we are the whole Acropolis, the
gigantic statue of Athena and all, will once more be gleaming, if not in
purple, then in terracotta, and gold which might quite possibly lead us to
revise some of our opinions about fifth-century taste. And in an atomic
age our remaining illusions are best hugged tight.

However, the traveller, disregarding these specialized disputes and
having absorbed the prospect from one or other, or better still from all three,
of these viewpoints, should be at last prepared for his visit and must now
select his route with exceptional caution. Avoiding, as though it were a
plague-pit, the official approach, he should advance from exactly the
opposite, that is to say the northern, direction. In so doing he will climb
up through the old streets of the Plaka, and emerge alongside a small
Byzantine chapel immediately beneath the Themistoclean wall which at
this point, so acute is the angle of vision, completely masks the buildings

on the summit. Turning to the right a path follows the contour of the rock, emerging slightly to the north of the Propylaea and opposite Mars Hill where St. Paul, and in recent years several historically minded Anglican Army Chaplains, so eloquently preached. Turning his back sharply on the pine-clad vista of the new by-pass, at this one point unavoidable, he should at once mount the steps of the Propylaea and immediately repair to the Parthenon, firmly resisting all temptation to turn aside to any of the other temples to right or left.

For not only does the Parthenon claim first attention in its right but it also provides a yardstick whereby to form some critical estimate of the Erechtheion and temple of Nike Apteros, and to maintain an attitude of uncritical admiration before the first of these buildings is to sidestep one of the most puzzling questions that arises in the whole history of Greek architecture. How could the Greeks with their clear, logical outlook and their unshakably humanistic standards of taste ever have tolerated, let alone evolved, the caryatid ? To them, more than to any other people it would, one would have thought, have been obvious that to employ a naturalistic three-dimensional rendering of the human form as an architectural unit was to invite disaster. When the Baroque architect of the seventeenth century, whose aims were anyhow completely different, flanked a doorway with a pair of groaning Atlases he had an expressionist justification ; the over-life-size figures with exaggeratedly bulging muscles do at least empha-size, as they were intended to do, the weight and mass of the architrave or balcony which they supposedly support. But here these elegant flower-maidens simper as unconcernedly as if they had never been called upon to balance two and a half tons of Pentelic marble on their pretty little heads.

The remaining buildings on the Acropolis are likely neither to produce so overwhelming an effect as the Parthenon and the Propylaea nor to pose such awkward questions of taste as the Erechtheion. The little temple of Nike Apteros, re-erected by French archaeologists at the beginning of the last century on its original site which had been used by the Turks for a mortar battery, seldom fails to evoke that enthusiasm which British art-lovers reserve for the very small. Supremely elegant and in perfect taste, there nevertheless clings to it, due perhaps in part to its elevated position, a faint air of Buzzards. Immediately below the rock itself lie the two theatres of Herodes Atticus and Dionysus. The former, built by that celebrated Philhellene Roman millionaire, the Lord Nuffield of the first century, whose gilt-edged spoor we shall come across all over Greece, is a fine dramatic structure that still serves a useful purpose. Acoustically nearly perfect, it provides during the summer months a Piranesi-like setting for the concerts of the admirable, but usually indifferently conducted, Athens State Orchestra. Architecturally, however, it is not much regarded by the *cognoscenti*. Incidentally it is interesting to note how persons who at home will think nothing of dragging one for a six-mile walk across the downs in pouring rain in order to inspect some third-rate fragment of poorly preserved provincial Roman pavement, in Greece will not bother to cross the road to glance at anything, however fine, later than the third-century B.C.

For those with that highly specialized taste for Greek theatres well developed the theatre of Dionysus is scarcely of less interest than Epidauros itself, but the attention of the ordinary visitor is likely to be chiefly focused on the front row of the stalls, on each seat of which is engraved the style and titles of the ecclesiastical dignitary for whom it was reserved. The auditorium in its present form only dates, however, from the third century, so that any Agate-like musing on the vanished glories of Aeschylean first-nights would be misplaced. The stage itself is later still and is chiefly remarkable for a supporting figure of a Triton in whose hirsute features a former generation of Conservative tourists were gratified to detect a striking likeness to the late Marquess of Salisbury.

The remaining classical antiquities of Athens are almost all situated to the north of the Acropolis. Of these the best known is the so-called Theseion, which, although supremely uninteresting in itself, poses a question which could we but answer it satisfactorily might well provide a firm and lasting basis for a rational system of aesthetics. Why should this temple, the best

47

preserved of its date in the world, built within a few years of the Parthenon and embodying all the same principles, remain by comparison so devastatingly boring? True, it lacks the advantages of a noble site, but nevertheless there exists no single fault of proportion or design on which to put a finger. And yet, however receptive one's mood, it produces less effect than many a Doric corn-exchange in an English provincial town.

The Temple of the Winds and the Choragic monument present no such difficulties. The former, to which the elements it symbolizes have been markedly unkind, must, I fancy, to any visitor unbiased by antiquarian obsessions compare unfavourably with James Wyatt's version of the same theme in the observatory at Oxford. The latter, the interior of which in the days when it was embodied in the structure of a Franciscan convent served Lord Byron for a study, is of considerable interest for the influence which, thanks to the careful engraving of 'Athenian Stewart', it exercised on the architecture and decoration of late Georgian and Regency England. Indeed, so popular did this early example of the Corinthian order prove, so readily adaptable its form, that to-day when one sees it first one is almost surprised not to find its summit surmounted by a gigantic ormolu candelabra tastefully draped with Waterford glass pendants.

There remain the Kerameikos and the Agora. Of these the cemetery will be found to be of considerable interest to those, among whom I am proud occasionally to number myself, who enjoy tracing out the lines of long-vanished gates and fortifications. To the amateur of burial-grounds it is liable to prove a disappointment as the finer memorials have all been removed to the safety of the museum. The market-place, on the other hand, it is difficult to contemplate calmly when one realizes that in order to lay bare this dreary bomb-site industrious and heavily subsidized American archaeologists laboured long years pulling down the greater part of the old Turkish quarter, the few remnants of which that still stand are yet sufficient to indicate the extent and nature of the loss. When one gazes on this vast expanse of antiquarian rubble and reflects on what it has displaced, one gains a new respect for the sound judgment of the great Duke of Wellington, who, on being informed that a Roman pavement had been laid bare on one of his estates, at once gave orders that it was to be covered up again without delay. The only find of any general interest which has so far emerged from all this destructive quarrying is an inscribed tablet, of the sort on which voters were accustomed to write the name of their candidate for impeachment, which is thought to provide direct confirmation of a well-known anecdote of Plutarch.

Aristides, surnamed the Just, was, according to this author, walking in the Agora on the eve of his proscription when he encountered a worthy artisan who was obviously having some difficulty in spelling the name he was putting down on his voting tablet. The renowned legislator could not resist asking the fellow whose name it was which he found it so hard to spell, and was promptly told 'Aristides'. On inquiring why he had selected this respected figure to be proscribed he received the eminently reasonable reply that it was because the writer was sick and tired of hearing him called 'the Just'. Whereupon the magnanimous old busybody insisted on writing the name down himself. When, therefore, the industrious Americans turned up a tablet with "Aristides" misspelt and crossed out at the top and rewritten in another hand at the bottom, the excitement was intense and it can, I think, safely be said that no archaeological discovery in recent years has given more pleasure to trivial minds.

It is only fair to point out that the Americans enjoy no monopoly in this species of learned vandalism and that at Delphi a far more difficult feat of ruination has been achieved by those paragons of taste, the French. The truth of the matter is that the average archaeologist of any nationality being almost invariably totally deficient in visual sense is about as safe a person to have around a well-conducted city as a bomber-pilot or a by-pass builder.[1]

There remains the temple of Olympian Zeus, the alpha and omega of Athenian antiquities of the classical period. Begun under the Pisistrati on what was then the Agora the site was abandoned after the fall of the tyrants and it was not until Hellenistic times that work was resumed on this gigantic project. It was finally completed by the Emperor Hadrian, whose arch with its insufferably complacent inscription still stands a little to the west, when its scale and magnificence caused it to be generally regarded throughout the Empire as an eighth wonder of the world and among contemporaries who have left some record of their astonishment and admiration was the celebrated architectural publicist Vitruvius. To-day it has suffered not a little in the popular estimation, along with all other monuments of its period, from the prevailing anti-Roman snobbery, and admittedly it must when complete have been of an almost overwhelming vulgarity. Nevertheless, in their present condition the remaining group of columns (on one of which during the Middle Ages a celebrated stylite had his perch) make an impression which even if it owes something to Pannini, is not easily effaced. And while it is chiefly the enormous scale which compels admira-

---

[1] An honourable exception to this general rule was the late Humphrey Payne, whose greatest triumphs as an archaeologist depended to a very large extent on his possession of the one faculty for the lack of which the majority of his fellows are justly notorious.

tion it is worth pointing out that the proportions are excellent and the carving of the capitals betrays no faltering or sign of decadence.

The temple of Olympian Zeus was the last great Athenian building to be erected in classical times. After its completion the city gradually lapsed into a condition with which we to-day seem likely to become all too familiar. Bureaucrats and taxes increased, trade declined and initiative withered away, and while to a casual observer the streets and market-places would doubtless have seemed as animated as ever, Athens in fact was living on capital and the tourist traffic. Statues and trophies were still erected on the Acropolis and a cosmopolitan throng of students still crowded into the lecture rooms of the University; but everywhere the shadows were lengthening. And this decline, occasionally arrested for a brief space by some sporadic recrudescence of national spirit, frequently accelerated by barbarian inroads, continued for the space of a millennium.

It should not, however, be assumed that these centuries were devoid either of incident or interest, simply that they have left scant traces in the Athens of to-day. The transfer of the capital of the Empire from Rome to Byzantium and the consequent renaissance of the Greek power in the Eastern Mediterranean did not produce that revivifying effect on the ancient Greek capital that might have been expected, for its importance was almost immediately eclipsed by its old rival Thebes and the comparatively new city of Thessaloniki. Christianity succeeded paganism as the official religion of the Empire and in the sixth century the philosophical schools which had until then somehow managed to maintain a precarious existence were finally closed by an edict of the Emperor Justinian. By way of compensation the Parthenon had been converted to the use of the new religion and its ancient fame combined with the lavishness of the fittings with which the great Bulgar-slaying Emperor later provided it (including a golden dove that fluttered above the high altar in perpetual motion and a miraculous lamp in which the oil was never exhausted) gained it a measure of respect in the Orthodox world second only to that accorded to the church of the Divine Wisdom in the capital. Of all these ecclesiastical glories the only trace which remains to-day is a fragment of fresco on the west wall of the cella.

However, the Athenian hierarchy did not long rest content merely with the adaptation of pagan temples to the Christian rite (the Theseion was now the church of St. George) but soon set about the erection of new shrines. Of these, three dating from the earlier period of Byzantine rule survive in something approximating to the original condition—the Kapnikarea, the church of the two Theodores and the old Metropolis. These three little buildings all exhibit much the same architectural features and exercise a similar charm. With slight differences they are all fairly straightforward examples of that cross-in-square plan which by this date had become almost obligatory on the Greek mainland. In the Kapnikarea, the oldest of the three traditionally founded by the Empress Eudoxia, an Athenian by birth, in the ninth century (though almost certainly rebuilt in the tenth), it is probable that the original plan was cruciform and that the angle chapels are a later addition, while in the Two Theodores, in which incidentally the dome rests directly on the crosswalls instead of the more usual support of four pillars or two pillars and two piers, the original plan has been somewhat obscured by the addition of a later narthex and parecclesion. All three, however, are crowned by typical examples of the Athenian form of cupola with a high eaveless dome resting directly on the arches of an octagonal drum.[1]

While the whole trio are of great beauty and interest it is undoubtedly the old Metropolis which best repays detailed examination. Built entirely of Pentelic marble which has weathered to a pale reddish ochre, it holds its own in the most extraordinary and praiseworthy fashion alongside the cliff-like walls of that monstrous masterpiece of Byzantine Revival, the New Metropolis, with which it shares the Cathedral Square. At first sight one is prompted to deplore the all-too-close proximity of this nineteenth-century horror, but familiarity encourages the belief that the excellent proportions and jewel-like decoration (for once, I think, the adjective is justified) in fact gain by the contrast. Certainly on a night of full moon, when the poverty-stricken mouldings of the larger building are all flattened away while the deeply-cut details of its diminutive rival hold the shadows like printer's ink, the effect, if theatrical, is immensely impressive. It is, indeed, these details which give to the whole building what is, perhaps, from the architectural point of view, its chief interest. On all four sides the external walls are enlivened by the introduction of fragments of classical frieze, sculptured panels of Eastern origin, Hellenistic votive tablets and every possible variety of small-scale relief likely to turn up on an Athenian scrap-heap. Formerly, when the Byzantine achievement was obscured by a fog of classical and Gothic prejudice, the presence of these alien elements embodied in a later structure was taken to indicate the prevailing poverty and ignorance of the period, and even to-day one may occasionally hear hoots of donnish laughter as some cultured tourist delightedly discovers a

[1] As with most Byzantine antiquities, it is almost impossible for the layman to gain any clear idea of the age of these buildings as all the authorities are entirely and vindictively contradictory. When in doubt stick to Millet.

classical inscription upsidedown. In fact, this system of decoration, so far from being haphazard, represents one of the very few examples of that artistic development that came to be known during the 'thirties as ' collage ' manifesting itself in architecture. The skilful disposal of the various fragments should, one would have thought, have made it obvious that the architect's intention was as considered as that of Picasso or Braque when they enlivened their canvases with cuttings from the newspaper and samples of graining culled from builders' pattern-books.

Beside these three churches there are others here and there in Athens dating from the same epoch but in every case so changed in character by later alterations and additions as to exhibit little of interest to the present-day visitor. Chief among them is the Russian church in Odos Philhellenou, a complete but careful reconstruction of the old church of the Panaghia Lycodemou which was erected on the site of the Roman baths. Alone among Athenian churches of this period, its plan is not the usual cross-in-square but approximates rather to that of Daphni and Hosios Loukas. However, its present occupants, with typical Slavonic caution, seem always to keep it tightly shut and despite several attempts I personally never succeeded in getting behind this ecclesiastical Iron Curtain.

Of the state of Athens on the eve of the Latin Conquest a vivid picture has been preserved for us by the cultured and public-spirited metropolitan Akominatos. According to this the scene which presented itself to the earliest recorded English tourist, a certain John of Basingstoke, Archdeacon of Leicester, must have been fantastic in the extreme. Already that process of shrinkage which was by the beginning of the nineteenth century to have reduced the city to a huddle of cottages clinging to the north slopes of the Acropolis, was well under way. Although at this date all the principal monuments of antiquity were still intact, everywhere the old villas and palaces were falling into ruin. On all sides long perspectives of pillared streets, grass-grown and deserted, stretched away into the countryside, as empty of life and full of menace as the colonnades in a painting by Chirico. Thanks to the incompetence of the central administration and the rapacity of its local representatives, the reduced population of these echoing ruins existed in the most miserable condition of want and misery, and on occasion, we are told, such was the general poverty that only a handful of the wealthiest inhabitants could afford bread. In these circumstances it is not surprising that after the fall of Constantinople the Franks acquired the province almost without effort.

Few episodes in European history are less familiar than the Frankish dominion in Greece and none more romantic. Here, beneath a semitropical sun and against the most renowned of classical backgrounds, the familiar institutions of medieval life in Northern Europe—feudalism, heraldry, jousting, the Courts of Love—all flourished with the luxuriance of those English cabbage roses that to-day cover many a Peloponnesian cottage. Indeed, seen in this exotic setting, the colours appear brighter, the strongholds more awful, the heroes more chivalrous, the tyrants more bloody ; everything is, as it were, slightly larger than life. The very names of these Dukes and Despots, Counts and Triarchs—Othon de la Roche, Erich von Katzenellenbogen, Oberto di Biandrate, Thomas de Stromoncourt and the rest—carry with them faint echoes of the Castle of Otranto. And it may well be that that process that is so readily observable at work to-day, whereby the personality of the foreigner, particularly one from northern Europe, is intensified, his idiosyncrasies rendered more marked, his natural reticence diminished under the influence of this extraordinary climate, was already operating at that remote period.

However, despite the fact that this highly developed culture was maintained for close on two hundred and fifty years, virtually no trace of it is to-day visible in Athens. Both the French Dukes and the Catalan adventurers customarily directed the affairs of the Duchy from Thebes, where they had their principal residence, and it was only the last dynasty, that of the Florentine banking-house of Acciajuoli, who ruled their reduced dominions directly from the ancient capital. It was they who restored the defences of the Acropolis and converted the Propylaea into a castle, erecting on the bastion opposite to that supporting the shrine of Nike Apteros, a tower eighty-five feet high which stood until 1875 and figures prominently in all the engravings of the early nineteenth century.

If the Frankish rulers of Athens are to-day unrepresented by a single monument, the Turks who succeeded them and maintained their sway for almost four hundred years, during which they accomplished far more in the way of destruction, produced little that now bears witness to their long sojourn. A couple of mosques, one of them the work of a Greek architect, a doorway hard by the Tower of the Winds bearing a carved Kufic inscription, a few place-names, and that is all. Of all nations the least creative, for ever borrowing and never producing, the Turks are represented in the long roll of Athenian monuments by gaps rather than additions ; innumerable masterpieces vanished beneath their tender care, and thanks to their lighthearted disposal of ammunition dumps combined with an unexpected accuracy of aim on the part of a Hanoverian gunner in the Venetian service, the Parthenon was, in the late seventeenth century, reduced to a ruin. There do exist, it is true, even in Athens a few so-called ' Turkish houses ', but these, like the 'Turkish bridges' one finds all over Greece, have, as one's Greek friends are tireless in pointing out, no connection with the Turks save that they were built during the period of their rule.

In 1829 a large portion of the Greek mainland was finally declared independent of the Sublime Porte, but some years had yet to elapse before the capital of the new kingdom was transferred from Nauplia to Athens. When at length this move was made the authorities found themselves possessed of a capital city rich beyond any in the world in historic associations but as completely devoid of all the necessary amenities of a metropolis as any bog village in Ireland. The Athens which Stewart and Revett drew and in which Byron resided, smaller in population and extent than the average English market town, was practically confined to the northern slopes of the Acropolis, and the Temple of Zeus, Mount Lycabettus, the site of Ommonia Square were all miles out in the country. The history of the next hundred years affords us one of the most extraordinary and enlightening examples of urban development in the whole dismal panorama of nineteenth-century expansion.

The peculiar atmosphere that prevailed throughout his capital at the time of King Otho's arrival in Greece may still be sampled in the half-dozen streets lying above and slightly to the east of the Agora which have as yet escaped the maw of transatlantic archaeologists. Here small houses, the upper stories, if any, of wood, and minute Byzantine churches are crowded together on widely different levels and divided by narrow alleys that unexpectedly turn into dilapidated stairways round every corner. Thanks to the innumerable small courts and gardens planted with cypresses and vines, the completely unselfconscious and successful use of colour-wash and the Greek passion for 'petrol-can gardening', the total effect is charming, picturesque and unsanitary. (It should in all justice be pointed out in this last connection that, despite a total absence of plumbing, this neighbourhood, even in the heat of an Athenian summer, is considerably less offensive than the old quarter of St. Ives, let alone its Mediterranean counterparts.) However, it was not to be expected that the westernized Corfiotes, the magnates of Hydra nor the new King's innumerable Bavarian hangers-on who now flocked to the capital would tolerate the primitive conditions prevailing in this humble residential area, and the first of a long series of building drives was soon under way. Of the few remaining houses erected at this early date the best surviving example is probably No. 2 Odos Palaeologou Venizelou, which Athenian cab-drivers seldom pass without informing one is the oldest house in Athens, the sole piece of historical information which any of them have been known to acquire, and incorrect

at that. A two-storeyed stone-built house skilfully filling an awkward site with frontages on three streets, it obtains its effect solely by the excellence of its proportions and a very restrained use of classical detail. By way of contrast, immediately opposite the end of this street there stands an admirable example of the type of house which No. 2 displaced, with ramshackle wooden balconies and Turkish style sash-windows that possesses, incidentally, an additional interest for the English passer-by as it is the house which sheltered our unfortunate Queen Caroline during the ill-starred visit she paid to Athens in the company of the notorious Bergami (q.v. p. 56).

Provincial simplicity was not, however, destined to be the keynote of the new Athens, for King Otho came fresh to his capital from the rarefied aesthetic atmosphere prevailing at the court of his Philhellene father. King Ludwig I of Bavaria was an aesthete and a romantic, and if his architectural fantasies were less spectacular than those erected by his successor and namesake fifty years later, it is only due to the fact that the neo-classical dream-world of his preference provided less scope for the more theatrical flights of royal fancy than the Wagnerian Middle Ages. Under this monarch's enthusiastic direction the Munich in which his son had been born and bred was being rapidly transformed from a typical south German town of the Biedermeyer period into that extraordinary hotch-potch of Greek Revival and Florentine Renaissance which survived until the coming of the R.A.F. To such a monarch the establishment of his family on the

throne of Greece presented itself almost exclusively as a Heaven-sent opportunity for a re-creation (if possible on more up-to-date and correct lines)
of the vanished glories of the age of Pericles, and in order that it might in
no degree be missed or bungled, the best obtainable architectural advice
was made constantly available to the scarcely less-enthusiastic Otho.   Given
the time and place, it was not perhaps surprising that this advice should
have been unmistakably coloured by the theories and practice of Herr
Schinkel, the greatest of the German neo-classicists whose undoubted genius
was, perhaps, scenic rather than architectural and who is best remembered
to-day for his magnificent settings for *Die Zauberflöte* piously preserved, at
least until 1939, and on occasion used, by the Berlin Opera.   The most
ambitious and among the earliest of King Otho's proposed improvements
was a scheme of this master which, perhaps fortunately, the chronically
embarrassed state of the Greek exchequer prevented from being realized
save on paper.   This was nothing less than the restoration and conversion
of the remaining buildings on the Acropolis to form a palace worthy of the
dignity of the Wittelsbach monarchy.   Some of Schinkel's elevations for
this project have survived and undoubtedly constitute one of the most
extraordinary documents in the whole history of the Picturesque.   After
studying them one finds oneself at a complete loss to decide which is the
more remarkable—the skill with which the architect has, from a purely
scenic point of view, utilized the available material or the sublime self-
confidence which allowed him ever to embark on such an enterprise.

The existing royal palace (the ' old palace ') with which the ambitious
monarch had finally to rest content, is a fair example of the official style as it
flourished in the early years of the century.   Academic and almost self-
consciously restrained, it avoids vulgarity at the price of a certain dullness ;
admittedly there clings to it an inescapable air of the barracks, but it is well
sited and it is difficult to-day to understand the reasons which prompted the
invariable abuse heaped on it in the older guide-books.   The architect was
Von Gartner,[1] one of the busiest of the German imports who established
themselves firmly in Athens where half the nineteenth-century public
buildings comprise a monument to their laborious talent.

It is not, however, the showpieces of the period that are likely to hold

[1] Von Gartner was *hofarchitekt* to King Ludwig until their close friendship was clouded
by a difference of opinion as to the frescoes decorating the arcades of the Hofgarten in
Munich.   His masterpieces in his native town include the Ludwigskirche, the Wittelsbach
palace, and that strange exotic the ' Feldherrnhalle'.   After studying for a time in Paris
under Percier and Fontaine he spent a year in London with his compatriot Hullmandel,
the lithographer who was responsible for the productions of Shotter Boys, Cattermole,
and other topographical artists.

57

House in Plaka

the attention of the modern visitor, but rather the less pretentious examples of domestic architecture built in that style which has come to be known as Othonian and which provides the closest parallel to contemporary domestic

architecture in England to be found anywhere on the Continent. Time and again in Athens one is confronted with a row of stuccoed façades in which monotony has been avoided by a pediment above a central window, a wrought-iron balcony at first-floor level, a little rustication at the basement,

58

a well-placed pair of pilasters or a welcome strip of balustrading, and for a moment the sky darkens, the palms and pepper-trees are transformed into Wellingtonias and monkey-puzzles and one is back in Cheltenham or Maida Vale. This is not, I think, the outcome of a purely personal nostalgia, for there exists many an Athenian house of this epoch which, were the French windows replaced by sash and the inevitable row of palmettes removed from the eaves, anyone less knowledgeable than Mr. Summerson could easily attribute to Cubitt or Basevi. This Othonian style held its ground throughout the century, although as time wore on the freshness and spontaneity were dimmed and the late examples tend to suffer from just that heaviness and monotony which renders Bayswater so depressing ; nevertheless, one not infrequently comes across a small house here and there in Athens exhibiting all the good qualities of the early period which, on inquiry, proves to be not more than twenty years old.

One of the reasons for the remarkable longevity of Othonian, which flourished long after the monarch who lent it his name had returned an exile to his native Bavaria (there to astonish peasantry and tourists alike by his frequent appearances in the *gemütliche* countryside around the Starnberger See clad in all the Byronic panoply of an Evzone), must be attributed to the almost total absence, until the tentative appearance of Art Nouveau, of any serious rival. The Athenian architect, more fortunate if less adventurous than his English colleague, was never faced with the difficulty of deciding between the rival claims of Pont-Street Dutch, Norman Shaw Queen Anne or Bedford Park Cottages styles ; his clients, staunchly nationalist, were perfectly content with a house that showed the requisite number of palmettes and acknowledged, even if it did not always observe, the classical orders. Above all, the relaxing breeze of the Gothic Revival never blew across these unwelcoming plains (however, when one observes what the Byzantine Revivalists could do, unaided by the Camden Society and unencouraged by any native Ruskin, one's feeling of relief is qualified). Nevertheless, central Athens is not quite innocent of pointed arches, and the heart of the British traveller is lifted up on emerging from the Zappeion gardens into Odos Amalias by a splendid view of the east end, uncompromisingly E.E., of the English Church.

The whole subject of English places of worship abroad is one that it is to be hoped, as soon as foreign travel is once more permitted, will at long last find its qualified historian. No more striking testimony to the self-confidence and unshakable convictions of the Victorian Age exists than that provided throughout the Continent of Europe by these innumerable examples of Anglo-Saxon mediaevalism standing where they ought not :

59

nothing demonstrates more forcibly the woolliness and love of compromise of a later generation than those pathetic monuments of nervous instability which, in a desperate effort to achieve ' good taste ', vainly seek to establish an unworthy and unattainable harmony with their exotic surroundings. In the former category one recalls particularly Sir Gilbert Scott's splendid spire raising, as it were, a reproving finger above the Mansard roofs of the Avenue Georges-Cinq ; that Perpendicular, West Country tower which on the skyline of Florence provides so unexpected a contrast to Giotto's campanile, the Embassy church in Copenhagen (E.E. and Sussex Flint) dominating from its nobly prominent position the alien waters of the Skaggerak. In the latter class the most terrifying example is provided by the new cathedral in Cairo, a sprawling specimen of the British Empire Exhibition Style (Near-Eastern Section), looking for all the world like a maiden aunt who, although unwilling to put on fancy dress, has yet consented to don a comic hat ' for the sake of the children '.

St. Andrew's in Athens makes no greater concession to local taste than that provided by a cruciform plan, a pleasing gesture acknowledging the mutual recognition of each other's orders existing between the Anglican and Orthodox churches ; in all other respects it is demonstratively British. It is no fault of the designer that the Aberdeen granite of which it is built, imported from Scotland at immense expense, should have weathered to a texture to-day almost indistinguishable from the local limestone. Built from funds collected by C. H. Bracebridge, Esq., of Atherstone, Warwickshire, it was consecrated by the Bishop of Gibraltar in 1843. If Murray's Handbook of 1897 from which I have extracted this information is correct and the building has undergone no radical restoration since, it is a very remarkable achievement for that date. The interior, in an austere version of Trans with plain continuous mouldings round the Chancel Arch, is entirely devoid of frills and seems to foreshadow with its marked emphasis on height the work of Comper. The name of the architect I have, unfortunately, been unable to discover.

There exists, so far as I know, only one other example of Revived Gothic in the whole of Greece,[1] an unfinished palace on the slopes of Penteli built by that singular woman the Duchesse de Plaisance. In a period remarkably rich in female eccentrics of the more affected sort, this worthy contemporary of Lady Blessington, the Duchesse de Berri and Caroline Lamb, more than held her own. The daughter of the French Consul at Philadelphia married to a duc de l'Empire, she combined in an extraordinary manner the keep-

[1] The Averoff gaol, thanks to its pointed windows and toy-fort crenellations, might perhaps be included in this category.

sake silliness of Romantic Europe with the bogus culture of a transatlantic blue-stocking. After a stormy youth which included a tender episode with that decidedly minor poet, Casimir Delavigne, she descended on Athens with an adored daughter and a firm determination to wave the torch of European culture in the provincial darkness of the Othonian court. As so often happens in these cases in Greece, her enthusiasm was soon turned into other channels by the prevailing atmosphere, and it was not long before she was demonstrating to an astonished Athens the depth of her Philhellenism by a series of costumes in the antique style carefully copied from Tanagra statuettes. She still retained, however, the fashionable love of solitude which led her to pitch her tent in the remoter environs of the capital. As these were at this period infested by the most ferocious brigands, her choice of residence argued a sublime indifference to a fate worse than death ; a fate, it was sometimes unkindly suggested, that she on more than one occasion suffered with remarkable fortitude. Two of these rural retreats survive to-day ; one is now the Byzantine Museum in Kifissia Street, occupying a site that was well outside the town at the period it was built, the other an unfinished palace in the Gothic style a little above the monastery of Penteli. Confronted with this latter building, the English visitor of sensibility finds himself a prey to most extraordinary emotions ; isolated among the pine-trees and overlooking the wide expanse of the Saronic Gulf with Aegina on the horizon, these echoing castellated walls, so suitable and expected had one come across them in some dripping Irish demesne, seem to retain in this crystalline atmosphere a more than Celtic twilight, preserving within their compass all the steel-engraved melancholy of nineteenth-century romanticism. When in 1845, murmuring some appropriate verses of Lamartine, the Duchess died, this, her final monument, was still unfinished (like many of those afflicted with building mania she was superstitiously averse to final completion), but she was nevertheless buried in the grounds and still lies beneath a marble mausoleum in the classic style rapidly falling into ruin with its once-white surface purple stained with political and amorous *graffitti* scrawled in indelible pencil by generations of Athenian picnickers.

At the beginning of the present century Athens was halfway in the history of its development between the clustered village of Byronic times and the sprawling metropolis of to-day. On the one hand, Lycabettus was still outside the town and its slopes free of villas ; Piraeus was another city separated from the capital by miles of olive groves ; and on the east the Palace gardens gave on to the open countryside. On the other hand, the area lying to the north of the Acropolis and to the west of Lycabettus was already laid out on a grid plan ; Syntagma Square in front of the palace was a dignified open space worthy of a small capital, in fact a great deal more dignified than it is to-day when so many of the old Othonian houses have been replaced by hotels and office-blocks in an international version of Businessman's Functional ; and a series of wide traffic arteries, Athena, University and Stadium Streets, radiated out from Ommonia Square.   This square was intended to balance Syntagma, to which it is joined by two of the city's principal thoroughfares, but while Stadium Street and University Street (or to be up-to-date Churchill Street and Venizelos Street) indeed form the principal axis of the capital's life, owing to the fact that in Athens, almost alone among European cities, the social drift is not from east to west but in the contrary direction it never seriously threatened the pre-eminence of its older rival.   Even in its heyday, during what we might perhaps call the early Compton Mackenzie period, it could never be rated above the shabby-genteel, and to-day its sordid expanse, which even the presence in the centre of a flower-market fails to enliven, is the stamping-ground of the cheaper sort of whore and the starting-place for all the more violent communist demonstrations.   During the December revolution it formed a dangerous no-man's-land between the furthest outposts of Government Athens in University Street and the EAMite strongholds to the west, and was from time to time occupied by British troops who were, however, unable ever to establish a firm hold owing to the fact that the Underground system, which has an exit in the middle of the square, was in the hands of the communists.

To the north of Ommonia lie the depressing residential steppes of Patissia which owe their origin to a remarkable demonstration of that rugged individualism which makes the Greek planner's lot so hard.   It had been intended by the city fathers that the future development of Athens should be an orderly southward expansion, eventually linking the city with the port of Piraeus, and plans to this effect had in fact been drawn up.   Before, however, they could be carried into effect a shrewd Athenian of the period (the

grandfather of that eminent publicist, George " Colossus " Katsimbalis), operating along lines exactly opposed to those which have been so successfully pursued by land-speculators in our own country, bought up all the land he could lay his hands on to the north of the town.   As he had anticipated the Athenian public, the moment it was suggested to them by the powers-that-be that they should dwell to the south, straightway rushed out and bought building sites in exactly the opposite direction, and the psychologist's fortune was made.   The results of this manœuvre were, however, except to the Katsimbalis family, depressing.   In the long monotonous streets which lie around the National Museum the inoffensive if slightly arid classical detail of the Othonian style has been softened and twisted by the debilitating influence of *art nouveau*, or to be strictly accurate, the *Jugendstil* of the early Teutonic nineteen-hundreds.   Water-lilies in beaten copper twine round the wrought-iron balustrades of balconies, and from the volutes of Ionic capitals depend fungoid growths which first sprouted in the studio of Walter Crane.   Socially as well as aesthetically the neighbourhood proved a disappointment, for the larger and more imposing mansions were all bought by the *nouveaux riches* of the Balkan Wars and one of the few taboos still rigorously observed in a city that is not markedly snobbish is that which postulates the existence of an unbridgable social gulf running roughly along the line of Hippocrates Street.   To-day there prevails in the whole district an atmosphere somewhat akin to that investing the Fulham Road–Redcliffe Gardens neighbourhood ; the feeling engendered by a grand social gesture which has not ' come off '.   The profiteers of forgotten wars have long since vanished, having either sunk back into their original obscurity or climbed successfully into the paradise of Kolonaki and their place has been taken by minor civil servants, small businessmen and respectable artisans. It occasioned some surprise, therefore, when during the civil war the champions of democracy massacred so many, and carried off as hostages still more, of the inhabitants of the district while leaving the ' monarcho-fascists ' and millionaires of Kolonaki, a large portion of which was at one time in communist hands, almost completely unmolested.   The reason in fact was not, for anyone acquainted with the firm realism of your convinced Marxist, hard to discover ; at that stage in the revolution it was obvious that the attempt to seize power by force having failed, the next effort would have to be made by constitutional means and that, while however many atrocities were committed on the idle rich it was unlikely that they would ever be sufficiently scared to vote against their own interests, the petty bourgeoisie might well be terrorized into toeing the party line at the next election.

Stadium and University Streets, which run parallel through the centre of the town, are the typical main thoroughfares of any continental city. Wide, shop-lined and tram-infested, they owe whatever specifically Greek character they possess to the overwhelmingly neo-classic buildings of the Academy and University, where the illusion of antiquity is only slightly marred by the presence of Mr. Gladstone in a marble frock-coat, and to the typically Athenian wrought-iron awnings, glazed and gilded, projecting over the pavements from the exceptionally high shop-fronts. In both streets the social standards are steadily lowered the farther away one gets from Syntagma ; through exactly what physical agency the awareness of this progressive degradation reaches one it is almost impossible to say. The pavements are as clean, the shops apparently as smart a hundred yards to the east or west of any given point, and yet one is sensible of a marked decline. This phenomenon, however, is not peculiar to Athens and may as easily be investigated at the point where Oxford Street becomes New Oxford Street or where the Boulevard des Capucines merges into the Boulevard des Italiens. Aeolus Street, on the other hand, which runs at an acute angle from near the west end of Stadium Street to the foot of the Acropolis, maintains its extraordinary character throughout its length. To drive down this thoroughfare at any hour of the day is torture, for no understanding of the western European conception that there exists some functional difference between the pavement and the roadway seems ever to have been granted to the innumerable passers-by. The character of the street is entirely commercial, but commerce is by no means confined to the shops ; every few yards a seller of cakes, cigarettes or sweets has set up his stall, and in the winter their ranks are swelled by the hot-chestnut merchants, and in Holy Week, the best time of all for a visit, by the retailers of fireworks, holy transfers, and decorated Easter candles. Towards the Acropolis, where the street emerges into what is left of the old Turkish bazaar, the shops both in the main road and in the innumerable side-turnings tend to fall into trade-groups ; to the left are the shoe-makers busy manufacturing *tzarouchia* soled with the hard-wearing products of Messrs. Dunlop and Goodyear (exactly how acquired many a M.T. officer would dearly like to know) ; to the right are the copper-smiths, in the main road itself the toyshops, and finally, beyond the cobblers, away to the east, the antique-dealers. This tendency whereby the merchants of the same class

collect in the same streets is not peculiar to this district but is general throughout Athens. Thus all the flower-shops are in a row under the Old Palace, and in Hermes Street one passes from the watchmakers' to the drapers' enclave, where whole rows of windows devoted to buttons of all colours and sizes produce the most extraordinary *pointilliste* effect. This system, which in mediaeval times was common to all Europe, is here for some reason always regarded by the tourist as peculiarly Oriental—a reflection which one imagines seldom occurs to the passers-by in Great Portland Street.

In 1922 occurred a disaster which not only completely, and it is to be feared permanently, upset the national economy of Greece, but entirely modified the whole character of the capital. By the treaty which brought to an end the disastrous Turkish war, a crack-witted enterprise for which the idiocy of King Constantine, the optimism, to call it by no harsher name, of Mr. Lloyd George, the incompetence of the Greek General Staff and the insane jealousy of the French were all in part to blame, an exchange of national minorities took place. By this agreement, which was hailed by international planners, liberal intellectuals, and *New Statesman* readers generally, as a triumph of peaceful co-operation and a sure presage of the new era dawning in international relations, an already overcrowded Greece was landed with one and a half million refugees from homes which they had inhabited since at least as early as the eighth century B.C. and which they had maintained against the Phrygians, the Persians, the Romans, the Goths, the Arabs and the Turks, only finally being forced to render them up at the command of the League of Nations. The result was to saddle the state with a permanent burden of unemployment, to create what had never existed before, an urban proletariat, and to ring round the principal cities with a girdle of slums ; and furthermore, ironically enough, to turn into an uncultivated waste what had hitherto been the richest districts of Asia Minor.

In dealing with this appalling problem the government, notably General Plastiras, displayed a praiseworthy resourcefulness, transferring the wretched newcomers as quickly as was humanly possible from the squalid encampments and hut-settlements in which they had sheltered on arrival into new housing estates on the outskirts of Athens, Salonika and the larger provincial towns. In Athens these ' Asia Minor ' suburbs—' Athens' crown of thorns ' as a British divisional commander aptly but, perhaps, in the conditions of December 1944 a little unfortunately described them—produce on the foreign visitor unacquainted with the circumstances in which they were built an impression of unrelieved horror which is apt to find expression in an unqualified condemnation of the government responsible. In fact, a settlement such as Kaisariani on the slopes of Hymettus is not badly planned, but a chronic lack of funds, a tendency ineradicable in the Greeks to make even such matters as draining, paving and lighting serve their purpose in the never-ending game of politics, and the sturdy if misguided individualism of the refugees themselves have all combined to produce the prevailing atmosphere of unfinished squalor.

Not all the refugees, however, were destitute, the Greek colonies of Constantinople and Smyrna were second only to the community in Alexandria in point of wealth and many of their shrewder members had succeeded in transferring considerable capital ahead. Moreover, the Greeks of Asia Minor had since classical times been notoriously the ablest of their race in all matters of finance and commerce, so that for a time, on the rising market of the 'twenties, the full extent of the disaster was in some degree masked by an increased activity in the business world and the creation of a host of new enterprises. This naturally resulted in further expansion and many prosperous quarters of Athens are, in their present aspect, as much the products of the Asia Minor disaster as Nea Smyrni or Nea Kokkinea.

The extension of the city at this time developed in two directions; first towards the Piraeus in accordance with the original plan frustrated by George Katsimbalis' grandfather; second along the line of the Leoforos Basileias Sophias or, as it is invariably called, Kifissia Street. This thoroughfare, which runs from Syntagma alongside the old palace out towards the village of Kifissia, was hardly developed before the first German war beyond the point where the palace gardens are now bounded by Herodes Atticus. The gardens themselves, laid out by Queen Amalia and an excellent example of mid-nineteenth-century romantic gardening, were handed over to the public when the monarch moved from the old palace, the original inconvenience of which had been considerably increased by a disastrous fire, and installed himself in the new palace in Herodes Atticus (a four-square building of small architectural merit decorated in the international Casino style of the early 1900's). Normally the resort of amorous Evzones from the nearby barracks and Kolonaki nursemaids with their repulsive little charges, in December '44 the Gardens served a grimmer if more useful purpose. No other open space existing in the tiny area of the city controlled by the Government, beneath these pleached *allées* and serpentine paths were hastily buried, or as time went on just dumped, the innumerable corpses of the victims of the fighting; fortunately for those of us who lived down wind the weather remained remarkably cold and dry.

Opposite the gardens the street is lined by a series of imposing public buildings in a variety of interesting styles. The Foreign Office, strict neo-classic ; the Ministry of War, Greek traditional ; the French Embassy, pure Deuxième Empire ; the Egyptian Legation, a Cairene version of Italian Renaissance ; the palace of Princess Nicholas, very late Othonian, and most remarkable of all, the Skaramangar House used during the Regency as the official residence of His Beatitude. The full beauties of this perfect example of Hollywood Balkan are only suggested by the exterior, from which, striking as it undoubtedly is, the passer-by can gain no hint of the wealth of peasant oak, the splendour of round-headed arches resting on squat pillars crowned by debased but gilded Byzantine capitals that lie within. With extraordinary good fortune I was privileged to see it first in ideal conditions which are unlikely ever to be repeated.

Without the night was stormy and the sound of heavy firing was carried on the wind from the direction of Pankrati, muffling from time to time the cries of the sentries challenging the occasional passer-by ; within, all the electricity in the city having long since failed, the only illumination came from a roaring log-fire in the immense, heraldically-canopied open grate and an excessively ecclesiastical candelabra standing on a refectory table. In a throne-like oak chair by the fire I could discern the robed immensity and noble beard of the Regent-Archbishop ; behind him the gold lace and buttons of the Evzone in full uniform shone and twinkled in the firelight. Somewhere in the shadows lurked a liveried footman in white cotton gloves. At any moment, I felt, the Princess Flavia would with incomparable grace come down the wide staircase, passing that curtained alcove which, for all I knew, might well conceal the redoubtable Rupert himself. It was one of those very rare moments when life beats art in a canter, for no more appropriate setting could have possibly been devised by the ablest scene-designer in Hollywood for an ecclesiastic who in appearance so admirably filled the supreme executive position which he had so reluctantly undertaken in a crisis that nicely combined the more picturesque elements of the Prisoner of Zenda with the half-baked ideology of *For Whom the Bell Tolls*.

Beyond the Skaramangar the street begins to lose interest, being given over almost entirely to blocks of flats in the Mitropa style of the 1930's. Self-consciously devoid of decoration and looking, with their rows of walled balconies, for all the world like so many chests of drawers of which alternate drawers have carelessly been left open by the housemaid, they owe their origin largely to the laws forbidding the export of capital enacted in the years before the last war. The wealthy Athenian at that time often employed his money to erect a block of flats, reserving for himself the top floor with its terraces and views, and renting, or more likely selling (for in Athens it is usual to buy the freehold of your apartment) the remaining floors to his friends and acquaintances. Heavy and monotonous as these cliff-dwellings undoubtedly are, they yet compare quite favourably in appearance with the streaky-bacon, neo-Georgian calamities that mock the decent stucco of our London squares and in convenience of arrangement are much superior. It was into the first-floor windows of a flat in one of these blocks on the south side of the street, at that time occupied by M. Papandreou, that an unarmed leftist skilfully tossed a hand-grenade as he marched by *en route* for the fatal demonstration of December 3rd ; an incident which was tactfully overlooked by the majority of British correspondents, confidently assessing the blame for the subsequent bloodshed from the secure vantage-point of the Grande Bretagne Hotel.

The only remaining buildings of interest in the street are the Officers' Club, which might have been built by a Greek architect with a nodding acquaintance with the later works of Norman Shaw, the Byzantine Museum, mentioned above as being one of the numerous homes of the Duchesse de Plaisance (and, incidentally, one of the best arranged small museums in Europe), and the British Embassy. This last was originally built as a present for the late M. Venizelos by his wife, who spared no expense in its design and decoration. An imposing block in the neo-Classic manner it is to-day chiefly remarkable for its colour, a pale cyclamen of a shade that is now known throughout Athens as ' Palairet pink '. A former Ambassadress, so it is said, one day chanced to be driving through a village south of Thebes well known for the bright colour-wash with which the inhabitants are accustomed to enliven their homes, and being much struck with the picturesque appearance of the hamlet she decided, the time having come round for the repainting of the Embassy, to follow the example of the simple cottagers. The experiment was undoubtedly bold, for a colour which lends a gay air to a two-roomed cottage in the country can prove a trifle overpowering when applied to a fair-sized palazzo in the principal residential quarter of a modern city. However, there is much to be said for a building which houses the representative of His Britannic Majesty possessing a character of its own, and this no one could be found to deny our Embassy in Athens. Indeed, at a time when the houses on the opposite hill seemed to be exclusively occupied by the champions of the ELAS rifle-ranges its character was, if anything, almost ostentatiously recognizable and the then Ambassador was heard on occasion, as he skipped nimbly across that area of his study covered by the French windows, to refer to his predecessor's wife with a warmth of expression uncommon among colleagues in the diplomatic service.

A few hundred yards to the north lies the monastery of the Asomatoi which retains the only good wall-paintings to be found in Athens itself.

These admirable specimens of the mural art of the sixteenth century are confined to the bema and apses, the only portion of the church to survive restoration ; the nave and narthex are an unusually depressing example of nineteenth-century ecclesiastical decoration. The whole assembly of buildings, however, forms a fascinating architectural *mélange*, for the church, part eleventh century, part nineteenth, is surrounded by a two-storied cloister giving on to a series of cells of very recent date, which by making no attempt to achieve an impossible stylistic compromise and remaining firmly and unmistakably of its period deserves to be considered as being among the best Greek buildings of the last twenty years. Similar though less-studied contrasts are to be observed throughout this neighbourhood caused by the survival here and there among the vast apartment blocks of small cottages and shops dating from the not very distant period when all the lower slopes of Lycabettus were covered with vineyards and small olive groves.

Beyond 'the rose-red pity', as opponents of British policy in Greece occasionally allude to the Embassy, Kifissia Street loses much of its character, becoming unpicturesquely slummy in the neighbourhood of the Alexandra Boulevard, and on reaching Psikiko traversing for some miles an Athenian equivalent of Metroland enlivened by all the architectural delights usually to be found alongside a by-pass before finally climbing the hill to the fashionable suburb of Kifissia. Kifissia, unlike Hampstead, which in situation, or Wimbledon, which architecturally, it somewhat resembles, owes its rich suburban character to an immensely old tradition. In the first century B.C. the inevitable Herodes Atticus built himself a summer villa on this cool hill-top, the lavish decoration and fittings of which have been exhaustively described by a sycophantic contemporary. From this account one might well imagine a species of Beverley Hills nightmare crammed with the costliest junk obtainable in the Empire but one would, I think, be wrong,

for what we know of this Ur-millionaire encourages us to believe him to
have been rather a ' cut above ' Sir Gorgias Midas and to have approximated
more to the type so well represented to-day by Lord Blank.   If this were so,
then the whole decoration of the villa would have been handed over to some
smart Greek decorator from Alexandria or Antioch, who could be trusted for
an immense sum to produce a setting in as perfect taste as that which Messrs.
So-and-So have achieved at his Lordship's little place at Sunningdale.   The
statues, the vases, the murals, the furniture would all have been genuine
period pieces ; nothing would have disturbed the perfect aesthetic harmony of the ensemble and the total effect would have been as characterless
and lifeless as a showroom in a department store.

To-day the tradition started by Herodes Atticus and carried on by the
Frankish lords and Turkish pashas who succeeded him, for the neighbourhood never lost its charms for the Athenian upper class, is supported by the
cotton magnates of Alexandria and the bullion brokers of the Phanar with
an enthusiasm and open-handedness that render Kifissia not only unique
among suburbs but also a ' folk-museum ', as it were, of the more extravagant
examples of twentieth-century domestic architecture without rival in Europe.
Along these shady suburban lanes the amateur of villa design will discover
specimens of styles almost totally unrepresented in the other great collec-
tions.   Where else, one may ask, can one find ornamental barge-boarding
and the classical orders freely employed in the same building ?   Is there
anywhere in Europe, save perhaps Mytilene, where that excessively rare
style, Turkish Art Nouveau, can be studied to such advantage as here ?
There is even a single specimen of that okapi among architectural modes,

70

Minoan Revival. The majority of these fantasies, built by men to whom money was no object, acquainted with foreign countries but temperamentally cut off from what they would still speak of as ' Western Europe ', and completely uninhibited by any middle-class anxiety as to what their housemaster or the neighbours would think, tend to display three main influences —the Hellenistic temple, the Monte Carlo Casino, and the Swiss chalet. In some of the more recent additions to the neighbourhood a fourth, that of peasant art, is also discernible ; one or two of these elaborately simple cottages *ornées* in what is optimistically known as ' Island Style ' can in fact trace their descent from the Red House at Bexley through Sir Edwin Lutyens and Hollywood.

The contemporary expansion of the city southwards was of a more strictly utilitarian character ; the goal of the great new road, Leoforos Singrou, which now shot out in this direction was not a smart villa-colony of Kolonaki but the third largest port in the Mediterranean. The Piraeus is almost entirely a creation of the last hundred years, for of the classical port nothing remains save some remnants of wall, the foundations of a mole and the fragmentary outlines of the Periclean shipyards, and until the middle of the last century the port of Athens was the island of Syra in the centre of the Cyclades where the traveller abandoned his steamer for a small caique.

To-day this sprawling conglomeration of dusty slums, bombed warehouses and shabby office-blocks has a population second only to that of Athens. While there is admittedly little enough to attract the attention of the cultured tourist on an Hellenic cruise, the city nevertheless possesses a tremendous character of its own and displays on occasion a queer surrealist beauty for which it is not difficult to acquire a lasting taste. The two small harbours of Aslan Limani and Turko Limani possess the usual charm attaching to small ports, but the particular quality of the Piraeus is more readily to be detected on the headland which divides them from the modern harbour. Here runs a coast road, unpaved and impassable for vehicles, flanked on the landward side by some ruined villas and the crazy shacks of an Asia Minor settlement and on the other by a cliff falling almost perpendicularly into the sea and honeycombed with caves that long remained a favourite resort for hashish smokers. Here one summer evening when the sun had already dropped behind Salamis but the whole gulf still retained in its waters and headlands some inner source of light stored up, perhaps, from the superabundance of the day, I experienced one of those rare moments when for no ascertainable cause a scene takes on an indefinable significance quite unrelated to its intrinsic beauty which renders it for ever after unforgettable and, in some strange way, a source of strength. The road, mounting sharply on rounding a sudden bend, presented a sharp horizon against the lemon yellow of the western sky, on which rested, at eye level, a row of those wooden café chairs that one finds in every corner of Greece, all unoccupied. Somewhere out of sight to the right a cracked gramophone played an endlessly repetitive Turkish song. For a few seconds nothing in the world existed except the rocky road, the sky and the pattern of the chairs hanging, as it were, in the luminous void.

The modern harbour to which the road, as yet unfinished, was originally intended to lead obeys that universal rule which decrees that all ports, once they have exceeded a certain size, lose much of their own proper character and become as unromantic as power-stations or stockyards. At the moment some of the macabre beauty of ruination clings to these wharfs with their warehouses and cranes, shattered and twisted by the blast of an exploding ammunition ship in 1941. (The result, incidentally, of a piece of light-hearted British bungling with which, much to the credit of their national magnanimity, the Greeks have never in my hearing reproached us.) Luckily, however, the holocaust which then swept along the quayside spared, as did the subsequent bombing, many of the remarkable Piraean brothels. These establishments, to which, for all signs of their purpose visible in the café which occupies the ground floor, one could unhesitatingly take one's maiden aunt, are notable not so much for the beauty of their inmates as for the dancing which takes place nightly. The music, which is supplied by a mandoline and a guitar, occasionally reinforced by a clarinet, is traditional and as far removed in character from the Judaeo-Haarlem rhythms of our western dance-halls as it is from the blameless jog-trot of the Morris. The dancers, seldom more than three in number, are ordinary members of the local public, dockers, ship-hands or the like, who go through the intricate mazes of the *hassariko* or the *slaviko*, which both involve a remarkable number of concerted bendings and leapings, with tireless agility and grace, their excessively proletarian aspect and costume not infrequently enlivened by a camellia tucked shyly behind the ear or a rose held between the teeth. On no account should anyone with an interest in Greek dances fail to visit one of these resorts, for these burly toughs display a concentration and a spontaneity that is to-day all too frequently to seek in the elaborate,

costumed *festas* of the countryside faintly coloured, as in all but the most remote districts they almost invariably are, by the not quite disinterested enthusiasm of the Ministers of Popular Culture and of Tourism. However, it were best not to go unaccompanied by some knowledgable Greek, for as the majority of the patrons have certainly been drinking heavily for hours and almost as certainly smoking hashish, slight differences of opinion are apt to find violent expression which sooner or later involves the appearance of the police. With this possibility in mind the wise customer will always select one of the marble or metal-topped tables in preference to the wooden variety, a certain number of which are usually provided by the thoughtful management.

The Singrou Avenue itself, linking this fundamentally different world with Athens, is a fine piece of road-building running from the temple of Zeus for six [miles in a dead straight line to the seashore at Phaleron; unfortunately the buildings which adorn it are singularly devoid of any architectural merit, and were it not for the extraordinary clarity of the atmosphere which enables one clearly to distinguish traffic advancing from one end of the highway to the other, one might well imagine one-self on the Great West Road. The principal landmark along its length is

73

Lycabettus

the brewery of Messers. *ΦΗΞ*, the Hellenized rendering of Fuchs, an honest Bavarian brewer who accompanied Otho to his new kingdom and by his industry assured the Athenian public of a constant supply of excellent lager. During the revolution it was strongly held by ELAS, which rendered each journey to the airport, along what for several weeks remained the only line of communication between the garrison in central Athens and the outside world, individually memorable. The defenders were not finally driven out until attacked by rocket-firing Typhoons of which the pilots, with a devotion to duty that has never received its due measure of praise, never faltered in their aim, although fully aware that their target contained the last remaining stocks of beer in all Greece.

On driving along this road back to Athens one is confronted the whole way from Phaleron, until it finally drops behind the roof of the old palace, by that singular elevation, Mount Lycabettus. For some reason this remarkable mountain, which dominates every view of the city and is quite unparalleled in any other capital of Europe, is almost invariably ignored in all modern accounts of Athens, and there exists, I believe, but one passing reference to it in the whole of classical literature. To gain some idea of the fantastic impression it creates the Londoner should picture to himself a steep, conical rock rising to the height of nearly a thousand feet with its southern foot in Grosvenor Square and falling away on the north in a series of precipitous drops to Wigmore Street, its spiky summit crowned with a small chapel. One reason that perhaps accounts in part for the prevailing silence on this subject lies in the fact that the majority of Athenians do not like Lycabettus ; they regard it as ' un-Greek ', and indeed not altogether unreasonably, for its extravagent silhouette, together with the ridiculous little pines with which that indefatigable romantic gardener Queen Amalia planted the lower slopes, give it a quite unclassical, northern air, as of an illustration to Grimm by Arthur Rackham. Nevertheless, undeterred by one's Greek friends one should most certainly climb to the summit not so much for the sake of the little chapel, a picturesque but not remarkable specimen of very late Byzantine style, as for the panorama.

From nowhere else does one gain so extensive or so enlightening a view of this extraordinary city as from this little terrace. Immediately below, the foot of the mountain is ringed round by the luxury flats and imposing villas of Kolonaki, the British Embassy blushing prettily in their midst ; to the east rises the great mass of Hymettus, the suburb of Kasiriani clinging like a scab to its flank, its foothills dotted with houses and domes, finally falling away to the distant sea in the neighbourhood of Glyphada. Close-at-hand to the south lies the heart of the city clustering round the great rock of the Acropolis, traversed by the parallel canyons of Stadium and University Streets and bounded in the foreground by the tree-tops of the palace gardens and the vast pillars of the Temple of Zeus whence Singrou Avenue, as straight and gleaming as the mercury in a thermometer, shoots across the slums and marshes to Phaleron and the sea. To the north and west the suburbs have spilt out in a great semicircular wave stretching from the coast to the hills near Daphni, which must, one feels, in a short space engulf the whole plain of Attica. As one looks more closely at this crowded prospect one notices that what at first had seemed a solid undifferentiated mass of housing is in reality a conglomeration of separate units, their focal centres marked by a neo-Byzantine dome, their boundaries indicated by a sudden outcrop of rock, some tributary of the Ilissos or even by a simple change of level. This, one realizes, is not so much a vast city as a collection of villages and small towns hastily united by force of circumstance. To a certain extent this is true of all great cities, of London more than of most, but with us the process of accumulation has gone forward over a long space of time, whereas here it has been accomplished in two decades. It is this fact which, combined with the intense local patriotism of the Greeks, gives to Athenian life its peculiar quality. It explains how it is possible for there to exist in the midst of a metropolis of over a million inhabitants a community living in a mile's radius of Syntagma of which almost every member, regardless of occupation, social position, or politics, knows every other ; in which the world of politics, law, journalism, the arts, finance are mingled and interlocked at every point, much to their mutual advantage. So it was up to the late war in Vienna, still is in Dublin, but has long since ceased to be in London. In Athens the old man selling filthy post-cards in the bars in Bucuresti is on Christian-name terms with half the Cabinet; the leading exponent of modern art is the son of that political Admiral whose face has launched a hundred coups; the nephew of the prominent shipping magnate is a leader of the Communist Party. 'Vous savez, mon cher, c'est une de mes cousines' is the theme song of Athenian social life in every class. Piraeus, Patissia, Ayios Iohannis, all the names on the buses are separate worlds with their own shops and taverns for whose inhabitants life centres round their own *platia*, quite uninfluenced by that of the next-door community and only slightly affected by that of central Athens. So firmly do these various districts retain their own individuality, so worthily do they maintain the tradition of the city-states of antiquity that it is no unusual thing to find oneself at the distance of one bus-stop from a notoriously Red centre in a neighbourhood where every other house displays the slogans and symbols of uncompromising royalism.

As one gazes down on this expanding confusion of yellow-washed slums, modernistic apartment houses, Byzantine churches, macadamized streets that start with the surface of a billiard-table only to revert to ochreous, naked rock after the first three hundred yards, smart avenues that change to raging torrents at the first rain-storm, ruined temples and bombed gas-works, *art nouveau* palaces and wooden shacks, one gradually realizes that the inhabitants of this town-planner's nightmare have preserved not only a few shattered columns and weatherbeaten porticos from the ruin of their ancient civilization but also one of its greatest discoveries—how men can live a communal life in a great city and yet retain their own individuality. Whether in the century of the common man they will be able to continue safeguarding this sane parochialism, which nine-tenths of European and American city-dwellers have lost, remains, of course, to be seen.

Chapter 3

ATTICA

Tourist, spare the avid glance
    That greedy roves the sight to see :
Little here of ' Old Romance ',
    Or Picturesque of Tivoli.

No flushful tint the sense to warm—
Pure outline pale, a linear charm.
The clear-cut hills carved temples face,
Respond, and share their sculptural grace.

HERMAN MELVILLE

ATTICA is approximately a triangle confined by two mountain ranges and the sea and dominated by three prominent peaks, Parnes, Penteli and Hymettus. Of these latter, almost the same height respectively as Ben Nevis, Snowdon and Scawfell, it is the last which in Athens imposes itself most immediately on the attention. The other two remain in the background, beautiful but a trifle remote, closing an urban vista as effectively and inevitably as do the Dublin Mountains, but Hymettus stands firmly in the foreground, its lower spurs running right down into the outer suburbs, its presence, even when it is invisible, impossible to disregard in any quarter of the town. Roughly triangular in plan, its silhouette bulky and couchant, the mountain makes its formidable impression by virtue of sheer mass, unconcealed by vegetation and unrelieved by the romantic trappings of crags and precipice. In this it is aided by the manner in which it takes the light that renders it unique among the mountains of Greece and, so far as my knowledge goes, without parallel in Europe. The fantastic colour which it assumes at sunset, due one imagines to the angle of refraction, and which gave rise to the epithet ' violet-crowned ' as applied to Athens, has been referred to already ; what is no less worthy of notice,

77

though less immediately dramatic, is the way in which the sun, once past the meridian, shades the innumerable shallow valleys running up from the sea with an ever-increasing intensity, progressively emphasizing the formal significance of every spur and ridge.

Incomparable as are the peculiar beauties of Hymettus, they are best appreciated from a distance. Once one is on the mountain the colour drains away, the surface which from Athens appeared as smooth and rounded as the South Downs turns out to be everywhere encumbered with large grey limestone boulders between which grow tough little clusters of thyme and camel-thorn, and the general effect of austerity is nowhere relieved, as it so frequently is on Penteli, by sudden plane-shaded combes and unexpected streams, grass-bordered and cheerfully noisy. Even the bees which once produced the most famous of honeys have now moved off to neighbouring heights. However, it is this very grimness of aspect to which Hymettus owes perhaps the most remarkable of its attractions—the painted churches, which both for number and quality no other district of Attica can rival.

When in the Dark Ages the fever of monasticism was first felt in Athens the peculiar advantages which the mountain offered to those desirous of leading the contemplative life were soon appreciated. Immediate surroundings which for discomfort and solitude compared not unfavour-

ably with the Syrian desert were here not so far removed from the
seat of a Metropolitan and a large centre of population as to nullify the
practical benevolence of the Church or to discourage the profitable
visitations of the pious laity. It was not, therefore, surprising that already
by the ninth century Hymettus sheltered a large number of monks,
some dwelling in communities, others living as hermits, and throughout
the period of Frankish rule and right on into Turkish times, shrines, chapels
and churches continued to be erected on its slopes.

Of all these little buildings certainly the best preserved and in many
ways the most perfect is the monastery of Kaisariani which enjoys the
additional advantage of lying within an hour's walk of the centre of Athens.
The Asia Minor slum which takes its name from the monastery ('the
Stalingrad of Athens' as in 1944 certain American journalists were inevitably led to christen it), stretches from the shabby-genteel residential district
of Pankrati on the one side to the lower slopes of Hymettus on the other.
It is traversed for a distance of half a mile or more by a wide, perfectly
straight avenue, devoid for most of its length of road-surface and pavement
alike and bordered by rows of once neat but now infinitely dilapidated
identical bungalows. When, quite suddenly, after one has been climbing
this depressing perspective for a seemingly endless tract of time it comes to
an abrupt end and one finds oneself transported in half a dozen paces from
the shabbiest of twentieth-century urban landscapes to the heart of a bleak
and quite unravished moor, the effect is exactly as if the Mile End Road
were to come to a full stop on the lower slopes of Snowdon.

From this point a rough track runs upwards to the shoulder of a steep
gully the head of which remains for some time invisible. When at length
it comes into view one is rewarded by the sight of a small cluster of honey-
coloured buildings, a handful of enormous cypresses and a couple of planes
grouped between the two converging flanks of the valley in a manner so
satisfying as to render picturesque an inadequate term of description.
Formerly the neighbouring slopes were covered with groves of pine and
olive, and although the contrast between the present bareness of the Attic
hills and their previous allegedly wooded condition is invariably overstressed
by Athenians, in this case photographs exist to prove the point. [1] Certainly
in classic times the undergrowth must have been considerably thicker hereabouts as otherwise it is difficult to credit the fatal error of Cephalus which
led to the earliest and most tragic of shooting accidents of which this glen

[1] Actually it would seem that where there are now trees, before the fearful winter of
'40-41 and the depredations of the Germans and a half-frozen peasantry, there were more;
and where there are now none, none flourished then, or probably even in antiquity.

is the traditional scene. Nevertheless, I for one would not have them back, for nothing surely could exceed the beauty of the existing contrast between this formal oasis and the bare bones of the mountainside behind.

To-day while the interest of the site is almost entirely Byzantine, still

Est prope purpureos colles florentis Hymetti
Fons Sacer,

and, though the only existing traces of the ancient temple of Aphrodite are a few columns built into the later work, the marble ram's head from which flowed the sacred spring and principal water-supply of Athens in classical times still exists a little to the right of the utilitarian iron pipe whence the water now gushes out. The church itself is of the greatest possible interest to anyone intending seriously to visit Byzantine buildings in Greece, not so much on account of its intrinsic aesthetic merits, considerable as these are, for they can be matched and on occasion surpassed elsewhere, but for its singular completeness. Nowhere else so far as I know can one gain so full and accurate an idea of how a provincial Byzantine Church appeared in the days of the Empire's greatness. The plan is a remarkably perfect example of the classic ' cross-in-square ' type with the dome supported on four free-standing columns with debased Ionic capitals, certainly lifted from the ruins of the old temple, while the series of paintings which decorate the interior are complete and ranged in strict accordance with the exigent requirements of the Orthodox liturgy. Thus the dome is occupied by the Christ Pantokrator with the prophets ranged round the drum and the four evangelists in the pendentives, while over the west door we find the Entry into Jerusalem and in the apse the Virgin and Child with the Divine Liturgy and the Communion of the Apostles. The paintings themselves, which are supposedly the work of a sixteenth-century Peloponnesian artist, are good examples of the Byzantine style in its last development without including any masterpieces. (Personally I feel that at least two hands have been at work, for the figures immediately beneath the dome in the narthex, a thirteenth-century addition to the main body of the church which dates from the tenth, are much freer and more lively in drawing than the better known, though more static, paintings in the apse.)

From the monastery upwards there leads one of those motor-roads so typical of the Greek genius which end long before reaching any recognizable goal and of which the beginning is approachable only on foot. This one, the work of General Metaxas, was intended to run right to the summit of Hymettus, but in fact peters out alongside the little monastery of Esteri. Here the original plan has been successfully obscured by later additions.

The few traces of painting, the best of which are in a refectory or *parekklesion* apart from the main church, are far more dilapidated than those at Kaisariani. From this small ledge on the mountainside, however, where in spring the snow still lies long after it has vanished elsewhere, the view of the plain below is superb. Slightly apart and easily distinguishable from the innumerable sanatoria, lunatic asylums, gaols and other witnesses to the march of culture which dot the flats on either side of the Marathon road stands the little fortified convent of St. John the Theologian. Its structure, already one imagines shaky, has recently been rendered even less sound by mortar fire and bombing, for the broken ground on which it stands solitary was the terrain over which one of the fiercest engagements between the ELAS forces and British troops took place in 1944. Within there remain some paintings in the apse which, though far less well preserved, still display an intensity for which one looks in vain among those at Kaisariani. (Female art-lovers should, however, be warned that there is in residence a dragon of an abbess who can be relied on to appear, as if by magic, when the space beyond the *ikonostasis* seems threatened by the sacrilegious intrusion of a feminine foot.)

Finally, on the last spur forming the north-eastern apex of the triangle stands the monastery of St. John the Hunter. This again is a cross-in-

square church, though the plan is hard to appreciate from without, so successfully has it been concealed by a quadrilateral of outbuildings. Its unrivalled site whence a wide view extends over the Meszogeion to the mountains of Euboea combined with the dazzling quality of the whitewash with which the whole range of buildings is coated has rendered it a favourite resort of amateur photographers, and many a suburban album to-day contains prints bearing eloquent testimony to what a little skill with a Leica and a yellow filter can here accomplish in the way of complete falsification of all tonal values. Within, the church has suffered heavily at the hands of the Greek equivalents of Scott and Street and contains little enough of interest. The monks have long since departed and the buildings are now in the care of a peasant, his numerous family and still more numerous livestock. Or rather were ; for according to his presumed widow the unfortunate man, like so many others of his class in this neighbourhood, was carried off by the ELASites as a hostage in December 1944 and has never been heard of since.

The seaward side of the Hymettan triangle, even more bleak in character than the rest of the massif, is entirely unrelieved by the presence of buildings. Grey and tawny ribs run down to the narrow coastal plain divided from each other by shallow, treeless, even shrubless, valleys ; recalling in some curious way the scenery of certain districts in Wales as they might appear under a blazing sun after a prolonged drought. Slightly forbidding, these slopes are nevertheless well worth climbing for the sake of the view southwards. Across the unproductive but villa-dotted plain at one's feet run two parallel roads ; one, keeping close to the seashore, starts from Phaleron, where Demosthenes once practised elocution on the beach, but which owes its present aspect to a visit to Brighton paid by that impressionable planner, the Katsimbalis grandpère in the late 'eighties ; the other runs inland, hugging the foothills and passing innumerable late classical burial-grounds, their sites still marked by fragments of massive masonry. Converging after some half-dozen miles, the two finally meet down on the coast at Glyphada, easily distinguished even from this distance by reason of its enormous modern church, one of the more surprising products of the Byzantine Revival. Hence the road runs along the coast past a string of rocky islets close inshore, allegedly the petrified wrecks of some Persian galleys escaping from Salamis (petrified, one assumes, by fear) ; past the Kavouri peninsula, as red and pine-laden as the Rochers Rouges near Antibes, where the remains of a small temple in antis, half buried in the sand of the narrow beach joining the peninsula to the mainland, marks the spot where Aphrodite, passing overhead to one of her numerous accouchements, loosened and let fall her magic girdle, so revered by the ancients on account of its remarkable aphrodisiac qualities[1]; finally coming to an end alongside the sulphur pool of Vougliameni, black and fathomless beneath its breath-taking cliff.

From this point a path runs up at right angles to the road and crossing the last seaward spur of Hymettus comes down on the rocky coast opposite the long beach of Varkiza; then, turning inland, it traverses a low culti- vated plain, where the olive trees are among the most beautiful in Greece, as thick and twisted but less melodramatic than those of Corfu, to the little village of Vari. At this hamlet, which is chiefly remarkable for the com- pletely rustic character it has managed to preserve, although but twenty minutes from the centre of Athens, two roads meet; that to the left, metalled

Glyphada

for the benefit of Athenian motorists seeking the bathing-beach at Varkiza, after passing some well-preserved fragments of cyclopean masonry near which in recent times much excellent Mycenean pottery has been unearthed, finally joins the coast road just below the luxurious villa of M. Canellopoulos where the negotiations bringing to an end the recent civil war were con- ducted in an atmosphere equally suggestive of Hollywood and a difficult session of the borough council. The one to the right leads to Koropi and the Meszogeion, but before following it some mention must be made of Vari's one remarkable memorial of antiquity.

About an hour's walk in the hills behind the village lies the so-called

---

[1] The sight of this beach on any summer evening encourages the belief that some, at least, of the remarkable virtues of this relic were transferred in perpetuity to the ground on which it fell.

Grotto of Pan, its entrance flush with the hillside and quite impossible to discover without a guide. Lowering oneself gingerly through a narrow hole in the ground, one discovers a flight of steps cut in the rock leading to a large underground cavern. Here may be detected with the aid of a torch the headless statue of a seated woman, a curiously primitive relief of a sculptor at work and an inscription, dating, one gathers, from the fifth century, stating them to be the work of one Archidamos who must, judging from his technique, have been singularly old-fashioned and from his chosen place of residence one assumes unsuccessful. There are also a large number of toads and a quantity of bats, all the work of nature.[1]

The road to Koropi from Vari, before emerging on to the plain of the Meszogeion, passes through a stretch of country that seems to be singularly little regarded but which to me is among the loveliest in Greece. It is a district of small valleys and miniature passes running between low hills in which the raw sienna of the earth is but imperfectly concealed by a top-dressing of grey boulders. Certainly harsh, its character is saved from the monotonous barrenness of Hymettus itself by scattered pines, a few hardy olives and, in the spring, an occasional patch of indifferent but brilliantly green corn. Small in extent it merges some time before reaching Koropi into a broad and comparatively fertile valley.

The Meszogeion, or Middle Lands, remain to-day, as they did in classical times though their population is considerably reduced, the chief source of agricultural wealth in Attica. This wide plain, its brilliant terra-cotta coloured earth dotted with olives and cross-hatched by long rows of vines is enclosed to the north-west by the high ridge of Penteli running down to the sea at Marathon ; on the west by the third and most precipitous side of Hymettus ; to the south-east by the mountains above Sunion ; and on the east by the gulf of Euboea. Chiefly prized for the sake of the large quantities of *retsina*, the best in Greece, which it produces, this astonishing soil is also remarkable for the number of works of antique art, statues, coins, and vases which have from time to time been discovered beneath it and the number which it seems probable it still conceals. One of the most beautiful of these, a marble Kouros of the very early fifth century, was chanced on by a peasant's plough during the Occupation and having been successfully hidden from the Germans for four years was triumphantly produced at the liberation.

Apart from its classical sites and its fortifying produce, this country is one which it is foolish to dash through in a frenzied hurry to get to Sunium,

[1] For a full account of these carvings see *The Technique of Ancient Sculpture* by the late Stanley Casson.

for even if one is unappreciative of the peculiar beauty of the landscape, rather in the style of Derain, it well repays exploration on account of its many churches.   These, which are scattered over the whole area, though thickest on the lower slopes of Hymettus, have little but their diminutive size in common ; they range from a pitch-roofed oblong, only distinguishable from the neighbouring cottage by reason of its apse, to quite elaborate examples of the cross-in-square complete with narthex.   Some have polygonal drums, others round ; some are whitewashed, a few are painted in broad horizontal stripes of yellow ochre and venetian red ; most are cruciform, but not all, and there even exists one on the road between Porto Rafti and Macropoulo which exhibits a most curious double basilical plan with two apses.   As always with the minor specimens of Byzantine church architecture, one is in most cases hard put to it to suggest even an approxi-

mate date, for so conservative has the Eastern Church always been that there here exist none of those useful pointers such as round-headed arches, window tracery or undercut mouldings which at home prove such a comfort to the amateur ecclesiologist.   Few of these buildings in fact date from before the fourteenth century and most of them, anyhow in their present form, are considerably later.   Often enough they contain some traces of painting,

infrequently of any great merit but seldom lacking a naïve charm.   But in one, at least, a whitewashed rather elaborate structure on the top of a hill half a mile south of Liopesi, there remain some single figures painted in a direct linear technique with black, ochre and earthy red which are distinctly impressive.

All, needless to say, in the absence of congregations (for they are seldom close to a village and no service is ever celebrated within their walls save once a year on the name day of the patron saint) are in a grievous state of disrepair.   Grass fringes their eaves and valerian sprouts from between their stones ; on the *ikonostasis* a few fly-blown oleographs curl with damp ; on the peeling plaster of the walls the outline of the red horse of St. Demetrius or the white horse of St. George is still faintly discernible, but the Pantokrator has long since flaked off the dome and the Panaghia vanished from the apse.   The wind blows through the glassless windows and the

Bema is covered with bird-droppings, but a pool of fresh wax beneath the embossed white-metal plaque through two holes in which gaze out the faces of the Virgin and her Child shows that the building's original function is not yet wholly exhausted. They are, in fact, almost exactly in the condition of so many of our East Anglian churches at the time when Cotman made his great series of etchings, and we who have seen the results of a century of restoration, preservation and high-principled scholarly consideration, may perhaps be forgiven a sentimental hope, which but a slight acquaintance with the Greek administrative machine encourages one to believe will almost certainly be fulfilled, that they may continue yet a little while in their present condition of unmerited but not unappreciated neglect.

South from Koropi, the last village in Attica to be burnt down by the Germans on their retreat from the coast, the road after traversing a rolling, upland stretch of country, climbs a pass, vanishes for a considerable stretch as the result of a more than usually successful piece of demolition, and appears again within sight of the sea in an improbable landscape of disused mine-workings and old slag-heaps, recalling, in its startling unlikeness to mining scenery as generally conceived, the district round Redruth. From here it runs along the coast to the mining town, famous since classical times for its silver deposits, of Lavrion.

Few Greek provincial towns have much claim to be considered beautiful, but Lavrion possesses a peculiar, slightly sinister ugliness all its own. Here, in a rather different sense from Tennyson's, it seems always to be afternoon ; the wide, ill-proportioned *platia*, which the presence of half a dozen wilting eucalyptus trees and a few aloes fails to adorn, is invariably deserted save for a frock-coated worthy in dazzling white marble, flanked by two depressed-looking palms, and an occasional yellow mongrel of repulsive appearance. Beyond, barren, metallic rocks run out into a hard, blue sea that stretches away, its surface unbroken save by the superstructure of a sunken tanker, to the waterless and uninhabited island of Macronisi. On the landward side above the dirty brick walls and dilapidated office buildings of the Societé Anonyme des Mines Metallurgiques de Laurion (in the Pas-de-Calais industrial style of the early 1900's) the skyline is broken by cindery slag-heaps and rusty derricks. Immediately ahead, dominating the town from a low hill, rises a large neo-Byzantine church, bright-yellow faced with white marble and crowned with an imposing dome of vivid electric blue. On all this the Attic sun beats down with the pitiless and revealing effect of an arc-light on the back row of the chorus in a provincial pantomime.

To go from Lavrion to Sunium along a road which in spring is bordered by a better display of wild flowers than any in Attica is like passing from some tropical slum of Mr. Graham Greene's to the Riviera of Mr. Dornford Yates. On romantic little headlands overlooking picturesque inlets stone pines enfold the red-tiled roofs of many an Athenian stockbroker's villa. Outside smart little *tavernas*, on the walls of which faded Gothic lettering still bears witness to the latest of the barbarian inroads, substantial Athenian families are eating a substantial Athenian lunch. On this railway-poster paradise looks down the celebrated temple of Poseidon, perched on the summit of Cape Colonna, the southernmost tip of Attica.

The temple, a Doric hexastyle of which barely a dozen columns are still erect, while creating a very fine effect from the sea is, as Lord Byron remarked, less impressive when seen from the land. Indeed, from the motor-road it appears, when silhouetted against the sun, remarkably like a half-finished hangar ; an unfortunate impression which the recent demolitions carried out by the Germans, who, with their usual enthusiasm for the treasures of antiquity, had maintained a large ammunition dump on the site, does little to diminish. Closer inspection reveals that the actual surface of the marble has suffered less from the ruthlessness of total war than from the exhibitionist tendencies of generations of tourists, for every available inch of smooth surface is covered with signatures ranging in interest from that of Lord Byron himself, very neat and tidy if rather large, to the ill-cut scrawl of some lovesick *feldwebel* from Düsseldorf. If antiquity can here excuse a habit we justly deplore in public lavatories, then the later culprits have a good case, for the seventeenth-century traveller, Sir George Wheler, records that even in his day the practice was well established.

From Cape Colonna to Marathon the north-east coast of Attica is comparatively low-lying and broken by innumerable small bays and inlets. To-day these natural harbours see little or no legitimate traffic, but their usefulness as secret ports of call, which was fully exploited both by the Greeks and ourselves during the Occupation, has recently been appreciated by those responsible for the illegal immigration of Jews from the Balkans, via Thessaloniki, to Palestine. In classical times the beautiful almost-enclosed bay of Porto Rafti was a harbour of considerable importance and the embarkation point for the annual pilgrimage to the shrine of Apollo at Delos. All that remains to bear witness to past glories is a gigantic headless statue of a woman crowning with a markedly surrealist effect a sugar-loaf island at the entrance to the harbour.

The plain of Marathon, a little farther up the coast, has become, naturally if irrationally, one of the principal places of pilgrimage for the modern tourist in the whole of Greece. One supposes that the heart of a

Clausewitz or a Liddell Hart may beat the faster for a sight of the mournful plains of Waterloo or the sudden Oxfordshire fields of Edgehill, but for the non-specialist an enthusiasm for battlefields is difficult to sustain. All immediate traces of conflict, the rusty pikes or the tree beneath which the hero breathed his last, have in most cases long since vanished, and as strategic advantage and natural beauty by no means invariably go hand in hand, pious memories of past slaughter alone remain to stimulate our interest. And for most of us, certainly in these present times, this is hardly enough. The physical aspect of the present site hemmed in between the last spurs of Mount Penteli and the salt-marshes, has been accurately and exhaustively described by Lord Byron. " The mountains look on Marathon and Mara-

thon looks on the sea " : when one has said that one has said everything. A certain interest, however, attaches to the mound on the east of the battlefield as being the occasion of a signal and enjoyable defeat for the more portentous and boring school of archaeologists. For years it had been strenuously and convincingly maintained by the leading Teutonic pundits that the popular tradition which held that this artificial eminence covered the bones of the Greeks who fell fighting the Persians was completely and laughably false, and that it was perfectly clear to the eye of anyone but a romantic tyro that it was undoubtedly of Neolithic construction. When, therefore, some years ago the mound was opened and the fragments of pottery unearthed proved beyond dispute that the bones among which they were mingled could only have belonged to the victors of Marathon, satisfaction was general and profound.

On the coast to the north-west, rendered strangely remote by a double barrier of mountains and salt-marsh, lies a classical site of considerably greater interest and beauty than Marathon. After crossing a little up-land valley, where the efforts at cultivation of the local peasantry appear to have been crowned with but indifferent success, one comes to the head of a steep ravine leading down to the sea, its flanks covered with shrubs from one of the most numerous species of which, Rhamnus, the place takes its name. Here two temples lying side by side, the larger of which once sheltered the great statue of the Rhamnusian Nemesis by Phidias, testify to the religious importance of the place in antiquity, while the considerable remains of a very solid-looking wall and one well-designed gate which crown a low hill at a point where the ravine runs down to the sea sufficiently display its secular grandeur. Indeed, one fancies there can have been few cities of Greece in which it would have been more agreeable to reside. Not too far from the metropolitan pleasures of Athens, yet adequately protected by the natural barrier of the mountains ; not large in size, but saved from

provincial stagnation by the wide celebrity of the local goddess (did not that ubiquitous old bore Herodes Atticus himself dedicate a statue of his daughter in the larger of the two temples up the hill ?) ; it enjoys a view unrivalled in Greece which must at that time have been animated by the constant passage of shipping up and down the Euboean Gulf, then one of the busiest of trade routes but where now the advent of a single caique occasions surprise.

Mount Penteli, of which the mountains overlooking both Rhamnus and Marathon are a final outcrop, differs in almost every respect from Hymettus. Its size, which is considerably greater, from afar makes no very formidable impression and its silhouette, recalling that of Mont St. Victoire as the genius of Cezanne has so frequently displayed it to us, has a dramatic and symmetrical beauty more elegant though less imposing. It is almost entirely composed of a marble, whiter than that of Hymettus though less chalky than Parian, possessing some metallic admixture which causes it to weather to a wonderful light-rust colour, which provided the building material for the Parthenon and which is still profitably exploited to-day. While nature, particularly on the western and southern slopes, has been noticeably kinder than anywhere on Hymettus, art has scored but few triumphs and the mountain can only boast of two monasteries. The larger of these, charmingly situated in a grove of planes a little above the Duchesse de Plaisance's

Gothic whimsy, is the richest in Greece, but is of little architectural interest ; the smaller, Daoua Penteli, is one of the most extraordinary, if least success-ful, buildings which the Byzantine genius ever achieved.   On an eccentric, and I fancy unique, hexagonal plan the architects have managed to exploit the Byzantine talent for domes to an extent which in so confined a space one would have considered impossible.   Looking up inside one's eye is caught and fascinated by large domes and small domes, by half-domes and full-domes, by domes on squinches and domes on pendentives, and one's mind saddened by the reflection that here the soaring imagination which conceived Santa Sophia has finally, after nearly a thousand years, exhausted itself in a dotty triumph of provincial virtuosity.   One recalls Sydney Smith's comment on the Brighton Pavilion, ' It is as though St. Paul's had gone down to the sea and pupped.'

    The third of the Attic trio, Mount Parnes, a massif or range rather than a mountain, runs north-west from the coast a little to the north of Rhamnus almost to the foothills of Kithaeron, forming the natural and easily defensible frontier with Boeotia.   At the point where it comes down to the sea there are the remains of the shrine of Amphiareus, an Argive soothsayer of con-siderable renown who took part in the expedition of the Seven against Thebes, from the unfortunate results of which disastrous enterprise he was miraculously preserved by the ground opening and swallowing him up, chariot and all. For some reason, not immediately apparent, he was credited as a result of this delivery with medical abilities second only to those of Aesculapius, and the Amphiareon, as his shrine is called, became a notable resort for the invalids of antiquity. And indeed one seems still to catch in the heavy oppressive atmosphere of this enclosed glen, with the ruins of a luxury hotel and an elegant little theatre, a faint lingering whiff of the smart Kurort ; to hear in the soft plashing of its medicinal stream echoes raised by long-vanished generations of overfed dowagers and retired centurions for ever describing, with a wealth of uninteresting detail, the exact state of their bowels or disputing the relative merits of faith-healing and homeopathy.

Daoua Penteli

The great barrier of Parnes, the upper slopes of which display a conventional, almost Tyrolean, mountain beauty with pine forests, Alpine meadows and even a skiing hut or two, can only be surmounted with anything approaching ease at three points, each of which was strongly fortified by the inhabitants of Attica at an early date in their history. From east to west they are, Dekelea, commanding the road from Tanagra ; Phyle, commanding the direct road to Thebes ; and Eleftherae, commanding the route by Plataea. The first gained a terrible notoriety on account of its betrayal to the Spartans by Alcibiades in the Peloponnesian war ; its loss not only deprived the Athenians of their principal safeguard on the north-east but provided their enemies with an admirable base from which to ravage the fields of Attica with a monotonous and damaging regularity.

To-day it is but a heap of masonry on a hill-top surrounded by almost the last pine-forest in this part of Greece which has so far withstood the ravages of fire, caterpillars and peasants. Below lies the royal palace of Tatoi, from the vineyards of which comes the best non-resinated wine that Greece produces, a very light white wine not unlike a young Moselle. The second, Phyle, though lacking so dramatic a history, is far better preserved, retaining three of its towers and, in places, walls to the height of seventeen courses. The mountain immediately above it that forms one side of the precipitous defile which it commands used in thundery weather to be watched by the augurs of Athens with apprehensive attention and as soon as the first flash of lightning was observed playing round its summit a messenger was instantly dispatched to offer a suitable sacrifice at Delphi. The third, Eleftherae, perched on a conical hill at the entrance to a narrow pass carrying the main road from Athens over Kithaeron, displays its importance and its strength at first glance to even the least-strategically minded. Its towers and walls, more numerous and better preserved than those of Phyle, are said to have suffered some slight and far from obvious damage at the hands either of the ELASites or the Germans ; a further demonstration of the deplorable fact that the military mind, once having grasped the tactical significance of a site, is unlikely to be deterred from using it to the best advantage by the reflection that its possibilities have already been exploited by the Athenians or the Thebans or any other interesting nation of antiquity.

Remarkable as are these three examples of ancient military architecture, more impressive by far is the great fortress of Aegosthenea that lies a few miles to the west. Leaving the main road half a mile or so beyond the pass, one reaches the little village of Vilia, notable in this barren land for the depth of green shade cast by its enormous plane-trees and the lushness of its cottage gardens. From here a new road, built by the Italians during the Occupation, descends in sweeping loops and curves through mountain scenery in the grand manner, slightly marred by large tracts of dead and blackened forest burnt by way of reprisal by the Germans, to a small bay on the Gulf of Corinth. Long before one reaches sea-level one's attention is caught and held by a vast enceinte of walls and towers of immense size rising above a sea of olives. So successfully has one been conditioned by early doses of Walter Scott and the posters of the L.M.S. that to-day the sight of curtain walls and barbicans at once induces a sternly medieval mood, and it is only by a conscious intellectual effort that one is able to grasp the fact that these fortifications, so admirably preserved and so much better built than any of the Frankish castles, are separated from the Tower of London by a tract of time almost twice as long as that which lies between the Tower itself and the

Admiralty air-raid shelter in St. James's Park. Closer inspection reveals the fact that what now remains above ground only constitutes the landward side of a vast military township enclosed by side-walls running down to the sea, and that the remarkable cleanness of the lines of its silhouette are in part due to the practice of incorporating a return a few inches wide at each angle of the towers. The great strength of this fortress, which was erected to guard against a sudden Spartan attack from the Gulf, appears never to have been put to the test, and in time most of its materials were employed for the erection of a Byzantine monastery which has now, in its turn, all but disappeared. There remain, however, two little churches with peasant paintings, dated as late as the first half of the nineteenth century, unvisited save by

bees and a few pink locusts zooming through the heavy thyme-scented air of the olive groves.

From the point where the track to Vilia leaves it the main road runs across a cultivated plain and a low range of mountains, passing an occasional Byzantine chapel and one group of buildings, a khan, grouped with a remarkably picturesque effect around some gigantic poplars, and begins the long descent to Mandra. All the way one is being constantly struck by the admirable emphasis a single tree can lend to a landscape, giving scale and distance to a prospect the immensity of which would otherwise be unaccented; an effect which in our own country, with great hangers of beech and thick groves of oak outlining without exaggerating the more rounded contours of the downs and hills, is rarely chanced on. (It is not, however, entirely unknown, as I recall some thorn trees in a hollow of the Berkshire downs immediately below the White Horse at Uffington which fulfil exactly this rôle.) Mandra, an Albanian village, is chiefly remarkable for the peculiar costume affected by its old men ; a pleated and smocked nightshirt, once the common wear throughout the countryside, and a curious peaked blue hat, a cross between the Chelsea pensioners' shako and a skiing cap. From here to Eleusis the road runs straight and level through the olives.

It can, I think, be said with some assurance that of all the major classical sites in Greece, Eleusis is infinitely the most boring. One proceeds round the base of a low conical hill through a cleft in which Persephone is thought by some to have been carried off by Pluto, through the remains of a Propylaea, dating from the reign of the Emperor Hadrian, the drums of its columns lying like sliced cucumbers where they were thrown down by an earthquake, and the decoration of which, judging from the existing fragments of sculpture, must have been in execrable taste, past another Propylaea of which only the foundations remain, and finally comes out into the Hall of the Mysteries. Doubtless for those with powerful imagination or well versed in the doctrines of the late Mme Blavatsky, this long oblong with its parallel rows of column-bases and terraced benches, where took place those sacred rites the exact nature of which has for so long exercised the curiosity of occultists and classicists alike, has a powerful appeal, but it has a stolid Masonic look to me. Even the view, which almost everywhere else in Greece provides adequate compensation for archaeological disappointment, fails at Eleusis. The great sweep of the coast-line round the overwhelmingly, if conventionally, beautiful bay of Salamis is from here broken by two cement factories and the armaments works of M. Bodosakkis, cunningly sited to effect the maximum aesthetic damage, while close at hand the scene is dominated by an ornamental concrete clock-tower, with which any seaside town-council in England would have been proud to have commemorated the Diamond Jubilee, generously presented to the town by one who, after Aeschylus, is perhaps the most distinguished of her sons.

General Pangalos was a resourceful and highly praxicopomatic [1] general who first came into political prominence (after a distinguished career in the

[1] From the adjectival form of the modern Greek word for *coup d'état*, meaning liable to *coups d'état* and used exclusively of generals and admirals.

first German war which gained him a K.C.M.G.) when, in the early 'twenties, he delivered his country by the usual methods from whatever form of tyranny it was under which she was at the time groaning. Having sworn to establish the rule of justice and democracy with no thought of private advantage, he soon found himself in the unenviable position, owing to the obstructive activities of various suspicious and far from disinterested rival saviours, of being forced to assume the supreme power. In due course he was elected to the Presidency by the voice of the people expressed in a vote the size and unanimity of which more than compensated for any disadvantage his cause might have suffered in the popular esteem from the grave necessity to which he had been put of having to arrest all the rival candidates some time before polling day. Once in power it must be admitted that those stern republican ideals which had hitherto always influenced his policy suffered some slight modification ; his installation of his wife in the Queen's apartments in the Royal Palace caused unfavourable comment among Republicans and Royalists alike, while his appearance in the royal box at an Opera ball clothed in a pink silk toga with his brow wreathed in roses shook the confidence of the more solid section of the electorate. Before rather abruptly leaving office, however, he initiated several sound and praiseworthy pieces of legislation, one of which, a sumptuary law establishing the exact number of inches from the ground the women of Greece would be permitted to wear their skirts, an edict that was rigidly enforced by a corps of inspectors equipped with tape measures, at the time attracted considerable attention in the world press. For his birthplace he always retained the liveliest affection which, together with some slight financial interest in a popular casino that he had established in the town, led him in addition to presenting the handsome clock-tower mentioned above, further to increase the amenities of the place by the construction of the magnificent motor-road which runs from here to Athens. This not only compares favourably with the most ambitious of continental autostrada but remains to-day the only stretch of road in Greece on which it is possible safely to achieve a speed greater than twenty-five miles an hour.

After his enemies had brought about his removal from power the general retired into an exile, enlivened by occasional abortive attempts at *coups d'état* (the competition in this line of business was, in the 'twenties and 'thirties, unfortunately considerable) from which he once more emerged into the light of history on being discovered among the collaborationists in the Averoff gaol shortly after the liberation. This unfortunate predicament was due, so he informed a correspondent (Mr. Richard Capell, to whose admirable volume *Simiomata* I am indebted for this brief account of the later phase of the General's career), to the fact that some days previously certain communists had lost their lives in a savage attack on his flat in Aristotle Street, an attack which would certainly have succeeded had he not, as one well versed in the uncertainties of Greek political life, kept beneath the upholstery of his sofa thirty hand-grenades, two pistols, a rifle and a tommy-gun. When some weeks later the Averoff was stormed by ELAS it was thought that the old campaigner had lost his life in the ensuing massacre, but I am glad to say that he was able, under cover of the disturbance, to make good his escape and is now once more living in a retirement which I have not the least doubt he is still prepared instantly to abandon at the first call of duty.

From Eleusis the patriot general's by-pass sweeps round the curve of the bay, where water, sky and islands seem all, particularly in the early morning, to have acquired a faint opalescent patina, following the route of the old Sacred Way along which the pilgrimage from Athens used annually to pass on foot ; past the market gardens which provide the people of Athens with a rather diminished supply of fresh vegetables since General Metaxas ploughed up so many of them to make way for his new airport ; past the pale viridian waters of the Sacred Lake, reedy and bird-haunted ; past the seaplane base at Skaramangar where no seaplane has touched down for many a long year ; past the rock-cut shrines which line the entrance to the low pass, to a point where the suspicious gendarmerie stand for ever poking the bundles of the indignant but not invariably innocent country-folk in a routine search for tommy-guns, hand-grenades, gold sovereigns and other rural produce with which a benevolent government consider the population of the capital to be already amply provided. On this eternal traffic-block look down the golden walls and miraculously balanced dome of the monastery of Daphni.

The church, which is all that remains save for a short stretch of cloister where the pointed arches speak clearly of the Cistercians who in Frankish times " liberated " the foundation from the schismatics, is certainly the best known and perhaps the most beautiful of all those in Greece dating from the days of the Macedonian renaissance in the eleventh century. It is probable that to-day it is chiefly celebrated for the magnificent series of mosaics ; which is very right and proper, but in-so-far as it may lead to a neglect or relegation of the architectural beauties of the place to a secondary plane of interest, a pity. For this church is not only one of the great buildings of Byzantium, but one of the great buildings of Christendom, and one which does not boldly assert its importance at first glance, but whose claims require study and consideration for their full justification. Luckily the appreciation of its architectural quality is rendered easier for the fact that all the marble panels and expensive decoration of the lower walls have long since disappeared, leaving the lines of the structure quite bare save for a narrow cornice or stringcourse, exquisitely carved with birds and flowers, running round the piers and walls at a point just below that from which spring the vaults of the squinches. As a result I know nowhere else where the simple, but frequently neglected, fact that architecture is primarily the art of manipulating space is so plainly and admirably demonstrated. Here, it is not the walls, nor the pillars nor the vaults, beautiful and matchlessly proportioned as they may be, that are of primary importance, but the space, the few hundred cubic feet of atmosphere, they enclose. Built on a curious octagonal plan with the dome resting on twelve piers and squinches (a reaction from the classic dome on pendentives which gained a certain popularity in Greece at this date, possibly because it was thought to afford a means of increasing the height without extending the floor space) it is only afterwards when one tries mentally, or on paper, to reconstruct it, that one realizes how complicated, subtle and ingenious are the means whereby this prevailing effect of extreme simplicity has been achieved.

The beauty of the mosaics is more direct and easier to appreciate ; which may in not a few cases be due to the fact that they have been recently and generously restored. As an introduction to the pictorial art of Byzantium they are, however, unmatched, for here the inevitable strangeness, of which at first approach those brought up amidst the post-Renaissance conventions of Western painting are always aware, is reduced to a minimum. Indeed, in certain panels, notably in the Crucifixion, one seems to be conscious of the first faint breath of the Florentine spring. How much this is due to the restorer one cannot, at this time of day, exactly say, but nevertheless one can, I fancy, cite these works as yet another, perhaps final, example of that dualism which runs all through Greek art ; of that never-ending motion of the pendulum swinging constantly between the representational, feminine genius of the Ionians and the formal, masculine conception of the Dorians. These elegant archangels belong clearly to the company of the mondaine priestesses at Cnossos, the softly smiling korae from Samos and the realistic, artfully draped, terra-cottas from Tanagra ; while their hieratic contemporary rivals, the grim fathers and martial saints at Hosios Loukas, are as clearly the descendants of the Calf-bearer and the formalized charioteers on the geometric vases, their blood, it is true, somewhat diluted by a Syrian admixture acquired in the intervening centuries. Moreover, it is as true of Byzantine as of classical art that it is when the pendulum is nearest the vertical or, to change the metaphor, when the tension between these two poles is at its greatest, that we get the supreme masterpieces such as the Delphi charioteer or the finest of the black-figure vases. And here immediately above our heads is one of them.

The Christ Pantokrator at Daphni, which as in all Byzantine churches occupies the space under the dome, is not only one of the greatest triumphs of religious art but also, to my mind, the most nearly satisfying portrayal of Our Saviour which Christianity has so far achieved. And one which at the present time, particularly in Anglo-Saxon countries with their genius for sentimentalization, might well accomplish that purging through pity and terror of which our religious life stands so sorely in need. Did there exist an Anglican equivalent of the Collegium Propagandae Fidei I should urge them to distribute reproductions wholesale as a much-needed antidote to the *Light of the World* and those regiments of ginger-bearded, whey-faced Scoutmasters which infest the Children's Corner in every church in the land. Thanks to the influence of such artists as Perugino, Thorwaldsen, Puvis de Chavannes and Margaret Tarrant, the Second Person of the Trinity has suffered so fearful a decline in Christian art that to-day there exists no painter, with the possible exception of Rouault, who could conceive such a representation as this Pantokrator, far less embody it on canvas.[1] It is only fair to add that this is in part due both to the breakdown of all generally accepted artistic tradition and the decay, or rather contraction, of religious faith, and it is obvious as one looks at this mosaic and recalls the hundreds of other Pantokrators all over the Orthodox world, all in identically the same posture with the features arranged in the same expression, how much was already settled for the painter before he even made his preliminary sketch. Indeed, nowhere could one find a more convincing demonstration that the most rigid convention so far from inhibiting the artist may well prove a source of strength.

Outside, the gendarmes are still noisily investigating the peasants' carts and the sun as it goes down behind the mountains of the Peloponnese turns an amber flood on to the whole plain of Athens stretched at our feet. Slowly the light dies and the violet-grey shadow creeps in from the coast, leaving the hills and ridges for a few moments more in a supernatural, rosy isolation. One by one these, too, sink into the dusk ; Observatory Hill and the monument of Philopappos ; the Acropolis, serene and powerful as a battleship in harbour ; Lycabettus, at this hour at its most fantastic and least probable ; the long hill of Turkovouni and the bare, contaminated slopes of

[1] At the time of writing I had not seen Mr. Graham Sutherland's *Crucifixion* at Northampton.

Haidari ; and finally the great slumbering ridge of Hymettus itself, turning faintly in its sleep as the last pink rays slip over the summit.

But behind us no change has taken place. The Church of Daphni still glows and pulses with the mysterious independent life with which the greatest works of art are invariably informed and will continue to do so long after the last green glimmer has faded from the west, long after to-day's tourists have gone the way of the monks. For it is of that small company of masterpieces which demand nothing from us save acceptance and are as indifferent to our response as the ocean itself.

*The deep pastures of Arcadia, the plain of Argos, the Thessalian
vale, these had not the gift ; Boeotia, which lay to its immediate north,
was notorious for its very want of it.   The heavy atmosphere of that
Boeotia might be good for vegetation, but it was associated in popular
belief with the dullness of the Boeotian intellect ; . . .*
JOHN HENRY NEWMAN

THE quality which, according to the Cardinal, Boeotia so markedly
lacked was " the special purity, elasticity, clearness and salubrity
of the air of Attica ", and to-day all good Athenians maintain
that on crossing over the pass of Kithaeron the prevailing clarity and
sparkle of the light are measurably dimmed by the heavier, more cloying
atmosphere of the plains ahead.   Be that as it may, the prospect which
opens out at the crest of the rise forms a sufficiently striking contrast to the
Attic landscape.   Immediately below a rolling plain stretches away to the
foothills of Parnassus, its reddish-brown surface unrelieved save where the
Boeotian lakes palely reflect the cobalt sky, and its expanse to be measured
only by the visible extent of the white ribbon of the great trunk road to
the north unreeling itself into the middle distance.   In the centre of this
panorama, though hidden from this point by a slight swell in the ground,
lies the city of Thebes.

To the name of no other city of antiquity does there cling so romantic,
albeit slightly sinister, an aura as to that of Thebes.   Thanks to a childhood
confusion with its Egyptian namesake, it was early invested with an exotic
air which the testified presence of sphinxes in the immediate neighbourhood
subsequently reinforced ; later the emotive power of that long monosyllable
was further increased by a knowledge of the Cadmean doom, the expedition
of the Seven and the extraordinary medieval resurgence.   The present
appearance of the town, however, does little towards sustaining the emotions
aroused by catching sight of the name on signpost or map.   A single
shabby street climbs and descends a low hill on which once stood the
Cadmeia, or Acropolis, of the ancient city which to-day only the presence
of a few planes and mulberries distinguishes from a hundred other such

thoroughfares in the Greek provinces, with the usual regiment of empty chairs outside the café, the cotton kerchiefs hanging in festoons at the drapers' doors, the extraordinary number of barbers' shops, and the inevitable sewing-machine advertisements.  And that, save for the massive remains of a medieval tower and a few pinkwashed cottages on the opposite hill, is all.

Nevertheless the past cannot be denied ; the pressure of history is here so great that even the most prosaic tend to grow reflective. These shabby shops and dingy villas occupy a site that can boast a longer history of continuous occupation than any other in Europe, perhaps in the world. Even after Chaeronea, when the vengeful Alexander laid the whole town flat, one house, that of Pindar, was spared to preserve unbroken the long tradition. In the very dawn of history Thebes was already rich and power-ful and with the overthrow of Orchomenos without rival on the mainland. In classical times, thanks to the extraordinary fertility of the Boeotian plain (an advantage which, according to Professor Toynbee, by providing an insufficient physical challenge insured that the inhabitants could never achieve a cultural response of Athenian magnitude), the city enjoyed an assured prosperity which was maintained during both the Persian and Peloponnesian wars by a policy so remarkably adroit as to be indistinguish-able from ' Collaboration '. Strangely enough, it was reserved for these hard-headed and singularly unglamorous people both finally to overthrow the Spartans on the field of Leuctra and to produce in the person of Epamin-ondas the last Greek hero of the antique pattern. After the disaster of Chaeronea, where the heroic tradition was gloriously maintained by the Sacred Band, the city, though soon rebuilt, lapsed into a provincial stagna-tion which in the time of Dio Chrysostom had become so complete that only one statue remained erect in the market-place and elsewhere the shoulders of a bronze Hercules were just visible above the tops of the long grass growing in the suburbs. Nevertheless this decay, seemingly so final, did not in fact mark the end ; for Thebes alone of the great cities of antiquity was reserved an extraordinary medieval renaissance.

In the seventh century of our era the silkworm was smuggled into the Byzantine Empire from China by two monks who combined missionary zeal with a practical devotion to the principles of free trade, and of all the cities of the Empire it was Thebes where its cultivation was most success-fully pursued. At the time of the city's sack by the Bulgarians in 1040 it had attained the position of the Lyons of the Byzantine world, and its source of wealth was so firmly established that it recovered from that disaster sufficiently quickly to render a far more business-like visitation by the Normans from Sicily a hundred years later a singularly profitable enterprise. When in the next century Greece was divided up among the Franks, Othon de la Roche, a Burgundian knight to whose lot fell the Duchy of Athens, made Thebes his capital, a position it retained under all his successors, attaining its greatest glory at the end of the thirteenth century during the administration of Nicholas de St. Omer who, thanks to the involved workings of feudal succession, shared half the city with his liege lord the Duke of Athens, at that time a minor.

The Middle Ages, anyhow in western Europe, were not a period of exaggerated cultural refinements ; the triumphs of the medieval spirit were all secured in the face of grave physical disadvantages, in the absence of adequate material means. As the increase of real wealth coincided with the beginnings of the Renaissance we cannot tell in what form that spirit would have manifested itself had the requisite conditions existed at a period when it was far from spent ; for no evidence exists which would enable us to reconstruct the shape that a medieval Versailles, a thirteenth-century Golden House, might have taken, for, with one exception, no society in the Middle Ages ever enjoyed the necessary wealth, security and leisure to embark on such an enterprise. The exception was the court of the Frankish Dukes of Athens residing at Thebes in the latter half of the thir-teenth century. Of this society Nicholas de St. Omer is perhaps the most typical, as he was certainly the most splendid, figure. The descendant of a penniless Flemish Crusader, his family had in the ensuing generations secured an unassailable position by a series of judicious alliances ; great grandson of the King of Hungary, grandson of the Queen of Thessaloniki, first cousin of the Duke of Athens, brother of the Hereditary Marshal of Achaia, he had further increased the considerable sum of his possessions by a marriage with the exceptionally wealthy Princess of Antioch. His immense riches he employed in building the great castle of Santameri (the corrupted form of the family name), a palace the size, beauty and luxury of which rendered it fabulous throughout Christendom. Here within walls frescoed with scenes of the Conquest of the Holy Land a society which retained all the religious and feudal usages of the West was able, thanks to the absence of any threat from a cowed but industrious native population of serfs and the far higher standard of material comfort prevailing in lands which had once been ruled from Byzantium, to cultivate the politer arts of the Middle Ages, minstrelsy, jousting, the courts of love, to a pitch of luxury and refinement quite unattainable in their native lands.

The culminating manifestation of this extraordinary and exotic culture occurred on the Isthmus of Corinth in 1305. Here on a strip of land which in classical times had been the site of the Isthmian games, the Prince of Achaia held a great tournament to which were summoned all the lords of Frankish Greece to try their skill against twelve knights from western Europe, acknowledged champions of the joust. The list of competitors, so fabulous are their titles, so intensely heraldic their names, reads more like the cast of some Pre-Raphaelite poem than a factual muster-roll ; Philip de Savoie, Prince of Achaia ; Guy de la Roche, Duke of Athens ; Nicholas de St. Omer, Lord of Thebes ; the Marquis of Boudonitza, the Duke of the Archipelago, the Count Palatine of Cephalonia, the three barons of Euboea ; all these and many more equally improbable paladins assembled to display their pride and skill on an occasion which in fact proved the last triumph of chivalry in Greece. For from the west a new menace was about to descend on a world where hitherto strife had been kept within the decent and enjoyable bounds of baronial wars occasioned by disputed successions. The Catalan Grand Company, a band of murderous and commercially minded thugs of low birth, and quite unaware of the correct usages of knightly warfare, were to prove opponents of a far more formidable type than the twelve champions of western Christendom. Less than seven years later the Duke of Athens, the Prince of Achaia and almost all their feudal lords, golden armour glittering, quartered pennants flying, charged and perished in a Boeotian bog behind which their unsporting adversaries had drawn up their ranks at the fearful battle of the river Kephissos. To-day all that remains to tell of that vanished, fantastic world are the corner tower of St. Omer's great Theban palace, a dozen or so craggy, excessively romantic castles, and strangest of all, the title of Duke of Athens, sure evidence both of the widespread fame of this civilization and the confusion it caused in the historical imagination of the west, with which in *A Midsummer Night's Dream* Shakespeare has ennobled Theseus.

North of Thebes the road runs across a wide and very fertile plain that was once the bed of Lake Copais. This shallow and seasonal sheet of water was finally drained some eighty years ago by a British company which has since intensively and profitably farmed the land thus reclaimed. It is, however, a chastening reflection that British enterprise was not in fact first in the field ; for when the engineers came to clear the underground channels which carry off the water to the Gulf of Euboea traces were discovered of a similar undertaking successfully carried out in what can only have been Mycenean times, a feat which classical tradition correctly maintained had been achieved by the Bronze Age rulers of Orchomenos. Today, if one concentrates on the foreground and middle distance, disregarding the chain of mountains on the horizon, the scene has far more in common with Cambridgeshire or Lincolnshire than anything one is likely to come across elsewhere in Greece ; immense fields planted with corn are bisected by straight reed-fringed canals, sluggish streams wind between pollarded willows and lose themselves in occasional patches of marsh, even the screens of planes and poplars planted here and there as windbreaks seem to have acquired an elm-like silhouette. At the southern end of the plain the

apparent familiarity of the landscape is somewhat disturbed by a low rocky hill that was once an island rising steeply from the surrounding flats, on which stand the remains of the mysterious fortress of Gla, the most puzzling of all early Greek sites, about which nothing whatsoever is known ; to the north rises a spur of Helicon crowned by the vast walls and ruined citadel of golden Orchomenos, once the capital of that strange race the Minyans and the wealthiest city of the Greek world. On the lush green meadows at its foot cattle and horses are grazing, though not now in the vast herds that existed before the Germans and the ELASites passed this way, in charge of wandering Vlachs whose little settlements of round huts built of pine-branches strike a strangely primitive note among the willows ; from the reeds and marshes an occasional heron laboriously takes wing and now and again a stork trails its long pink legs between the higher treetops and the chimney-stacks of the neighbouring village. And everywhere are quantities of magpies : a bird here so inevitable and frequent that it might well be the symbol of Boeotia.

At right angles to this road, immediately north of Thebes, runs another, the surface of which, difficult as it may be to credit, is even worse, along the flanks of the mountain from which the sphinx once descended to ravage the Theban plain, to the coast of Aulis opposite Euboea. Here the almost enclosed arm of the sea lying between the island and the mainland, where the Greek fleet assembled before the Trojan expedition, narrows at one point to a channel a few yards wide, known as the Euripus and celebrated since antiquity for the unpredictable behaviour of the strong current which

Mosque at Chalcis

is liable to change direction several times within the hour ; a phenomenon
which is traditionally alleged so to have preyed upon the mind of Aristotle
that in despair he committed suicide by flinging himself into the middle of
the stream.   To-day the straits are crossed by an ingenious wrought-iron
swing-bridge, the work of an Italian firm and a very pleasing example of
late nineteenth-century functionalism, guarded at one end by the ruins of
a Venetian fort and at the other by the town of Chalcis.

Forty years ago Chalcis had the reputation of being one of the prettiest
towns in Greece, but in the intervening period modern improvements have
effectively disposed of this claim ; the walls have all been destroyed, the
minarets cast down, and in their place now stand a singularly hideous
barracks and a quantity of shabby warehouses.   Nevertheless, the town
has retained two monuments of note, a mosque which though ruinous still
produces even to one completely ignorant of the niceties of Mussulman
architecture an uncommonly dignified and impressive effect, and a most
interesting church.   In one respect the latter is unique ; it is the only
existing example of Gothic architecture in Greece remaining intact.
Basilical in plan with the exceptionally broad nave common to all Franciscan
foundations from which the aisles are divided by arcades of pointed arches

surmounted for half their length by a clerestory, the only visible indications of Byzantium, apart from the modern *ikonostasis*, are the capitals of the pillars which were obviously lifted from some earlier building on the site. The chancel arch is enriched with a band of sculpture in the exquisite but slightly finicky taste of the French fourteenth century which is likely, one fancies, to have proved one of the very few pieces of handicraft in Greece which Ruskin would have found himself able unreservedly to admire, and of the two chapels terminating the aisles both are rib-vaulted, that to the north being sexpartite. And in the choir itself ribs are still dimly visible beneath the layers of plaster and the painting of the Pantokrator with which Orthodox zeal has attempted to disguise from the faithful that what custom demanded should be a dome is in fact a vault. Admittedly this is neither a very striking nor very important example of Gothic ; nevertheless few northern hearts can remain untouched by a certain nostalgia at the sight of these pointed arches chanced on so unexpectedly after a surfeit of pendentives and squinches.

The island of Euboea, or the Negropont as it was commonly known to earlier generations, is, save for a narrow coastal strip on the west, wild and mountainous ; its inhabitants, self-reliant and industrious, were among the first of the Ancient Greeks to embark on colonial enterprises and its capital, Chalcis, was the mother city of several of the Greek settlements in Sicily and gave its name to the district of Chalchidiki across the Thessalonian gulf. In later times it long remained the most important and highly prized of the Serene Republic's overseas possessions, while after the Venetian collapse its advantages were fully exploited by the Turks who here developed

a reputation for peculiar rapacity.[1] In the north of the island there still exists, reduced but undivided, what is in fact the last of the great Turkish estates in Greece, Achmetaga. After climbing a mountain range and descending a narrow, romantic gorge through which dashes a highly picturesque torrent, one at length emerges on a scene which approximates more closely to the conception of Arcady embodied in the paintings of Poussin than anything to be found in the Peloponnese. Across a wide and fertile valley through groves of plane trees, reputed to be even larger and older than those in the Vale of Tempe itself, flows a stream so broad and full as almost to deserve here in Greece the description of river. The wide meadows

[1] " From the Greeks of Athens, the Jews of Thessaloniki, and the Turks of Negropont, good Lord deliver us ! " a popular saying in pre-liberation Greece quoted by Gibbon.

and pastures on either bank are dotted with browsing cattle and toiling peasantry picturesquely grouped ; on the lower slopes of the encircling mountains, thickly wooded, are scattered white painted homesteads uncommonly tidy and well maintained. In the principal village the cottages are surrounded by gardens in the highest condition of productivity, tall groves of plane and poplar shade the roadway and on the banks of innumerable small streams infants of remarkable beauty play among the ducks and chickens. This idyllic condition of things is due neither to chance nor to the superior virtues of the local inhabitants, but to the fact that the estate was purchased on the departure of the last Pasha by a member of the Noel family, inspired by his cousin Lady Byron to try his fortunes in Greece, who here instituted a benevolent despotism which was worthily maintained by his descendants and is to-day admirably exercised by Mrs. Philip Noel-Baker, the present owner.

Compared to the great natural beauty of the place the architectural interest is small, though there are many excellent examples of traditional cottage buildings (the manor-house itself was burnt down by the Italians during the Occupation), but for keen hagiologists the little church, curiously nonconformist in its external effect, will prove singularly rewarding. For here are deposited the remains of one of the least known and most curious of the many St. Johns in the Greek Calendar. A Russian nobleman by

107

birth, this holy man had attained the rank of general in the armies of the Tzar when he was captured by the Turks at the Battle of Plevna ; being allowed by his captors a considerable degree of liberty, he never attempted

to break his parole, or return to his fatherland, an example of constancy which had it been displayed by a Russian general in more recent times we should perhaps have been justified in assuming to have been dictated by an enlightened self-interest but which in those more barbarous days was sufficient, apparently, to merit canonization. After his death his fame and miraculous powers earned the village in Turkey where he died a considerable local reputation and when in 1923 the Greek population were forced to return to the mother country his embalmed corpse, together with a lot of large and singularly unattractive ikons, was carried on the shoulders of the faithful a three days' march from the interior of Asia Minor to the coast. On arrival in Greece the Saint was temporarily deposited in the church at Chalcis, during which time his good offices were so highly appreciated by the local population that it was only with the greatest reluctance that they allowed his rightful owners to take him with them to their new home at Achmetaga. And, indeed, shortly after his departure from their midst the former organized a highly successful cutting-out operation to remove the relic in a lorry by night, and it was only after prolonged negotiations carried on under the threat of civil strife that the devoted villagers finally regained their property. Restored at last to what one hopes will prove his final resting-place, the Saint is now visible in a glass-topped coffin, dusky with age, but his tarnished epaulettes still gleaming fitfully in the candle-light.

The only other town in Boeotia of a size and importance comparable to Thebes is Livadia, which lies at the other end of the Copaic plain on the main road to the north. Clustered thickly on the slopes of the mountain which here comes right down into the plain, it is indistinguishable in appearance from innumerable other Greek provincial towns save in one respect. Turning sharply to the left at the top of the principal street one is confronted after two minutes' walk by a scene so truly 'awful' in the eighteenth-century sense of the term, so romantically grandiose, that it is

difficult to realize that one is still but a stone's throw from the main road of a considerable town. The road, as a road, here ends at a high-backed Turkish bridge, across which it continues in the shape of a mule track, disappearing after a hundred yards or so round the shoulder of a canyon. To the left an immense precipice towers above this narrow gorge which on the right is flanked by a rocky height, hardly less sheer, crowned with the ruins of a Catalan fortress. The narrow torrent which comes pouring down alongside the mule-track is here fed by several springs and streams which gush out from the face of the rock and empties itself, this side of the bridge, into a large mill-pond shaded by old plane-trees. The whole scene is one that would have been admirably recorded by such an artist as James Ward.

In classical times the place attracted a crowd of visitors quite uncon-cerned with its natural beauties ; for these springs, exactly which it is now, alas, impossible accurately to determine, are those of Mnemosyne and Lethe, Memory and Forgetfulness, and in the cavern above resided the oracle of Trophonius, second in fame only to that of Delphi itself. Trophonius was allegedly a son of the King of Orchomenos, with marked architectural abilities, who is credited with designing the earliest temple of Apollo at Delphi. For some reason that remains a trifle obscure, shortly after the completion of his masterpiece, the ground opened and swallowed him up and when some time later the Boeotians were suffering from a severe drought they were guided by a miraculous swarm of bees to this cavern, which was, presumably, as near the surface as the engulfed architect could get, where he gave them oracular but satisfactory advice in their trouble. The popularity of the oracle continued unabated down to the time of Pausanias, despite the fact that the ritual involved in its consultation was the most elaborate in Greece. Here the applicant could not get away with anything so comparatively simple as sleeping under a sacred oak or handing in a correctly completed questionnaire to the Pythoness, but was forced, after a long period of preparation, marked by frequent ceremonial washings in the correct streams, to descend feet foremost into a narrow pit whence he was sucked down into an underground channel, out of which he was finally ejected with considerable force upside down in an unconscious condition. It is not, therefore, surprising to read that the applicants were not infrequently in a very dejected frame of mind for some time after consultation. Apart from this remarkable gorge the only other points of interest about Livadia are the peculiar quality of the soil which, according to Pliny, renders the neighbourhood lethal to moles, and a handsome public clock presented to the town by the celebrated Lord Elgin.

Song for the brides of Argos
Combing the swarms of golden hair :
Quite quiet, quiet there.

Under the rolling comb of grass,
The sword outhrusts the golden helm.

Agamemnon under tumulus serene
Outsmiles the jury of skeletons :
Cool under cumulus the lion queen :

Only the drum can celebrate,
Only the adjective outlive them.

LAWRENCE DURRELL

THE coast-road from Athens to the Isthmus of Corinth is one of the most celebrated, as it must assuredly be one of the most beautiful in the world, but formerly its fame was due rather to the dangers with which the wayfarer was confronted than to the exceptional merit of the surrounding scenery.   The only town of any importance through which it passes is Megara, where all the women wear yellow headkerchiefs and on feast-days paint their faces (a custom which until very recent times was quite unknown elsewhere in Greece) in an elaborate and supposedly antique fashion which is held by the Megarans strongly to support their claim to be the last descendants of the aboriginal inhabitants of Attica.   Thence the road mounts and skirts a precipice overhanging the sea in so hazardous a manner as to have occasioned the unfavourable notice of the geographer, Strabo.   The Scironian rocks, as these heights are called, take their name from a celebrated highway robber who until his career was cut short by the heroic Theseus used at this point to toss unwary travellers into the sea below, where they were instantly consumed by a gigantic tortoise.   The large rock which is visible just offshore below the highest point of the cliffs is said by some to be the bones of Sciron which, rejected by both sea and land, hung suspended in mid-air until completely petrified ; others hold that it is merely the remains of the tortoise. Later, conditions were somewhat improved by a carriage road built by the Emperor Hadrian, but this did not long survive the Empire, and in the last century was only a mule-track, impassable for horses, and notorious for its steepness and danger : even a hardy and experienced Swiss traveller of the period records that he was here subject to a vertigo which had never assailed him among the passes and peaks of his native Alps. To-day a motor road and an electric railway run parallel along the cliffs, both easily and successfully blown out by German engineers but now, at length, restored by the British.

The isthmus of Corinth is one of the dreariest stretches of country in all Greece ; of exactly the right elevation and width to cut off all view of the sea, of so poor a soil as to support nothing but the most depressed-looking scrub, the motorist, enveloped (save immediately after a downfall of rain when he will find himself axle-deep in mud) in a cloud of dun-coloured dust of extraordinary penetrative power, is likely to find it as uninspiring scenically as Hartford Bridge Flats, which in many ways it much resembles. Although of no great extent, one still marvels at the apparent ease with which in the days before the canal whole battle fleets were rolled across this strip of land ; in the Peloponnesian war both Spartans and Athenians performed this feat, which was repeated after Actium by the Emperor Augustus in hot pursuit of the vanquished Antony and Cleopatra, and again in Byzantine times. Hardly less surprising is the lack of success with which a position, that one would have imagined to be easily defensible, has been held in the face of a determined onslaught from the north from the time of the Goths to that of Feldmarschall von List. The celebrated canal is to-day blocked at several points by demolitions (easy enough to bring about where the soil is so soft that even in peace time free passage was not infrequently hindered by landfalls), and at the eastern end by a sunk tanker reputedly so ingeniously set about with lethal booby-traps of all sorts that it is likely to remain where it is for some time to come.

The modern town of Corinth is situated in the angle of the isthmus and the northern coastline of the Peloponnese ; completely wrecked by a disastrous earthquake in 1928 it was entirely rebuilt in the period immediately following and now provides as nasty an example of twentieth-century urban architecture as can be found in Europe. Two miles further on and slightly inland are the ruins of old Corinth, where, with the aid of a map, the enthusiast may trace many of the principal streets and squares of a city which in the ancient world combined the opulence and financial importance of nineteenth-century Liverpool with a reputation for commercialized pleasure which in our own day only Atlantic City can rival. However, not even the fountain of Pirene, noticed and approved by Pausanias, nor the remains of the Doric temple, the oldest in Greece with capitals curiously squat and wide, nor even the memory of the Pauline sojourn, can invest this site with much glamour. For the Corinthians seem always to be among the least sympathetic of the ancients, the advertising men and motor-car salesmen of the Greek world, whose history and whose art (save for the earliest examples of proto-Corinthian pottery) both alike testify to the presence of an undeniably vulgar streak in the national character. Even the appalling massacre of the entire population by Mummius moves us less in retrospect than do many of the less drastic fates which overtook other cities of the ancient world ; and indeed on the numerous occasions in its long history on which the place was successfully assaulted one's sympathies seem invariably to be engaged by the attackers, notably by that Aratus whose daring capture of the town for the Achaean league is so movingly described by Plutarch. This lack of sympathy may perhaps be in part induced, as it is certainly increased, by the spectacle of Acrocorinth : no city, one feels, with so apparently unassailable a citadel as this should have been captured quite so frequently and easily as history tells us that it undoubtedly was. This majestic sugar-loaf, rising seemingly perpendicularly from sea-level to a height of eighteen hundred feet, is girdled at the summit by an extensive cincture of crenellated curtain walls and crowned by a massive keep. Fortified from the earliest times, the existing defences are largely Venetian with Turkish additions, though here and there are traces of both Byzantine and Frankish work. The top when one arrives there is of considerably greater extent than one would have imagined, and the baileys, barbicans and fortified posterns correspondingly more numerous. Incidentally it was here, in a then unravished meadow, that Pegasus was browsing when first discovered and captured by Bellerophon.

Past Acrocorinth the road to the south enters a landscape quite different in character from that of Attica or the Isthmus. Here the mountains immediately enclosing the valley are no longer naked and tawny ; their lower slopes are covered with a layer of yellowish soil curiously stained and blotched with patches of venetian red in a loose water-colour technique, while the rocks which thrust through towards their summits are a cold violet-grey dotted and mottled with dark-green shrubs. Alongside the road a stream has carved its way through the valley-bed so deeply and neatly as to recall one of those models employed by schoolmasters to demonstrate the facts of physical geography ; the water-course itself, through which, save after a phenomenal storm, no more than a desultory trickle of brownish water seems ever to flow, is choked with oleanders, while on the fields above the perpendicular cliffs of this miniature canyon, vines, maize and figs are more or less flourishing. In the immediate foreground planes and white poplars have replaced the monotonous eucalyptus whose meagre shade is all that Attica affords, and the middle distance gains character and emphasis from the ghostly hieroglyphics of the bare fig-trees and the black exclamation marks of innumerable cypresses. Lovely at all seasons, this country is at its best in the late spring when the oleanders are in bloom, bringing to the rocky river-bed an improbable flavour of the Edwardian conservatory : when the verge along the road is a mosaic of wild flowers and one may observe, if one is lucky, darting and swooping among the young vines in their extraordinary, erratic manner of flight a flock of that beautiful metallic bird, the bee-eater.

After a few miles the mountains press in on either side until there is barely room in the valley for the road and stream to run parallel, and the light railway is forced to cling precariously to the mountainside to the south until it disappears into the pass of Dervenaki where, during the War of Independence, a small Greek force under Kolokotronis ambushed a large Turkish army returning from an incautious expedition to the Argolid (a glorious victory which bulks large in the national saga but which the cynical Findlay considers to have been due rather to the dilatoriness and incompetence of the Capitan Pasha than to any outstanding display of skill or daring on the part of the Greeks). A little farther on the road forks ; to the left, mounting a narrow pass parallel to that of Dervenaki leading to the plain of Argos, to the right traversing a tract of rock-strewn downs to Nemea. From now on one is in the heart of the Hercules country ; at Nemea itself the hero disposed of the famous lion, while in the mountains immediately above lies the Stymphalian lake celebrated for its ferocious bird-life to which he successfully put an end. South of the pass is Tiryns, where his childhood was spent and where he strangled the serpents (the first incident in classical mythology of which I, and I suspect many of my contemporaries, were made aware, thanks to the spirited wood-engraving which used to testify on the bottle to the invigorating qualities of Woodward's gripe-water), facing across the bay the spot where in later life he overcame that more formidable reptile, the Hydra. To-day the hero's memory is only preserved at Nemea in the name of the local red wine, the powerful ' Lion's Blood ', for which this district is justly celebrated. Apart from Herculean associations the spot is of interest as having been the site of the Nemean games, one of the four great athletic festivals of ancient Greece originally founded to commemorate the death of a mysterious Argive worthy, the infant Archemorus who perished from the bite of a serpent when his nurse had incautiously laid him down on some sprigs of parsley, but which subsequently came to be connected more closely with the later and more active hero.   To-day there still stand in the midst of a saucer-shaped valley, where the cypresses are larger and more numerous than any I have seen elsewhere, a few columns of a Doric temple of Zeus, of a markedly slenderer form than is usual ; and many more lie shattered where they were cast down by an earthquake.

The view of the plain of Argos first seen from the narrow defile, or perhaps to even greater advantage from the hill of Mycenae, is assuredly one of the world's great views ; or would be so considered did we still continue to take that interest in views for their own sake which proved so absorbing to our great-grandfathers.   But to-day the grand panorama is out of fashion ; painters such as Utrillo and Sickert have shown us the beauty of the suburban street corner and the tram-stop by the canal, poets such as Eliot and Bet-jeman have cast their spell over the dingy perspective of by-pass and stucco, and we all seek refuge from immensities in the discovery of chance beauty in *intimiste* surroundings.   This development is by no means new but has been continuing for upwards of a century ; Tennyson's near-sightedness, the Pre-Raphaelites' preoccupation with detail, the scientific palette of the Impressionists, the cosiness of Birkett Forster, the colour prints of Hokusai, a half-baked anxiety for ' naturalness ' at all costs, have all contributed to the shift in our angle of vision and the resultant break-up of the splendid arranged scenery of Claude and the early Turner, and to confine a taste for panorama to the less sophisticated tourist and those responsible for the advertisements of the Southern Railway.   For my part I unashamedly confess to being a ' pushover ' for vistas ; no eminence so steep, no winding stair so tortuous that a promise of a view over seven counties will not get me aloft.   However, although an addict I am not uncritical ; demanding both form (foreground, middle-distance, and background) and extent in my views ; if the former be lacking the effect is as undramatic as a landscape seen from an aeroplane, while it is only the presence of the latter that differentiates a view from a picturesque peep.   The present prospect, nobly fulfilling both these con-ditions, is like some splendid water-colour by the elder Cozens.   The fore-ground is boldly filled in with a jumble of vast cyclopean limestone crags following the downward slope of the hill ; in the middle-distance the plain of Argos, framed on either hand by ranges of mountains, stretches away to where on the horizon the waters of the bay of Nauplia gleam palely blue beneath the vast rock of Palamidi, reduced at this distance to the dimensions of a sand castle.   It possesses, moreover, the additional merit, not absolutely essential but always welcome, of human interest, that is here provided by the cultivation in the plain and the ruins just visible on the summit of the high hill above Argos.

The citadel of Mycenae itself lies a mile or two off the main road to the left, occupying the summit of a low foothill guarding the mouth of a narrow cleft between two steep, conical and completely bare mountains. From a distance it makes no effect at all, so similar in shape and colour are the vast blocks of which it is built to the surrounding rocks, and it is not until one has rounded half its circumference and halted opposite the Lion Gate that one first becomes aware of the staggering impressiveness of the place. For of all the existing remains of remote antiquity this is surely the most moving ; compared to these few fragments of wall and half-dozen empty tombs the Pyramids are but a boring exercise in solid geometry carried out by an unimaginative totalitarian ; the Coliseum of no more interest than the Wembley stadium ; the great wall of China and the temples of Yucatan likely to prove too far removed from our own past for proper comprehension. Closer, in the feelings they arouse, are Stonehenge and Cnossos, but of the former we know too little and of the latter too much ; in Wiltshire the imagination has too great a freedom, peopling that majestic circle with Druids and Celtic chieftains, a host of shadows clad in indeterminate garments performing ill-defined ceremonies ; in Crete the elaborate restorations, the store-cupboards and the water-closets set too strict limits to the play of fancy. But here just sufficient evidence has been dug out of the soil, and tradition and poetry have preserved just accurately enough the figures of the Atridae, fully to engage our sympathies without overwhelming our interest with a superfluity of detail. Moreover, when one has circulated the citadel itself, climbed the grooved ramp along which passed the chariot of the returning *generalissimo*, mounted the stairs once purple-carpeted by Clytemnestra against his return, observed where a corner of the great hall has long since crashed into the goat-haunted ravine below, there still remains the so-called Treasury of Atreus, which is from the purely structural point of view, apart from all else, the most remarkable monument remaining to us from the Bronze Age in any country in the world. Through the slope of a low hill runs a level, unroofed trench or *dromos*, lined with well-cut masonry leading to a gateway, to-day impressive solely by reason of its size and proportions, as the decorated pilasters that once flanked it have long since been whisked away to Bloomsbury,[1] surmounted by a triangular opening in which it

---

[1] The return of these pilasters, whose empty sockets are a standing reproach to our nation, might far more easily be effected than that of the Elgin marbles. Uninteresting in themselves, they should be removed from their pointless isolation in the British Museum and restored to the setting away from which they lose all significance.

is probable that there once stood a sculptured group similar to that above
the Lion Gate. Over the threshold one finds oneself in a seemingly enormous circular chamber of which the walls gradually incurving at last come
together to hold in place the large key slab high above our heads. What
immediately impresses in this interior is not the extreme simplicity, for this
is largely fortuitous, the gold rosettes that once adorned these walls having
long since vanished along with all other traces of decoration, but the immense
technical skill with which each individual block of masonry has been cut,
the mathematical ability displayed in their grading and, above all, the
constructive imagination required ever to have conceived so ingeniously
planned a structure on so large a scale. Is this the outcome, one wonders,
of century after century of practice and experiment, the final triumph for
which all those round tombs with trench-like approaches roughly constructed in unhewn slabs, from Sardinia to the Hebrides were but fumbling
and barbarous essays? Or are these latter rather to be regarded as but the
feeble expression of some dim memory of this past glory haunting the racial
consciousness of the scattered and degenerate descendants of the Mycenean
masons? This is a question to which doubtless the archaeologists will
one day find an answer; but whatever that answer may be, it can in no way
affect the spell which these ruins cast, for they are among the very few works
of man which have attained an existence outside time, as unaffected by
the processes of human thought as the sea or the mountains. On leaving
this valley, particularly at evening, one is assailed by that feeling which
many buildings of great age and beauty produce as one quits them, though
never in my experience in such intensity as here, that the sentiments which
the sight of them has aroused are not altogether subjective; that throughout
the coming night, and the next day, and the next, for centuries to come, a
mysterious and to us incomprehensible life will continue in its own rhythm
which our visit was as powerless to interrupt as was the passage of the panzer
divisions five years gone by, or of the Turkish armies hurrying north, or
Mr. Gladstone being shown round by Schliemann, or as are the dogs barking
in a far-off farm or the nightingales singing overhead . . .

> . . . and sang within the bloody wood
> When Agamemnon cried aloud
> And let their liquid siftings fall
> Upon that stiff dishonoured shroud.

To be situated halfway between Mycenae and Tiryns would impose a
certain strain on any town, but Argos, even if it did not enjoy the close
proximity of two such monuments would still fail to impress. Having been

almost completely destroyed during the War of Independence it retains to-day no character of antiquity and suffers furthermore from the presence, in the centre of the principal square, of a more than usually large and hideous Neo-Byzantine Church. Like Corinth, it is in its present condition overwhelmed by the magnificence of its citadel, perched on the top of the conical hill known as the Larisa which, though less than half the height of Acrocorinth is by reason of its exceptional steepness hardly less impressive ; here too the summit is crowned by a ring of medieval fortifications, part Byzantine, part Frankish, which seem, however, to have been defended by the Argives with a tenacity that was seldom displayed by the Corinthians, notably in the thirteenth century when under Guillaume de Champlitte the town sustained a prolonged siege by the Byzantine forces, and again in the early nineteenth when it was successfully held against the Turks by Ypsilantis. Outside the town on the road to Tripolis lies an immense theatre largely cut out of the side of the hill which, when complete, is considered to have seated no less than twenty thousand spectators. Alongside it are the ruins of a mysterious Roman building in brick of the exact nature and purpose of which I have never discovered any satisfactory explanation, and in the cemetery near by is a cross-in-square Byzantine church overrestored but externally of considerable beauty and interest which for some reason escapes notice in all the text-books.

The Argolid, as the plain round the city is called, is fertile and celebrated since antiquity for the merit of the horses which are bred there. To-day it is not so much the horses as the carts they draw which are worthy of note. These are high, two-wheeled affairs not unlike elevated costers' barrows, elaborately and traditionally painted, and it is the familiarity of the style with which this decoration is carried out which renders them so remarkable. For these floral patterns, landscape motifs derived from picture-postcards, and grouped horses' heads enlivening the dashboard, have for us nothing of the exotic, for they can be almost exactly paralleled in their treatment and disposition with similar decorations not only on our few remaining costermonger barrows but also on barges, ice-cream carts and caravans. The reflection which the spectacle of these Argive carts arouses (in fact they are general all over Greece, but the specimens to be seen round Argos are more numerous and more elaborate) is one of doubt whether perhaps the interest which, thanks to such tireless researchers as Miss Barbara Jones, has recently been taken in the surviving popular art of our own islands has not been a trifle too insular ; one wonders whether all those carefully collected examples of still happily unselfconscious rustic adornment, so far from being so peculiarly local as is generally supposed, may not merely be Anglo-Saxon variants on a widespread international theme.   If this is indeed the case, the original place of origin of the style is still to seek, but as to the method of its dissemination over an area stretching from Donegal to Crete it is possible to hazard a guess.   The fact that it is almost always found to flourish most vigorously in districts connected with horse-breeding, and elsewhere in fair grounds or on canals, stamps it as a nomad art, and it is surely not too fanciful to suppose that for its wide but incidental dispersal we have in fact to thank the Gypsies.

Gypsies are to be found all over Greece, closely resembling in appearance and behaviour our own variety, but displaying in the costume of their womenfolk a marked difference.   Instead of the plumed hat and sealskin jacket so popular on Epsom downs, the women here effect ankle-length petticoats, elaborately ruched and frilled, worn without a skirt, and a loose short-sleeved cotton blouse or *bolero*.   Their heads are covered with a handkerchief arranged, in most cases, not in the manner of the Greek peasant woman with the two ends crossing over the lower part of the face and tying behind the head (a mode which is said to have come down from Byzantine times), but rather in the style of the English gypsies made familiar to us by the paintings of Mr. John.   In their taste for brilliant colours they are the equal of their English sisters, the shades most favoured being a pink more ' shocking ' than any devised by Schiaparelli and a vivid chrome yellow.   The males are usually  attired in much the same fashion as elsewhere, even retaining, in a countryside where every peasant who is neither too old-fashioned nor too poor has acquired a cloth cap, a characteristic preference for the slouch hat.   Their speech, so I was informed by a philologically inclined companion who chanced to overhear the conversation of some children by the wayside, is undoubtedly a variety of Romany, but differing considerably from that still current in western Europe.

Halfway between Argos and Nauplia, a few yards to the left of the road, there rises casually and undramatically the fortress of Tiryns.   Larger than Mycenae, of greater antiquity and better preserved, whether because of its less dramatic situation or the fact that the careers of its inmates have not been immortalized for us by the poets, it yet fails so overwhelmingly to impress.   Of the interest of the site, however, there exists no doubt for nowhere else, even at Mycenae, can one gain so adequate an idea of the extraordinary civilization which flourished in this plain from the middle of the fifteenth century B.C. to the middle of the twelfth. Protected by these immense walls, in places twenty-five feet thick, dwelt an aristocracy enjoying a manner of life which, if rather less refined, was distinctly more robust than that of the Minoans and of which the like was not to be seen again in these parts for centuries to come. The founders of this civilization came, not as was once thought, overseas from Crete, but down from the north. On arrival they were certainly at a far lower stage of development than the mixed population of Pelasgians and Cretan colonists whom they discovered in possession of all the more readily accessible stretches of the coast, but they must undoubtedly have been exceedingly quick-witted and assimilative, for not only did they readily absorb all the cultural refinements of the Minoans but also developed a nautical ability sufficient to enable them within a century of their first arrival to sack the great city of Cnossos itself and bring that age-old civilization crashing down, never to rise again. To-day all that remains of all that complex glory, apart from a half-dozen sites such as this, are some fragments of fresco similar in style to those at Cnossos but portraying a people subtly different in costume and physique, a handful of gold ornaments wherein a highly evolved technique has not suppressed a barbaric grandeur of conception, some of the finest pottery ever made and vague rumours of the lives and actions of its shadowy princes embodied in the Homeric sagas.

No greater contrast in the nature of the historical interest aroused by two almost contiguous sites could be found than that existing between Tiryns and Nauplia lying but a couple of miles apart. In the former, the last flicker of human activity faded away almost three millennia ago ; the culture that produced it is almost as remote from ours in time as it is possible for a civilization to be, and of all the intervening ages between the Bronze and the Atomic the only trace left on these gigantic blocks is a slit trench blasted through a section of the wall by the Germans. Nauplia, on the other hand, bears architectural witness to an activity dating from no earlier than the sixteenth century ; here, as nowhere else in Greece, it is possible to shake off the illusion, for it is an illusion, that time, after gradually slowing down for centuries, finally stopped somewhere around the middle of the eleventh century and only resumed its march in the middle of the nineteenth. This comparative familiarity in time is paralleled in space for many of these buildings—the town hall with its arcades and subtle window-spacing, the high stone-built mansions which stare blankly at one another across narrow streets—represent a tradition from which even we ourselves, from the day when the Queen's House was built at Greenwich to that

which witnessed the completion of the Travellers' Club, have profited.
Thanks to the Venetians, the atmosphere of Nauplia is, as the Greeks
would say, decidedly western European.

The town first passed into the hands of the Serene Republic by cession
on the decline of the Frankish power in 1402, and they managed to retain
it until 1540, when it fell to the Turks. In 1686, however, thanks to that
last spasmodic twitch of Venetian imperialism, the Turks lost the town to
their old rivals under Morosini, who held it until 1705, and it is during this
final period that the elaborate fortifications, both of the citadel on Itsh-Kaleh
and the great stronghold on the summit of Mount Palamidi (recalling in their
austere functionalism, heraldically relieved by escutcheons and winged lions
over the various gateways, the illustrations to a treatise of Vauban) were
built. The Turks as usual simply took over for their own use what others
had constructed, and to-day the only visible traces of their presence are a
fountain, a mosque where the anti-representational prejudices of the Prophet
are now nightly flouted by the animated shadows of Lana Turner and Clark
Gable, and the wide eaves with which many of otherwise strongly Italianate
houses are furnished, decorated in some cases with folk-paintings of considerable charm. When at last they were finally disposed of a new period in the
town's history, brief but glorious, began ; for seven years, 1827 to 1834,
Nauplia was the capital of the newly liberated Greece. This distinction it
largely owed to its situation, which was almost equally convenient for the
magnates and shipowners of Hydra and Spetsai, the Kapitanos, such as

Kolokotronis, operating in the northern and central Peloponnese, and the feudal lords of the Mani, the three elements who between them divided the control of the national movement. However, although the new capital served well enough to unite them physically its deceptively Western atmosphere did not prove sufficiently powerful in effect to counteract the national genius for discord, and it was outside the principal church in the town that Capodistrias, the remarkable Corfiote who after a successful career in the Tsarist diplomatic service became the first head of an independent Greek Government, was assassinated by George Mavromichaelis, the most important of the Maniote chieftains. This short period of metropolitan glory left its mark on the town in a large number of good Othonian-style houses which contrast not unfavourably with the pseudo-*palazzi* of Venetian days, although to judge by the incidence of bomb damage their construction was considerably less solid. Whether the phenomenal number of wrought-iron balconies, projecting from every type of house, are attributable to Venetian, Turkish or Greek influence I am unable to say, but, together with the extraordinary richness and beauty of the innumerable tiny gardens, often no more than three whitewashed petrol-cans alongside a doorstep, attached to the cottages clustered round the foot of Itsh-Kaleh, they serve to lend a charming air of light opera to the whole town. With the removal of the capital to Athens a decline set in and the only building of note of more recent date is a Mycenean Revival bank in the principal square, a rare example of a style to which one understands the late General Metaxas to have been peculiarly attached.

The country to the east of Nauplia, through which the modern traveller usually tears to get to Epidaurus, is by no means without interest. Some short distance out of the town on slopes of that range of hills of which Palamidi is the most conspicuous, stands a singularly beautiful little convent dating from the eleventh century. The exterior provides an excellent example of the decorative use of brick in conjunction with stone, the surrounding buildings, though severely plain, are harmonious and the garden in which they all stand is one of the most beautiful in a completely unpretentious way I have ever seen. The interior of the church, however, to which we had been drawn by the guide-books' mention of '*peintures exceptionelles*', proved to have been richly frescoed with the most painstakingly repellent nine-

Nea Moni, near Nauplia

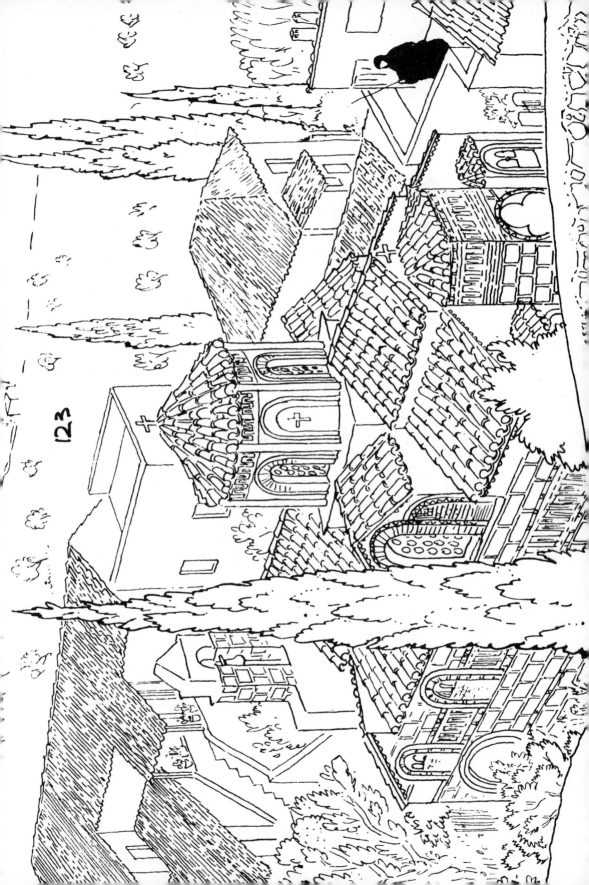

123

teenth-century *bondieuseries* in the whole of Greece. The abbess, who was responsible both for the charming garden and, as she proudly admitted, the murals, was a woman of considerable character. Close on eighty at the time of our visit, she was soon to celebrate her jubilee as a nun and spoke movingly of her deep appreciation of the blessings of the contemplative life. It had afforded her, she explained, many opportunities for tranquil reflection on the eternal verities which for her included, strangely enough, the present strategic situation in the central and eastern Mediterranean. As a result of her long cogitations she was able to reveal, without fear of contradiction, that it was manifestly the will of God that Russia should be wiped off the map as soon as possible. The stern glance with which she accompanied this conclusion awoke in me an uneasy feeling that the least I could do was to go out and set about the Lord's work personally and at once. Fortunately she soon embraced the opportunity which the presence of outsiders provided for discussing the affairs of the world which she had so long ago renounced, and in particular she spoke of the drama to which she had always had a strong attachment, the result, she told us, of a performance of *King Lear* by a Turkish repertory company in Smyrna that she had witnessed in the 'eighties of the last century and which had left an ineffaceable impression on her mind.

On the sea-coast to the south of the mountains behind Nauplia lie the remains of another Mycenean citadel. Asine, smaller, and far less elaborate than Tiryns or Mycenae, yet possesses a strange, individual aura of its own. In part, no doubt, this is due to the remarkable beauty of its setting

on a low mound directly overlooking the sea with a small rocky bay on
the one hand and a long sandy beach on the other, but the very obscurity
which surrounds its rulers and its history and the miniature scale, when
compared to Tiryns, of both its walls and its surroundings (the mountains
hereabouts are steep but not high and the landscape generally recalls the
small canvases of Patnir) are not without their effect. During the second
German War the place was once more fortified, this time by the Italians,
and if one walks along the crumbling slit trenches one finds oneself in places
ankle deep in potsherds, both Mycenean and geometric. In one place the
floor of a gun-site has been laboriously laid out in an amateur mosaic pavement of pebbles of which the principal decorative motif is the dreary exhor-
tation ' Combattere, laborare, etc.' Curiously enough the presence of these
vulgar platitudes in such a situation does not, as one might have expected,
arouse any feeling of indignation ; the effect they produce is rather one of
pathos inspired by the picture of some miserable little Wop trying in vain to
keep up his spirits in these heroic surroundings by giving concrete form
to these ridiculous but familiar maxims : (the Italians are really a very
humourless race). To-day, despite his still existent handiwork, this unknown soldier and all that he represented have vanished more completely,
have become, in these surroundings, infinitely more shadowy than the
original ruler of this coast of whom we know nothing but that he once, more
than three thousand years ago, existed.

> Et le roi d'Asiné que nous cherchions depuis deux ans
> Inconnu oublié de tous même d'Homère
> Un seul mot dans l'Iliade et ce mot douteux
> Jeté ici comme un masque d'or tombal
> Tu le touchas ? te rappelles-tu sa résonnance ? creuse dans la lumière
> Comme la jarre désséchée dans le sol excavé ;
> Et résonnance pareille dans la mer sous nos rames.
> Le roi d'Asiné sous la masque un vide
> Qui partout nous suit partout nous suit, sous un nom :
> Ασινην τε, Ασινην τε. . . .[1]

Farther to the east, just inland from the coast, is Epidaurus, where in
classical times the great shrine of Aesculapius combined for the Hellenic
world the dramatic attractions of the Salzburg Festival with the therapeutic
advantages of Aix or Harrogate. To-day there remain the finest Greek
theatre in existence, as perfect, as functional and as unromantic as a well-
designed gasometer, the foundations of several smart temples and luxury
hotels, some traces of Roman baths and a most curious building, known as

---

[1] Ο Βασιλιας της Ασινης, Y. Seferis, trans. by Levesque.

the Tholos, surrounded by two concentric colonnades of which considerable fragments of the inner, in a beautiful and very early Corinthian style, are preserved in the museum, and concealing in its midst an elaborate system of trenches which may once have served, it has been suggested, as a ritual snake-pit. In medieval times the neighbourhood was chiefly celebrated for the presence of a remarkable hermit whose piety was so phenomenal and who had achieved such a degree of sanctity that even the forces of nature were compelled to pay attention when he spoke, as was dramatically demonstrated when on the occasion of the neighbouring village being threatened by inundation from an exceptionally high tide, he addressed the waves in much the same terms as did King Canute but with exactly contrary results. Of these stirring times no monuments are to-day visible at Epidaurus itself, but a mile or two back along the Nauplia road, close to the village of Ligourio, are three small Byzantine churches, all very ancient and all of interest. In the largest, situated in the village itself, are some remarkable wall-paintings, including a doxology in which a large number of animals, clouds, trees and mountains are all shown in attitudes of ecstatic and animated praise. Unfortunately the interior of the church is very dark and the paintings very begrimed, so intensive study is difficult. One section of the frescoes has indeed, as the local worthies were at pains to point out, recently been cleaned ; a process which, if continued, will undoubtedly ensure the total dissappearance of the lot in a matter of months.

The strip of country across the bay of Nauplia, hemmed in between the mountains and the sea, fertile though it is, has little enough to show to compensate for the appalling state of the road ; nevertheless, round Myli, where Hercules overcame the Hydra, the landscape has a character of its own, thanks to a stream, the ancient Lerna or Amymone, that here divides into innumerable channels winding through the water-meadows to the sea in so serpentine a manner that the late Professor Tozer was led to identify them with the innumerable heads of the legendary monster overcome by the hero, a typically materialist and unimaginative example of the higher criticism which would, if accepted, reduce a notable exploit to a pedestrian level of a commonplace feat of hydraulic engineering. In later times the place was celebrated as being the site of one of the more heroic and successful actions in the War of Independence.

As the road leaves the coast on its long climb over the mountains to Tripolis one notices in the few villages *en route* a change in the architecture of the cottages. Gone are the one-storey shanties with single-pitched roofs, their walls colourwashed and windows boldly outlined in white, and in their place one sees more two-storied buildings with a projecting wooden balcony in front of the entrance on the first floor to which leads a rickety outside staircase. The ground-floor is here used as a store-room or pigsty, and beneath the floorboards of the balcony hang rows of indecent-looking pigskins inflated with wine. As one mounts, the landscape becomes increasingly barren and depressing ; between high unfriendly mountains lie wide flat valleys, marshy and waterlogged. Here and there an acre or two of dwarfish oak forest has survived, but the scene, though almost invariably damp, is treeless. It is, therefore, a considerable shock to realize that one is now at last in a position to say 'Et in Arcadia ego'. Tripolis, the capital of this gladeless, nymphless province, where to-day Poussin would find little to occupy his talents, is a sprawling characterless town where on the only occasion that I visited it when it was not raining it was snowing, standing in the midst of a windswept plain the monotony of which is quite unrelieved by its reputed fertility. The mountains that surround it are high and wild, the habitat of wolves, polecats and even jackals, the westernmost point at which this last, essentially Asiatic, animal has been located ; and in the few

villages the men still not uncommonly wear the *fustanella* and invariably in winter a heavy, homewoven, lambskin coat. In happier times Tripolis was famed for its good-living ; on Easter Sunday travellers approaching the town by rail could locate its position long before it was actually in sight by the dense cloud of smoke hanging in the air above it that rose from the innumerable fat lambs being roasted in the streets ; of this fact I was assured by the bishop himself who, incidentally, even in these hard times, managed to maintain a table that was by no means to be despised. (In particular I recall some excellent Mantinea, a local white wine that had gained enormously from being kept for some years in the episcopal cellar, a happy fate that, alas, overtakes too few wines in this thirsty and impatient land. Also a heavier wine, nearer brown than red in colour, in body not unlike a very light port with a peculiar, nutty flavour all its own, that is grown in the immediate neighbourhood of the town and of which very little is ever allowed to leave it.) In Turkish times Tripolis was the capital of the Morea, though why the Pasha, presumably a teetotaller, should have chosen as his residence the coldest spot in the Peloponnese, lacking every advantage or amenity save one and of that he was precluded by his religion from taking advantage, is difficult indeed to understand. When the Greeks captured the place in 1821 they slaughtered every single Turkish inhabitant to the number of more than eight thousand, an extravagance for which they paid dearly a few years later, for when the redoubtable Ibrahim Pasha re-took the town not only did he repeat the massacre, but for good measure levelled every building with the ground. It is not, therefore, surprising that to-day the city should have absolutely nothing to show of the slightest architectural interest.

The road from Tripolis to Sparta leaves the plain soon after passing the site of Tegea and begins a slow ascent of the mountains separating the plain of Tripolis from the valley of the Eurotas. From the top of the pass one first sees the snowclad peaks of Mount Taygetus, perhaps the most beautiful of all the Greek mountains, the vast bulk of which gradually reveals itself as one descends to the valley. The town of Sparta, despite the fact that it enjoyed, in the days of King Otho, the rare advantage of being laid out by a professional German town-planner, and a baron to boot, to-day, perhaps because the implementing of the plan was left to local talent, creates an even more dismal effect than Tripolis. In fact, this noble and carefully studied plan may well have proved a disadvantage by imposing an unnaturally tidy lay-out on elements which remain as squalid as usual, for the poverty of the average Greek provincial shop-front that in the picturesque confusion of a tortuous bazaar can easily be overlooked, is only too apparent when lining a broad, processional way (leading from the rubbish-dump to the slaughterhouse) inspired apparently by the Ludwigstrasse in Munich. Fortunately, by way of compensation for the more than usually disappointing aspect of the modern town, one is here quite free from that sense of guilt which the presence in the neighbourhood of antique remains that one has no intention of visiting usually induces. The happy certainty that the Rugbeian Commissars of antiquity were unlikely to have left behind them any architectural or aesthetic traces that could possibly engage the attention of a person of sensibility is more than justified, and one can hurry away to Mistra with a clear conscience.

There can be few cities in the whole world with a more remarkable situation than Mistra ; none with a more curious history. At the beginning of the thirteenth century a certain Geoffroi de Ville-Hardouin, returning from a brief Crusading outing in the Holy Land, stopped off in the Peloponnese. Noting the exceptional wealth and prosperity of the country (this part of Greece was at that time far more populous and highly developed than it is to-day or has been within living memory) and encouraged by the example of those more prominent Crusaders who had recently decided at Constantinople that there was really no essential difference between infidels and schismatics, he profited by an opportune squabble at that moment raging between two of the Greek barons in the south profitably to intervene and carve out for himself a substantial fief. In the course of time Geoffroi died and his estates passed first to his son of the same name and then to his nephew William. The latter was a ruler of remarkable abilities and un-limited ambition who at once set about increasing the limits of his princi-pality of Achaia (his uncle's original acquisition had by a most capable combination of conquest and diplomacy already been considerably enlarged) until they embraced the entire Peloponnese. This done, he proceeded in exactly the same manner as had his Norman forebears two centuries pre-viously in England to secure his conquests by the erection of a number of castles. One of the first sites he selected was this rocky spur of Mount Tay-getus rising abruptly from the Spartan plain and divided from the main mass of the mountain by a deep ravine, and on it he constructed as elabor-ate a fortress as his considerable skill in military architecture allowed. How-ever, the Prince of Achaia's conquests had been made with suspicious ease ; the Byzantine military machine in these parts, rusted from long disuse, hamstrung by a highly organized but incompetent bureaucracy and oper-ating under remote control, had proved easy game for the tough old buc-caneers of the Fourth Crusade. But William should have realized (and doubtless would have done had he had Professor Toynbee at his elbow) that the pressure of disaster, provided it is not of too overwhelming a nature, not infrequently calls forth a proportionate response. Ignoring this possibility, however, he embarked on an ill-starred invasion of the Byzantine dominions on the mainland which resulted in his capture by the Emperor and in order to secure his release he was forced to cede three of his principal strongholds to the Greeks, including Mistra, and in their hands the city remained until the time of the Turkish conquest.

In the course of the next two hundred years Mistra became the cultural capital, not only of Greece, but of the whole Empire. This Peloponnesian hill-town, with its innumerable churches and monasteries, was the very centre, as it has remained almost the sole monument, of the final flowering of the Greek genius, the scene of that strange isolated Renaissance which in so many ways foreshadowed what, on a continental scale, was shortly to come elsewhere. In many of the wall-paintings which here survive in better condition and greater numbers than anywhere else in Greece, there is a new lightness of touch, an increase in sensibility more full of promise and more Western in character than the rather over-sophisticated refinement of the later work at Daphni. Particularly one notices the bolder, less inhibited use of colour which yet remains entirely expressionist and as far from naturalism as ever.

Although the general impression one gains from these paintings is of a school rather than of a succession of individual masters, the imprint of certain distinct personalities operating at various periods is clearly discernible. Thus the artist (or artists, for there were probably two) at work in the Peribleptos was a subtle colourist with an inner intensity of vision that can, without undue straining, properly be described as Giottesque ; in the Pantanassa a master was at work whose genius found expression in an architectural marshalling of his various elements and a complete control over the disposition of elaborate and closely observed detail ; while whoever was responsible for the very late work in St. Nicholas was the able exponent of a linear technique that had earlier found expression in the less well-preserved, but possibly finer, paintings in the Brontocheion.[1]

The new lease of life which the Byzantine tradition here enjoys in the realm of painting is equally noticeable in the architecture of the town. The cross-in-square plan which would seem to have become almost obligatory elsewhere is only represented by three of the smaller churches of which the Peribleptos is the most important. In its stead the Mistran architects experimented with various varieties of the cross-domed basilica, with the most resounding success in the case of the Brontocheion, where one is made aware of the importance of space as an architectural element almost as vividly as at Daphni, and with the most consummate mastery given the difficult nature of this site, in the Pantanassa. Not all the new developments to which these buildings bear witness can, however, be attributed solely to the inventive genius of this last generation of Greek architects. Here and there exist visible signs—the trefoils at the east end of the Peribleptos, the arcade of pointed arches surmounted by a curious, almost ogival, fleur-de-lys-crested string-course round the apse of the Pantanassa and, above all, the campanile of the latter church—that the close proximity of a Frankish culture had not remained wholly without effect. Similarly the

[1] At Mistra the visitor is in the unusual but stimulating position of having to rely entirely on his own judgment as the various authorities are hopelessly at variance. Thus Diehl and Millet both consider the Peribleptos to contain the finest frescoes ; Byron and Talbot-Rice, on the other hand, maintain those in the Pantanassa to be the supreme achievement of the Mistran school. While Muratoff, who has but a low opinion of them all, regards the Peribleptos master as charming but decadent, the paintings in the Pantanassa to be the merest hack-work, and can only detect merit in the early and almost invisible murals in the Metropolis.

façade of the Despots palace, the most considerable secular building of Byzantine construction which exists, exhibits a distinctly Italianate look.

To-day this last outpost of Hellenism is completely deserted. The houses which once lined the steep, winding streets are crumbling away each on top of its own long-dry cistern ; the massive walls of Villehardouin's great keep are garrisoned by lizards and tortoises ; the lamps have long

The Brontocheion

since gone out in the churches and a handful of nuns in the Pantanassa are the only inhabitants of what was once the very centre of Orthodox Christendom. As recently as the beginning of the last century, when Leake visited the place, a Turkish Pasha dwelt in the palace of the Despots and the town was the administrative centre of a considerable area, but with the coming of King Otho a misplaced historical sense triumphed and the city down in the plain was galvanized into a ghastly parody of the life which had there been mercifully extinct for a thousand years. On looking out from the terrace of the Pantanassa over this wide idyllic valley, with its thick groves of olives, its orchards and its vines, one cannot help reflecting on the relative fame and achievements of medieval Mistra and ancient Sparta. Down there where the hideous campanile of the new cathedral juts above the tree-tops a race of warped and sadistic scoutmasters, undisputed lords of the fairest valley in Greece, protected from assault on all sides by mountain chains, possessed of unlimited leisure (thanks to the presence of a far more numerous race of deliberately degraded serfs) flourished for close on half a millennium. In all that time they never produced one single work of literature or art of more than purely local or temporary significance ; never once rose above the cultural level of an old-fashioned sergeants' mess. Yet to-day their name has become a byword for courage and endurance and the fortitude with which they were accustomed to bear ill-fortune is held up for the admiration of every schoolboy. That their trials were almost invariably the result of their own insatiable lust for power and dominance is seldom stressed and the bright glow of Thermopylae has blinded posterity to the fact that the Spartan virtues were inculcated by methods which bear an all-too-striking resemblance to those prevailing in the Hitler-Jugend. Up here, on the other hand, dwelt a people who were never in a position to echo the Spartan boast that their diminutive capital had no need of defences : during the brief two hundred years their city endured they were seldom undisputed masters of the valley beneath their walls. For the whole of this period the Peloponnese, formerly among the most prosperous provinces of the Empire, was in a condition of the most abject misery. The almost constant state of war existing between Greeks and Franks, the endless internecine feuds raging between the various claimants to the disputed succession of the Villehardouins, the economic imperialism of the Venetians, the raids of the corsairs and Catalans and latterly the steady encroachments of the Turks, all contributed to ruin the economy of the countryside, which was finally wrecked by the disinclination of a discouraged peasantry to sow where bitter experience had shown others would inevitably reap. And yet despite all this, despite the fact that they were fully aware that their empire and all that it stood for in the realm of culture was, in all probability, doomed, they yet succeeded in producing works of art of a serenity and accomplishment that only the Italian Quattrocento can rival, works which until very recently remained quite unknown save to a handful of scholars and enthusiasts. That such an achievement was possible in conditions so materially adverse is a chastening reflection ; and for the coming generation may well prove an inspiring one.

The chain of hills which shut off the valley of the Eurotas to the south are less lofty and more fertile than the surrounding mountains to the west and north. The pines and thorns that line the road from Tripolis here give way to avenues of mulberries and walnuts, acacias, olives and even such seeming exotics as the carib. Beside the road the whitewashed walls and wooden balconies of the farms and cottages are half-hidden by an inextricable tangle of vines and rambler roses, and on the higher ground flourish innumerable flowering shrubs of which the most remarkable is one that at first sight appears to be a species of holly, but which is in fact a diminutive oak on which live the minute red insects that produce cochineal, the cultivation of which provided, a hundred years ago, the principal source of revenue for the whole district. Beyond these hills lies the plain of Helos, of which the ancient inhabitants, enslaved by Sparta, have left us their

name as a synonym for serfdom. On the west this flat, malarial stretch of coast, to which brakes of immensely tall reeds give a Cretan look, is bounded by the mountains of the Mani, the central of the three prong-like peninsulas into which the southern extremity of the Peloponnese divides. The inhabitants of this district were formerly notorious for their untamable wildness and ferocious blood-feuds. Indeed, so thankless did the task of administering this area prove that the Turks were finally constrained to grant the Maniotes a very large measure of self-government, a privilege they only withdrew after the ill-fated Russian attempt to rally the local population to a war of liberation at the end of the eighteenth century. In a vain attempt to pacify the district and put an end to the ceaseless tribal warfare the government of King Otho decreed the destruction of the fortified towers which the head of each family was accustomed to erect as a stronghold from which to harry his neighbours and attempted, with but indifferent success, to enforce this edict with the aid of Bavarian troops. Even to-day the neighbourhood is remarkable in a country where daily life is seldom uneventful for the rugged nature of the prevailing social code, and it is no accident that some of the most individualistic, not to say reactionary, of latter-day Greek politicians are natives of this region.

133

At the point where the mountains meet the plain lies the small port of Gytheion, the principal town of the Mani. Close inshore and forming part of the breakwater of the harbour is the island of Marathonisi, crowned by a castellated Turkish tower that the then Pasha was building for himself when Leake visited the place at the beginning of the last century, for which a single incident has secured a lasting fame :

> Here first the happy Paris stopp'd
> When Helen from her lord elop'd.
> With pleas'd reflection I survey'd
> Each secret grott, each conscious shade ;
> Envy'd his choice, approv'd his flame,
> And fondly wished my lot the same . . .[1]

To-day the town is more remarkable for its inhabitants than its historic associations, the majority of whom, during the twenty-four hours I passed there, did not draw a sober breath. While the falsity of the frequent assertion of the stupider Philhellenes that 'you never see a Greek drunk' is manifest after a very short while in any part of Greece (the Greeks, as has been stated above, are a formidably intelligent race not given to any profit-less austerity), nowhere else have I had the experience of going to a *taverna* for a not very early breakfast and finding the next table still occupied by the same party who were well launched on a steady drinking bout when I left the place some twelve hours previously, singing as lustily in the sunshine as they did by lamplight. There is one further distinction enjoyed by this otherwise unremarkable town ; it has the highest murder-rate in Greece.

At the end opposite to Gytheion the coastal plain is closed in by another range of mountains, less rugged than those of the Mani but still sufficiently barren, which run down the easternmost of the Peloponnesian prongs to Cape Malea, the most southerly point of the European mainland. On their further side, where they fall steeply away to the sea, rises the impregnable rock of Monemvasia, a name which in its anglicized form of 'malmsey' makes so improbable but dramatic an appearance in our own history. Originally one of the principal Byzantine fortresses in the Morea, it was finally captured by William de Villehardouin in 1250 after a three years' siege (it was never, in all its stormy history, taken by assault), but did not long remain a part of his possessions as it was one of the three strongholds which the Prince of Achaia was forced to give back to the Emperor by way

[1] These lines were actually inspired by the sight of the island of Cerigo, the poet erroneously supposing that island to have been distinguished by an event which in fact took place at Marathonisi.

of ransom in 1263. Greek it remained for the next two hundred years, but after the fall of Constantinople the inhabitants placed themselves under the protection of Venice as seemingly the only Christian power sufficiently strong to afford protection against the Turk. Their faith was justified until 1540, when the Venetians by the treaty signed that year were compelled to surrender this last outpost of European civilization on the mainland of Greece to the infidel.

First seen from the mountains above, this precipitous rock, rising sharply from the sea less than a quarter of a mile off the shore, appears completely barren and deserted. A few scattered cottages at the landward end of the narrow causeway joining it to the mainland are the only human habitations on what would appear to be as barren a stretch of coast as any in Greece, but on crossing the causeway one follows a road raised some twenty feet above sea-level that half circulates the rock before coming to an end in front of a fortified gateway in a wall running at right angles from the mountain-side to the sea. On entering, one finds oneself immediately in a setting that would not appear out of place at the other end of the Mediterranean but which here in Greece wears an exotic air. Narrow streets and alleys curve and wind between stone-built houses, dive beneath low archways and mount unexpected flights of steps in a way that recalls the hill-towns of southern France or Italy, such a village as Roquebrune for instance, and it is only the lettering over the shop fronts that serves to remind us we are still in Greece. Tucked away in this labyrinth hemmed in between the sea, the mountain and two parallel stretches of wall are a number of churches of considerable interest, though their identification is rendered difficult by the fact that the dedications listed in the various guide-books agree neither with one another nor with local usage. The largest, which the presence over the door of a Byzantine sculptured slab ornamented with peacocks mentioned by Leake enables one to recognize as the metropolitan church, is a basilical structure much restored. On the *ikonostasis* hang some remarkable ikons in which the Venetian influence is so strong as almost to remove them entirely from the realm of Byzantine painting. Further on are two large churches, very similar in style, in which a more balanced compromise between East and West has been achieved ; domed cruciform in plan, the western arms of the cross have here been so prolonged as almost to be classed as naves, and the domes rest on pointed arches. (This last feature provides a curious example of provincial longevity as at the time of their erection the pointed arch had been almost completely abandoned in the West itself.) On the outside the domes are covered with cement, a practice common enough in Crete and the islands where, however, it is seldom employed on so large a building, but rare on the mainland, which together with the grey, unpainted stone of the walls gives both buildings a curiously gaunt un-Greek look. The fourth church in the lower town, of considerably later date, is far more familiar in appearance, cross-in-square in plan and gaily painted in yellow, white and blue. Inside is preserved a miraculous ikon that was drawn up out of the sea in a bucket,

one of the innumerable *chefs-d'œuvre* of that tireless artist St. Luke, for which even the sophisticated, English-speaking young school-marm confessed a considerable respect.

Up the face of the cliff at the back of the town climbs a precipitous path, elaborately walled and provided with countless unexpected turns and exposed positions for defensive purposes, leading to the small plateau on the summit of the rock on which the deserted ruins of the upper town are slowly crumbling away in the brilliant sunlight. At the very top stands the church of St. Sophia, dating from the earliest period of the town's history, similar in plan to Daphni, where the only signs of Western influence are the square Renaissance windows, now blocked up, which on the gallery level once connected the main body of the church with the much later narthex. The carved stonework that still remains in places inside the church is particularly fine, while from without the drum and dome, that slowly rise up glowing and tawny against the skyline as one comes over the brow of the hill, are as lovely as any in Greece. What, however, gives to the place its unique quality is the fact, of which as one approaches one can gain no hint, that it hangs on the very edge of an immense precipice and that from the narrow terrace at the back one can by merely extending one's arm let fall a pebble into the peacock sea eight hundred feet below.

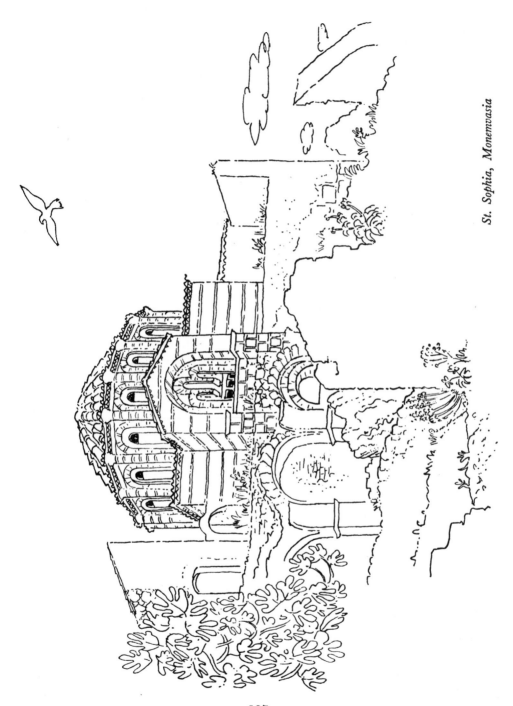

St. Sophia, Monemvasia

To-day Monemvasia is slowly dying. The production of the celebrated malmsey which gave the place its medieval fame has long since been abandoned (though the local wine remains excellent). An impregnable fortress commanding a sea-route that is no longer threatened and which, since the cutting of the Corinth canal, few use is not worth the expense of a garrison ; cut off both by distance and a range of mountains from the nearest town of any size, the most flourishing Byzantine centre south of Mistra is now a decaying fishing village which seems likely soon to be as completely deserted.

Beyond the range of Mount Taygetus and its prolongation in the Mani peninsula lies a fertile valley leading to the important port of Kalamata, at the head of which, in almost the exact centre of the Peloponnese, once stood the great city of Megalopolis. Founded by Epaminondas as the capital of the Achaean League, the comparatively brief history and present melancholy condition of this once vast city (the circumference of its walls was not less than six miles) provide a striking example of the fate that seems invariably to overtake artificial foundations that spring up, fully developed, at the bidding of some powerful ruler. To-day the sight of these few frag-ments of temples hidden in the corn, the tree-covered semi-circular ridge that was once the largest theatre in the world, lying on either bank of the Alpheus, inevitably gives rise to gloomy speculations as to the probable fate of New Delhi and Canberra. Whether or not these imperial cities will go the same way, the fate of Megalopolis affords a useful reminder, to a gener-ation obsessed with the beauties of planning and convinced that the creation of satellite towns is the only sure means of salvation, that cities which have been deprived of a period of incubation and organic growth are frequently as difficult to keep alive as a seven-months' baby in an oxygen tent.

The Alpheus flows west along a wide bed from Megalopolis towards the mountains through which it cuts its way in a long steep-sided gorge, dominated by the craggy fastness of Karytaina. This small mountain village clustering on the upper slopes of the precipitous conical mountain hugs the walls of a castle which is to-day the most picturesque, as at the time of its building it was the strongest, of all the Frankish keeps in Greece. One of the twelve original baronies into which the principality of Achaia was feudally divided by the original Villehardouin, Karytaina passed from the family of Brouyêres to that of Brienne and then by marriage to the Dukes of Athens, who finally lost it to the Greeks. In later times it pro-vided a secure base for that colourful but all-too-frequently ineffectual hero of the War of Independence, Kolokotronis, whose heavily moustachioed features, eagle glance and high-crested Dragoons' helmet, imperfectly

lithographed, adorn the walls of almost every *taverna* from Patras to Cape
Matapan. To-day, with the castle walls ruined but in appearance still
formidable, hanging in mid-air above the narrow gorge through which the
Alpheus, no longer the broad and placid stream it was at Megalopolis,
rushes to Olympia and the sea beneath the arches of a medieval bridge,
the place presents as romantic an appearance as any in the Peloponnese.
The village itself, exceedingly poverty stricken even for this hard country,
is made up of high stone-built houses, rising above one another on the steep
slopes of the mountain-side, dour and forbidding and very different in
appearance from the cottages and farmhouses in the valley below, which
with their upturned eaves and the lattice work of their wooden balconies
have a curious, almost Chinese charm. Of its three churches, two are
noteworthy ; Ayios Nikoloaos preserved a series of wall paintings which
although frequently repainted in places, are almost complete, and the
Zoodhikos Piyi, surprisingly enough, is distinguished by an untouched
Byzantine campanile.

From Karytaina the road winds upwards above the gorge of the Alpheus
to the remote hill-town of Andritsana. The place itself, pretty enough with
its plane trees and fountain and tiny *platia* through which wind continuous
caravans of mules and where, once a day, a steam-wreathed motor-bus
comes pantingly to a halt, owes its fame to its proximity to the temple of
Bassae, three hours on horseback over the mountains to the south. For
centuries the very existence of this temple was forgotten save by a few local
peasants who referred to the whole district as the ' columns ', and it was not
until almost the end of the eighteenth century that it was rediscovered by

a French traveller. For accurate measurements and a detailed description
the world had to wait until the visit some years later of the industrious
Cockerell, afterwards professor of architecture at the Royal Academy, in
whose design of the Ashmolean at Oxford certain details—notably the
engaged Ionic columns on the St. Giles elevation—may perhaps have been
inspired by memories of his youthful discovery. Architecturally the temple
is of considerable importance as embodying several notable variants from
what we have come to consider the standard plan of a Doric temple. The
cella is so narrow as to preclude the presence of the usual internal colonnades and their place is taken by two rows of engaged Ionic columns, of
which the pair farthest from the entrance are set at an angle, while between
them in the centre of the aisle rose a single Corinthian pillar, the earliest
known example of this order yet to be discovered. Of an austere, close-
grained grey limestone, with the majority of its columns still in position, this
temple, whence one obtains a view stretching from the island of Ithaca as
far south as Mount Ithome, on the flat top of which the Messenians were
formerly accustomed to sacrifice to Zeus, which now reveals no single sign of
human activity of any sort, achieves an effect that no other classical site can
rival. Of the once-flourishing city of Phigaleia, whose inhabitants erected
the temple as a thank-offering for delivery from the plague, not a trace
remains. Nearby is a cave originally dedicated to the worship of the
black Demeter, a mare-headed goddess whose cult was probably already
old at the first coming of the Achaeans and whose primitive abode seems
somehow less unexpected and more suitable to these remote mountains
than this incredibly accomplished building by the greatest of Greek architects. Nevertheless, it is largely this very contrast between the temple and
its setting which to-day renders Bassae the most fascinating of all the temples
in Greece.

Formerly it was a comparatively easy matter to cover the dozen and a half
miles from Andritsana to Olympia along a road that crossed the Alpheus,
a short distance up stream from the latter place, but the destruction of the
only bridge by the Germans now enforces the adoption of a circuitous route
via Dimitsana that passes through country justly remarkable for the rugged
drama of the scenery but almost devoid of architectural interest. Dimitsana
itself, the principal town of the region, is a typical mountain village, clinging
to the face of the rock above a funnel-shaped chine, where a small terraced
platia, some cast-iron benches and a lamp-post or two seem to bear witness
to a municipal yearning after better things and to indicate that someone
at some time or other entertained visions of raising his native place to the
dignity of a ' resort '. Beyond and above lies a strange region of upland

valleys where the surrounding hills, albeit that they are, in relation to sea-level, the summits of considerable mountains, form but a low horizon to wide meadows strewn with grey limestone boulders and crossed by shallow, marshy little streams, where the prevailing sense of space and elevation after hours spent among the gorges and inclusive cliffs of the Alpheus valley is strangely exhilarating. From here the road drops down to the valley of the Ladon, which stream it follows until its junction with a much-enlarged Alpheus a few miles above Olympia.

Among the great classical sites of Greece, Olympia is, in respect of its setting, unique. Completely out of sight of the sea, unshadowed by mountains, it lies in a flat, well-wooded plain bounded on one side by low hills and on the other by the broad and shingly bed of the Alpheus. In place of the few twisted olives and tough little clusters of thyme which elsewhere are all that provide a contrast to the stones of the ἀρχαῖα, great pine trees, very different from the usual ragged dwarfs, shade the remains of the temples and treasuries the foundations of which are lost in the long grass. The general effect is romantic and park-like rather than classical.

The immediate impression produced by the ruins themselves is one of surprise at their extent. The scale on which this athletes' paradise was conceived and laid out is something of which the usual accounts, both ancient and modern, give no hint. To a certain extent this feeling is commonly aroused by most Greek antiquities, for one is so accustomed to the emphasis which, not perhaps entirely disinterestedly, dons and schoolmasters lay on the smallness, austerity and simplicity of the Greeks' material achievement (taking care to underline the favourable contrast to the colossal size, vulgar ostentation and effeminate luxury of the Roman and eastern Empires) that the lavishness and scale on which they were accustomed to conceive and carry out their more important undertakings come as a revelation : but here it is more than usually immediate and apparent. The immense drums of the Temple of Zeus, the long line of national treasuries, the gymnasia and competitors' quarters, the extensive hotel accommodation, the countless bases which once supported a whole population of statues, all effectively prove how far the reality of the Olympic festival was removed from the simple, manly ideal which provided such a welcome inspiration to the late Victorian generation of public-school masters. The actual prizes may only have been simple crowns of laurel or olive, but it would appear that amateur status could be as profitably exploited in ancient Greece as in modern America, and that well-publicised athletics could be made to play as useful a rôle in building up the tourist industry in the fourth century as in the twentieth. While a proper sporting spirit received its due measure of respect in contemporary literature, the first contest of which we have any record and in commemoration of which the festival was instituted, the victory of Pelops over the King of Pisa was gained in a manner which would to-day undoubtedly debar that legendary hero from any further appearance on the race course. That this pretty example of 'fixing' aroused no general disapproval in the Greek public is shown by the flattering likenesses of all those concerned with which the pediment of the Temple of Zeus was so magnificently adorned.

The crowd which assembled in this spot every fourth year on the first full moon after the summer solstice would, one fancies, after one had got over the initial strangeness of costume and appearance and abandoned the preconceptions engendered in the classical Sixth, have gradually revealed itself as strangely familiar in all its diversity. The athletes themselves, as quarrelsome and self-conscious as prima-donnas, fresh from a training as specialized and prolonged, if in theory more intellectual, as that to which professional baseballers are subjected; the old *afficionados*, forever recalling bygone triumphs whose whole life consisted in a constant pilgrimage from Delphi to Nemea, from the Isthmus to Olympia; the horsy contingent who came solely for the chariot racing and the maiden gentlemen whose interest in the competitors was not entirely inspired by a passion for sport; for all these it would not be hard to find parallels at Newmarket or Lords. But in addition there would be a number of other types whose modern counterparts could only be found at St. Moritz and Le Touquet— the international good-timers, the " café society " of the Mediterranean world. Half-Asiatic princelings from Lydia and Cappadocia, the Maharajahs of antiquity, rich beyond dreams of avarice, with their hosts of hangers-on and strings of the most expensive bloodstock; Syracusan magnates with recently acquired fortunes and strong colonial accents; international bankers and financiers from Alexandria and Antioch and aggressive Roman tourists playing the rôle of the Transatlantic millionaires whom facially, to judge by the evidence of their portrait busts, they so strangely resembled : it was to the long-continued patronage of such visitors that the organizers of the festival were accustomed to look for their principal support. How munificent that support could on occasion prove is shown by the remains of the elaborate fountain, supplied with running water brought from a considerable distance and at immense expense, presented by that ostentatiously generous old culture-snob, Herodes Atticus. However, for all their seeming familiarity, this public was largely Greek, and in one respect, therefore, the atmosphere would have differed considerably from that prevailing at any Anglo-Saxon gathering; however various the reasons which had drawn all these patrons to the extreme west of the Peloponnese from all over the Mediterranean world, reasons of sport, of pleasure, of patriotism or purely snobbish, all would pursue in common an intense and insatiable passion for politics. The truce enforced by religious sanction that prevailed, no matter what contests were raging elsewhere, not only at Olympia itself but also for the period of the games along all the roads leading to it, provided the ideal opportunity for the representatives or agents of a dozen semi-independent cities and states to take soundings, cement alliances, dissolve coalitions, detach by persuasion or bribery a rival's supporters, and for a month the shady groves of the *altis* must regularly have witnessed as much undercover activity as the corridors of the Hofburg during the Congress of Vienna or the pump-room at Homburg in the days of Edward the Peacemaker.

In ordinary times the principal aesthetic importance of Olympia largely rests on the presence in the Museum of the sculptures from the pediments of the Temple of Zeus, the innumerable votive bronzes of all periods which still continue to be discovered from time to time in the neighbourhood, and the Hermes of Praxiteles. To-day it is only the first that is visible, the Hermes still being swathed in sandbags and bricks and the bronzes buried away beneath several feet of concrete, and this only partially as protective scaffolding provides a difficult but not insuperable obstacle to aesthetic appreciation. Even were this barrier removed it would still not, I fancy, be altogether easy to form a just estimate of the sculptor's (or sculptors', for Pausanias gives us two names) achievment, for although the whole composition of each pediment has been admirably arranged in the correct architectural setting, they can only be viewed from eye-level and we must rely on our imagination in assessing the effect they would have produced in their original position high on the terminal gables of this enormous temple. We are confronted with an exactly similar difficulty with the Elgin marbles, and it is only the practical impossibility of submitting either set of sculptures to the test that emboldens me to maintain the heretical view that the Olympian pediments (certainly the western) are, granted the specialized nature of the function that both series were designed to fulfil, superior. Let me say straight away that I am fully aware that many of the Elgin marbles have a rhythmic subtlety of which the Olympian sculptor was quite incapable and a grandeur of conception which here only the figure of Apollo on the western pediment displays. Nevertheless, Phidias, in pursuing this higher aim, has been forced in some small degree to sacrifice the monumental quality which the Olympian pediments so outstandingly possess and without which sculpture in relation to architecture invariably fails of its full effect. Could we see a single specimen from either pediment side by side in a

143

museum, it is to the representative of the Parthenon team to which, even after a century of London sulphur and the scrubbing-brushes of Lord Duveen, we should undoubtedly give the palm, but did both compositions still exist in their entirety, in their original positions against a painted background high above our heads, I am convinced it would be the Western pediment from Olympia that would produce the greater effect. Indeed, this temple may well have been the last building before the erection of Chartres in which the relation of sculpture to architecture was properly understood, and the Parthenon the first in which an almost infinitesimal sign is to be detected of the beginnings of a fatal misconception as to the nature of that relationship which was soon afterwards, and to an even greater degree in our own day, to produce such deplorable results.

The continuity with which the Olympic Games were celebrated over a period of nearly a thousand years is, when one considers the immense developments which took place in the ancient world during that period, astonishing ; in the words of Professor Clark : 'Amid all the intricacies or complications of policy, through all changes of fortune in the component States, in spite of pestilence and war, the Olympic festival recurred with the regularity of a solar phenomenon.' Nevertheless, even this institution came finally to an end, being suppressed by an edict of the Emperor Theodosius in A.D. 393. The new town which was then established in the sacred precinct did not, for all the massive walls with which it was encircled, flourish for very long. Within fifty years it had been sacked by the Goths, whose destructive handiwork was further extended in the following century by a disastrous earthquake that cast down many of the temples, and the only trace of this last period which remains to-day is the very curious little church that occupies the traditional site of the studio in which Phidias produced the great chryselephantine statue of Zeus that ranked among the seven wonders of the world. This building, which is usually ascribed to the fifth century and may well be the earliest existing Christian church in Greece, is of the highest interest, though not of remarkable beauty. Basilical in plan, with a single apse, it retains an ambo, a pierced marble screen of elaborate workmanship and the fragments of some unusual Ionic columns, oval in section, with their fluting enriched by scrollwork in relief. The design and workmanship of all these details bear clear witness to the indecisive and transitional character of the art of the early fifth century and to the desperate efforts which were then being made by elaborating an already over-sophisticated tradition, by ringing the changes on the combination of certain established elements which had long since been exploited to the full, to conceal the vacuum that the fully developed art of the Byzantine Empire was shortly to fill. These fragments of columns are decadent in exactly the same way as the façades of the late Sir Reginald Blomfield are decadent, and serve equally well to emphasize the often-neglected truth that, lacking inspiration, scholarship and inventiveness are, whether singly or in combination, powerless in themselves to produce a work of art.

The flat coastal plain which stretches round the north-west corner of the Peloponnese from Olympia to Patras is scenically dull but historically interesting. Soon after leaving the modern town of Pyrgos one arrives at the village of Gastouni, on the outskirts of which stands a cross-in-square Byzantine church of, I imagine, twelfth or eleventh-century date, with

excellent decorative brickwork. Here the principal treasure is a miraculous ikon attributed to St. Luke, though the gold and silver plates with which almost the entire surface is covered make identification on stylistic grounds difficult. The history of the relic is exhaustively but rather confusingly described in ' strip ' form on a large illuminated banner hanging in the *bema*, from which one gathers that it was discovered up a palm tree by a pious Ethiopian together with whom it was wafted through air, finally descending on a small town which from the painstakingly accurate delineation of the church is clearly Gastouni. There also appears to be a mysterious sub-plot involving a richly clad Pasha that in default of more exact knowledge is difficult to relate to the main narrative. On the outside of the north wall is an ogival arch dating from the period when the building was taken over by the Latins for the celebration of their own rites. Away on the coast, but visible from here, stands a more remarkable memorial of Frankish rule, the great keep of Chlemoutsi, the Chateau Gaillard of Greece, occupying the flat top of the promontory of Glarentza. (It is one of the more enjoyable freaks of history that the names of this, the most north-westerly of the Peloponnesian strongholds, and that of Monemvasia, the most south-easterly, should both be familiar in their anglicized forms, thanks to an incident in which the Duke of the former was drowned in a butt of the latter.)

While Glarentza remained the principal fortress of the entire district—the key to the Peloponnese as it was called—in Frankish times the capital of the principality of Achaia was at Andravida a few miles further on the main road to the north. To-day this rather depressed looking little town has nothing to show for its past glories save the ruins of the church of St. Sophia which despite the dedication was a Frankish foundation in the Gothic style. Of this the choir and two side-chapels alone remain, all three rib-

vaulted ; the chancel arch is well proportioned but plain and there is no trace of the lavish carving with which the rather similar, though later, church at Chalcis was enriched. As far as it is possible to judge from the existing portions and the ground plan the church would appear to have been northern rather than Italianate in feeling and, indeed, the exceptional width of the central aisle may well have given it an almost English look. Elsewhere in the town were also churches both of the Teutonic Knights and the templars, but these have long since been utilized for building materials by the practical inhabitants and now it is only with the greatest difficulty that the lines of their foundations can be traced.

Between Andravida and Patras the only building of interest, save for a village where the demonstrative nationalism of the inhabitants has led them to paint every house in the main street in broad horizontal stripes of white and blue, is the little church at Manoulada standing by itself, half-hidden by reeds and long grass, a short distance from the main road. This decaying but picturesque little building, strangely austere in its lack of the usual brick-courses running between the masonry, is one of the very rare examples of an original cruciform plan remaining unmodified, for here the angles between the western and lateral arms of the cross have not been filled up with the usual side-chambers to make a cross-in-square. According to the representatives of the Fine Arts sub-commission of the C.M.F., the church when they visited it had grass and shrubs growing on the roof and windows which, through a desire not to offend the Virgin, the locals refused to cut down save after firm remonstrances. Judging by the condition of the roof when I

saw it some time later, consideration for the feelings of the Virgin has now once more got the better of the effect created by the ' firm remonstrances '. From this point the road runs, or rather would do so had it in fact any existence save in the imagination of the optimists who compiled the most recent map, through the principal hunting-grounds of the Frankish rulers of the Morea where the numerous fine oaks are so widely spaced over a grassy plain as to recall Richmond Park rather than the thickest forest which, doubtlessly erroneously, one always assumes a medieval game-preserve to have been, and finally reaches the northern coast a few miles to the west of Patras.

The largest town in the Peloponnese, Patras was originally founded by the Ionians and has changed hands a quite exceptional number of times (it was even once for a short period included in the Papal States) without ever very materially affecting the course of history. It was the scene of the crucifixion of St. Andrew, whose remains the inhabitants erroneously believe still to lie beneath the high altar of the principal church in the town. In fact they were carried off in the fourth century by a devoted Greek monk, who had been warned in a vision to remove them from a neighbourhood that was shortly to be exposed to barbarian inroads, to the greater safety of Fifeshire, where a magnificent cathedral dedicated to the Apostle was in course of time built to receive them and where they are to-day revered

147

by golfers of all nationalities. The other great event in the ecclesiastical history of the town was occasioned by the action of its bishop, who in 1821 first unfurled the banner of Independence, thus proclaiming the war of Liberation, a scene which, engraved or oleographed, is to be met with as frequently in Greece as is *The Death of Nelson* in England or *Washington crossing the Delaware* in the United States. Cynics maintain, however, that in one important particular all these representations are inaccurate, as none of them show the gun which more stout-hearted patriots were forced to thrust into the back of their ecclesiastical companion before he could be induced to make his spontaneous gesture for freedom. In its present condition the town is a fair example of early nineteenth-century planning, laid out on a grid system of which the main axis is a wide street leading at right angles from the quays to the long flight of steps going up to the hill on which stands the castle, with the upper stories of the houses in the shopping district carried over the pavement on arcades. The most prominent landmark to be seen from the sea is the high dome of the unfinished cathedral of which the drum, encircled by a colonnade of Ionic pillars in the neoclassic style, provides a welcome variant from the current vernacular of the Byzantine revival ; a variant, however, which seems likely to prevent the ultimate completion of the building which in the view of the Holy Synod exhibits too 'Roman' an air for an Orthodox place of worship. The Synod has accordingly decreed the suspension of all further work for an indefinite period. The port possesses, at the moment, an illusory atmosphere of bustle and prosperity, due largely to the blocked state of the Corinth Canal, the original cutting of which worked in favour of the Piraeus at the expense of Patras which in normal times is now dependent solely on the currant trade and coastal shipping.

The castle, the sole remaining historic monument of the town, built by the Villehardouins and subsequently maintained and enlarged by the Venetians, is an uncommonly well-preserved specimen of Frankish military architecture. Over the principal gateway into the keep is a sculptured slab which nine out of ten passers-by assume to be a winged Venetian lion, but which closer inspection reveals to be one of those stylized contests between indeterminate animals which were such a favourite motif with Byzantine artists. From the walls above the view is singularly wide and grand ; immediately opposite across the Gulf, which here narrows to a strait, the precipitous northern face of the great mountain to the west of Navpaktos drops sheer to the waterside : beyond, the massed ranges gradually fall away to where a narrow, sandy spit runs out into the open sea in the neighbourhood of Missolonghi ; in the far west the silhouette of Cephallonia rises above the distant horizon. It is best inspected at evening, for Patras is traditionally celebrated for its sunsets, and in my experience has proved no exception to the rule which seems to decree that of all the natural advantages with which the compilers of guide-books are in the habit of endowing, in some superlative degree, a few favoured spots, such as exceptionally soft water or an unusually dry climate, a reputation for sunsets is almost the only one that is not invariably and completely unjustified.

From Patras eastward a coast road runs along the shore of the gulf to Corinth ; a road so dilapidated, though once so fine, so generally impassable and in places so dangerous, that its condition is symbolic of the whole present state of the Morea. This province, once among the richest in the Empire and later the most profitable *pashalik* in Greece, has now been reduced, after six years of war and rebellion, to a condition worse than that which prevailed in the last days of Frankish rule. With many of its towns, such as Kalavryta, burnt to the ground and their inhabitants slaughtered by the Germans ; and others, once prosperous, such as Pyrgos and Kalamata, now stagnating in the general decline of Mediterranean trade, the urban life of the Peloponnese is sufficiently depressing. But in the country districts conditions are, if anything, worse. Oil that cannot be marketed for lack of containers or that is being hoarded by speculators ; vineyards that lack the essential phosphates and artificial manures for their proper cultivation and of which the produce can no longer, thanks to the competition of the Algerian growers, find a ready market in France, are among the major sources of distress, but hardly less powerful for harm are the political dissensions with which the land is riven. In the south, traditionally royalist, the inhabitants, whose memories are long, still maddened by the savage massacres carried out by the Communists in the early days of the liberation, now pursue, regardless of the law, even the mildest Liberals with a comprehensible but deplorable vindictiveness. In the remote fastnesses of Taygetus and Arcadia communist bands still maintain themselves under arms and descend at intervals to carry out brutal reprisals on the conservative villages in the plain. An underpaid and ill-disciplined gendarmerie, whose average expectation of life in a region never celebrated for a respect for the law is short, cannot, despite the guidance and encouragement of British advisers, be expected to effect much improvement.

This state of affairs, which can be paralleled in other parts of Greece and is indeed surpassed in the north, is not irremediable. The Greeks, were they not distracted by events beyond their own frontiers, could, given time and a small measure of economic assistance, put their own house in order. Unfortunately they are all too aware (for even the average inhabitant of the remoter villages of Arcadia is invariably better informed about foreign affairs than the by-pass dweller in England) that their fate is not ultimately in their own hands, and that their country, lying astride the Iron Curtain, is likely to remain in the international limelight for an indefinite period. Economically this shrewd but dangerous awareness delays recovery by encouraging the belief that the Western Powers cannot afford to let Greece go under and that, therefore, it would be a pointless labour to swim to the shore when the kind Americans will, whether they like it or not, have to take one there in a comfortable lifeboat; psychologic- ally it induces a perilously *exalté* but highly congenial mood in every patri- otic Greek who derives considerable satisfaction from the thought that his country, historically so important, but economically so uninviting, is likely to provide the *casus belli* for the greatest of all wars.

THE great trunk road across the Boeotian plain divides at Livadia. To the right it continues north past the Lion of Chaeronea to the mountains behind which lies Thessaly ; to the left, after crossing an Alpine district of upland meadows, where in spring the large number of Judas trees strike a curiously exotic note, it follows the barren valley dividing the two great massifs of Parnassus and Helicon. Less than an hour from the town the latter route divides again at a depressing wind-swept cross-roads where, according to tradition, took place the unfortunate meeting between Oedipus and his father, *hinc illae lacrimae*, whence the main road continues on to Dephi and the fork to the left winds its wretchedly surfaced way to Distomo. This village, which must always have worn a sufficiently poverty-stricken aspect, is now a terrifying monument to human barbarity. In 1943 it was the scene of the most savage act of German reprisal and almost every house still standing amid the ruins exibits crosses scrawled in blue paint beside the door, together with the names of its inmates whom the Germans took out and shot in the market-place. At Distomo the road, as a road, comes to an end, but a mule-track continues south-eastward, climbing alongside a dry watercourse and finally vanishing altogether in a saucer-shaped and comparatively fertile depression high up on the Helicon range. On a shoulder of the surrounding hills, overlooking this valley to the south, stands the monastery of Holy Luke.

In the tenth century of our era, so insecure had existence in this part of the Byzantine dominions become that it was only in a few such remote spots that it was possible to lead a relatively tranquil life outside the strong walls of the larger cities. The northern plains were regularly and efficiently devastated by the Bulgarians and the coastal districts in the south were constantly subject to the incursions of Arab corsairs operating from their great base in Crete. It was not therefore surprising that it should have been the site first of a hermitage, then of a small community, founded by one of the innumerable orthodox ascetics of the period, Luke the Stiriote, whose family had been driven from Aegina by the Arabs and from Kastoria by the Bulgars, and whose final refuge on the Corinthian gulf had been laid waste by the Hungarians. What, however, was truly remarkable was the elevation of his shrine after his death to the dignity of one of the most celebrated places of pilgrimage in all eastern Christendom. Save for one single act the career of Luke, a man generally admitted to have been of great nobility of soul but guiltless of those more extravagant and spectacular feats of mortification and endurance which so powerfully impressed the contemporary imagination, was no more noteworthy than that of dozens of other monks and holy men. But his prophetic gift, which does not seem to have been so strikingly exercised on any other occasion, led him to foretell shortly before his death the recapture of Crete under an emperor named Romanus. Twenty years later, when Crete fell to the Emperor Romanus II, the prophecy was recalled by a grateful Empress, Theophano, who straight-way set on foot plans for the erection of a magnificent church on the site of the holy man's last resting-place. Architects, painters and mosaic workers were dispatched to Phocis from the capital, and the proximity of the ruined city of Stiris insured an adequate supply of building material. Unfortunately, on the death of Romanus, Theophano married his principal general, Nicephorus Phocas, a dour, parsimonious man, little given to ostentatious and expensive good works, and the project was abandoned. At the beginning of the following century, however, Nicephorus having been murdered by Theophano, who as a result was herself in close confinement in Armenia, the throne passed to her son, the redoubtable Basil the Bulgar-slayer. This ruler, the greatest member of the Macedonian dynasty, cultivated, in the intervals allowed him by his single-minded devotion to that task which gave him his name, an intelligent and fruitful Hellenism which found concrete expression in the realm of ecclesiastical architecture of which many of the finest examples in Greece date from his reign. It was only to be expected that on the occasion of his visit to Greece in 1019, besides adorning the church of the Mother of God at Athens ' which pagans call the Parthenon ' with the costliest decorations and fittings by way of thank-offering for his victories, he should also have ordered work to be resumed on the shrine in which his mother had taken so lively an interest.

The monastery contains two churches of approximately the same date, of which the larger has retained more of its original decoration than any other Byzantine church in Greece. That it should have done so is not perhaps the least of the miracles to be attributed to its patron, for the very presence of so rich a foundation in this wild situation successfully dispelled that immunity from raids which had previously constituted its main advantage. The Franks, the Catalans and the Pope all at one time or another forcibly relieved the monastery of various treasures, including the bones of Holy Luke himself, and where Christians had led the way the Turks in their turn were not slow to follow. During the War of Independence it served as an insurgent headquarters and the suspicion, quite unfounded, that it had resumed this function during the last war provoked a severe bombing from the Germans. Yet windowless and leaky-roofed as it is, the church affords a better idea of the actual appearance of a great Byzantine shrine of the eleventh century than one can obtain anywhere else in the world. In this lies its difference from the contemporary monastery of Daphni. Where there the walls are stripped of their marble panelling, the mosaics have been carefully, perhaps too carefully restored, and the general effect is well-lit and tidy, here the original sculptured slabs, cracked but *in situ*, still enclose the piers, the stern-faced saints and warriors in the dome and pendentives remain, though wanting many *tesserae*, much as their designers left them, and the general atmosphere is one of shabby but magnificent gloom. The plan of the church is similar to that of its Attic counterpart, but owing to the presence of galleries and the richness of the decoration more difficult to appreciate on first sight. The mosaics, on the other hand, though of the same date, are very different in inspiration and treatment. Here the pendulum is at the masculine, Doric extremity of its arc, and whereas the larger groups lack something of the rhythmic ease and subtlety of those at Daphni, the single figures, which are more numerous, have a formal, austere beauty that in most cases produces a less immediate but more powerful effect. The smaller church that conforms to the customary cross-in-square plan, which may or may not indicate a slightly earlier date, has long since lost (save on the pavement) the last traces of whatever mosaics or frescoes may once have adorned it, but by way of compensation the stone carving, particularly the capitals of the four pillars supporting the dome and the cornice of the *ikonostasis*, is of magnificent quality and certainly more easily studied than that in the larger church. Bombed, impoverished, sheltering but a handful of monks, with its interior marred by insecure but essential scaffolding, the present condition of the monastery of Holy Luke is lamentable ; nevertheless, the intensity of the original inspiration that still informs its sombre, battered mosaics, the beauty of its lonely situation and the considered ingenuity of its plan, all urge the acceptance of the verdict of that travelled and enlightened Caroline divine, the Rev. Sir George Wheler, sometime Rector of the parish of Houghton in Lancashire : ' And truly this is the finest Church I saw in all Greece next to Santa Sophia in Constantinople, notwithstanding it is very old and hath suffered much by earthquake and time.'

The right-hand road at the Oedipus fork climbs steadily up the flanks of the great massif to the south, overlooked for most its course by the snow-capped summit and numerous plateaux and spurs of Parnassus. At the col itself it turns away to the right and begins a long descent cut out of the seemingly vertical slopes of the latter range, of which the mighty presence is from now on continuously apprehended, though frequently invisible. Just below the top of the pass lies Arachova, a compact mountain village dominated by a campanile, long celebrated for the exceptional beauty of its women and the legendary bravery of its men. As in all Greek villages the female population when not working in the fields are firmly kept within doors, no opportunity is afforded the casual traveller of testing the accuracy of the former claim, but it is pleasant to recall that the latter was abundantly

justified during the Occupation, when the village acquired a noteworthy 'resistance' record. From Arachova onwards the road, keeping to the northern side of the valley, dodges in and out behind the various shoulders and ridges of the mountain, round the last of which there comes suddenly into view a glaring white sanatorium in the modern manner, the new museum built by the French as though with the express object of obliterating by violent contrast the weathered stones of the site itself, which to-day announces to all travellers from the east that they are now approaching the world's navel.

It is not difficult to understand how the ancients came to consider Delphi the very centre of the earth, for even had they not had Zeus's pair of eagles to guide them (that still wheel and circle endlessly above the cliffs), the whole conformation of these mountains gives to the landscape a magnificently ultimate look as of a point to which all the routes of the world must inevitably converge. The shrine itself, which with its various temples, treasuries and monuments fills a triangular space high up on the northern mountainside enclosed by the twin cliffs of the Pheidriades, overlooks the valley of the Pleistos which on the east runs down in a deep ravine from a vast amphitheatre of mountains and on the west broadens out into the olive-carpeted plain of Amphissa, ringed on one side by a further range and the other by the waters of the gulf of Itea. Immediately opposite rises the perpendicular face of Mount Kirphis, up which is scribbled the zig-zag of a mule track leading from the valley below to a little cultivated plateau a short way below the summit. In archaic times this focal illusion created by the surrounding scenery was supported by the disposition of the existing trade routes ; from the gulf of Itea, penetrating deep into the mountains bordering the Corinthian Gulf, ran ‗e shortest and only practicable road to the plains of Boeotia and Thessaly. It is not, therefore, surprising that even in the second millennium B.C. a Minoan cult should have been established at a spot which was not only obviously of a peculiar natural sancity but also commanded the only line of communication between the thalassocratic empire of Minos and the interior of the mainland. At first the presiding deity appears to have been female, the great Mother-Goddess of the Aegean world, but with the coming of the Achaeans she, or rather her daughter Themis, to whom in practice local worship was in fact directed, was dispossessed by Apollo, one of the most prominent of the deities of the patriarchal pantheon which accompanied the northerners to their new homes. The sacred navel stone and the Pythoness who exercised her prophetic powers in the service of the presiding deity were both appropriated by the newcomer who, in order to consolidate his power, did not hesitate to kill off Themis—a crime for which, it is interesting to note, the god was forced to go to Crete, for ritual expiation. Once firmly established under its new management the shrine rapidly became not only the foremost among all the sacred spots of Hellas, but a focal centre, in fact the only focal centre, for the national consciousness of the whole Greek race. To the oracle all the various cities and states looked for guidance in war, in foreign policy and in colonial expansion, and at the successful conclusion of any enterprise they were accustomed to express their gratitude and score off their rivals by the erection in the sacred precincts of monuments of competitive magnificence. Needless to say, the national character being even at this remote epoch in certain respects already very well developed, sanctity was made to pay by no means despicable dividends, and it was the Delphians' annoyance at their unjustified limitation by outsiders, in this case the inhabitants of Krissa, the city at the head of the gulf which had grown rich on the tolls it levied on the sea-borne pilgrim traffic, which led to the first Sacred War. As a result of this sacrilegious contest the administration of the shrine was henceforward entrusted to an Amphictyonic Council which, by including representatives of all the principal Greek states, would, it was hoped, not only protect this holy enclave from any further commercial aggression but would also ensure that the judgments of the oracle should be free from bias. In the event both hopes were falsified ; the supra-national character of the committee did not prevent a tendency for the will of God almost invariably to be intrepreted in a manner favourable to the Dorian tribes, a factor of no small consequence in the Peloponnesian war, and proved powerless to protect the temples and treasuries from the depredations of the Phocians, who made themselves masters of Delphi during the second Sacred War. When this disastrous contest was finally brought to an end by the intervention of Philip of Macedon, the reconstituted Amphictyonic Council became nothing but a docile and useful instrument of Macedonian policy until the final overthrow of that Empire by the Romans.

Despite the fact that the much-advertised disinterestedness of the oracle was often more apparent than real, the appearance of Delphi in days of its glory strikingly confirmed the international character of the shrine. The centre of the whole ensemble was the great temple of Apollo, above the portal of which was carved the useful but discouraging injunction, ' Know thyself'. This building, of which the podium and peristyle are complete and several columns replaced in their original position, runs parallel to the mountainside, supported on a magnificent wall of polygonal masonry, and conceals deep in its foundations the sacred chasm in which, seated on her tripod above a vessel containing the teeth and bones of the Pythoness, the priestess, having drunk of the waters of Cassotis, inhaled the stupor-inducing fumes rising from the centre of the earth preparatory to prophesying. Leading up to the temple from the road below runs the Sacred Way, a paved ramp bordered by the treasuries and votive offerings of various cities and states. Of these monuments many of the most remarkable have vanished ; the bases of the statues of the Argive worthies are untenanted and their great Trojan horse in bronze is now as legendary as the original ; of the noble hall filled by the Spartans with the trophies of the Battle of Aegospotami, only the foundations remain ; and even the site of the Athenian memorial of Marathon, with its statue of Miltiades by Phidias himself, is uncertain. Relatively complete and *in situ*, there only remains the Treasury of the Athenians, a small Doric temple *in antis*, on the walls of which is engraved the score of a hymn to Apollo which has proved the source of almost all that we know, and a great deal of what is surmised, about the character of ancient Greek music. Technically speaking, the treasury in its present shape is a reconstruction carried out by French archaeologists at the beginning of the present century, but owing to the fact that every stone of a Greek building of this date can go in one place and one place only, and that the majority of the original blocks were still available on the site, our confidence in the result is not subject to the unworthy suspicions which arise at Cnossos. The fragments of sculpture which have survived from the pediment and metopes, tantalizing but beautiful in their incompleteness, date from that miraculous period when the vigour and restraint of archaic art, though reinforced and rendered supple by a new freedom, had not yet been refined away by the influence of an all-too-accomplished naturalism.

From the other national treasuries various decorations and sculptures have survived and are preserved in the great white eye-sore of a museum. Of these a pair of caryatids from the Cnidian treasury are the earliest in date ; although to-day they display a certain simpering Ionian charm, they must when complete have been altogether too rich, for the surface of the stone was not only elaborately painted but such details as the eyes and ornaments were appliquéd in coloured glass and bronze. Better by far are the slightly later Siphnian caryatids, though even here the still far-from-naturalistic convention does not altogether save these elegant maidens from the essential ridiculousness of their functional position. At the time of its erection the Siphnians had recently discovered a gold-mine on their island and accordingly adorned their national shrine with all the extravagance of a South African millionaire decorating a newly acquired residence in Edwardian London. The magnificent frieze which encircled this Ionic temple is the work of two masters ; one who employs a deeply undercut technique is a straightforward, narrative artist with a keen dramatic sense, but the other, whose approach to his subject is perhaps graphic rather than strictly sculptural, is something more. These groups of horses, rhythmically so sure yet set down with such astonishing economy of means, are among the very greatest works of ancient sculpture, and in their special field not only surpass the horses of the Parthenon but may justly be compared to the finest paintings of Stubbs or the engraved stone funerary steles of the Tang dynasty. In the absence of the charioteer in Athens there is nothing else of quite this quality in Delphi to-day, although the sphinx of the Naxians, an unimaginative but undoubtedly striking archaic work, and a distressing acanthus column, surrounded by three dancing caryatids in whose all-too-naturalistic attitudes an infinitely more accomplished artist seems to have anticipated something of the peculiar sentiment of the late Albert Moore, have now been brought forth from their wartime shelters.

Terraced up the mountain-side behind the temple are the ruins of innumerable public buildings such as the painted Stoa, once decorated by the celebrated Polygnotus, and the well-preserved auditorium of the second-century theatre, as well as the plinths and bases that once supported a forest of statues, triumphal columns and votive monuments presented by potentates and communities whose territories were scattered all over the ancient world, from Cyrenaica to the Black Sea. Still higher up, immediately below the final barrier of cliff, lies the stadium, two hundred and twenty yards long, surrounded by twelve tiers of seats that remain intact, though the Pentelic marble enrichments of the Judges' rostrum, the gift, inevitably, of Herodes Atticus, have long since disappeared. The only subsequent addition is a pair of goal-posts erected by some British officer enthusiastic for Soccer. On the lower slopes of the ravine of the Pleistos below the main road are situated a further group of buildings in an enclosure dedicated to Athena that include the ruins of two temples to the goddess, the treasury of Marseilles and a circular Doric building, the Tholos, of which the exact purpose remains unknown. The earlier of the two temples was first overwhelmed by a landslide of which the divinely appointed objective, which it attained with complete success, was a Persian army marching on Delphi from the direction of Arachova (an act of God which was repeated with equal effect some three centuries later against a Gothic force), and the second was built to replace it on a site considered to be less exposed. The treasury of Marseilles is a very early example of the Ionic order, dating from the sixth century, enriched, particularly round the base, with mouldings of exceptional beauty and delicacy, and its columns, no longer standing, crowned with capitals formed of rings of palm leaves and innocent of volutes that are unique.

The Tholos, of which the base is complete and several columns have been re-erected, is a Doric building that for the purity of its details and excellence of its proportions is without rival in Greece or anywhere else. Even at the time of its erection it appears to have been regarded as an exceptional achievement, for the architect, Theodoros, wrote a long treatise on his work, an occurrence so unusual as to indicate a quite abnormal degree of public interest. To-day it demonstrates, as does no other existing building of antiquity, that the Doric style was not invariably confined by its nature to buildings of great scale and massiveness, but was capable, in the hands of a master, of achieving an intimacy and refinement as far removed from the over-delicate cosiness of the Ionic, on the one hand, as it is from that monumental austerity, proper to Doric, but which on a reduced scale is apt to appear empty, on the other. Immediately above this group the waters of the Castalian fountain, to wash in which was an essential preliminary of any visit to the oracle, fall from a niche-surrounded basin at the foot of a narrow but immensely high ravine into a modern cistern on the roadside where a group of peasant women are forever washing their linen. From the rocks above the Delphians were accustomed to throw down those guilty of sacrilege and other crimes, a fate which they accorded the celebrated Aesop, who had been so unwise as to make a few unfortunate though doubtless well-merited cracks about the local administration.

On the same level as the enclosure of Athena a little further to the west are the ruins of the gymnasium, half lost among the immensely large olives. This building, which, with its swimming-baths and lecture halls existed for many more purposes than just the convenience of the athletes competing in the Pythian games, fulfilled the function of clubhouse and general meeting-place for the more important visitors. Of these by no means all had come for purely religious reasons, for Delphi in the days of its greatness was something much more than a glorified Lourdes with a first-rate fortune-teller thrown in : they included merchants, artists and architects on the look-out for contracts, diplomats and international financiers making contact with their opposite numbers from the other end of the Mediterranean, philosophers in search of pupils and pupils in search of philosophers, and a large smart element who were accustomed regularly to visit Delphi during the season. Add to these the sporting visitors who, although the Pythian Games never compared in importance with the Olympic, were nevertheless numerous, the genuine pilgrims and the vast crowd of religious touts who derived a profitable livelihood from the interpretation of the frequently cabbalistic pronouncements of the oracle for the benefit of the less sophisticated consultants, and one will gain some idea of the extraordinary character of this place and the importance of the rôle it played in the life of Greece.

Standing on the terrace of the small inn in the village and looking out over the valley the impression of being at the very centre of things, both in place and time, remains curiously overpowering. Down below the vast unbroken sea of olives, lapping the lower slopes of the high ground and overflowing into the ravine of the Pleistos, stretches all the way from the real sea, that appears strangely solid and metallic by contrast, to the town of Amphissa clustering round the great ruined keep of the counts of Salona. Beyond, the barren and lofty mountains of Aetolia, whose scattered inhabitants still retain much of that rough, foreign quality with which they were credited in ancient times, stretch away down the Gulf to the little walled port of Navpaktos, whence the Turkish fleet sailed out to its doom at Lepanto.

The sky-line to the south is broken by the jagged peaks of the Peloponnese, among which Hercules hunted and destroyed the Erymanthine boar, and the mountains to the east are an outcrop of Helicon, sacred to the muses, where rise the waters of Hippocrene ; and the slopes on which one is suspended are those of Parnassus itself, of which the cloud-wreathed, snow-capped summit, from here invisible, dominates not just this wide landscape immediately beneath but the whole of classical Greece south of Olympus itself.

From the dark barriers of that rugged clime,
 Ev'n to the centre of Illyria's vales,
 Childe Harold passed o'er many a mount sublime,
 Through lands scarce noticed in historic tales :
 Yet in famed Attica such lovely dales
 Are rarely seen ; nor can fair Tempe boast
 A charm they know not ; loved Parnassus fails,
 Though classic ground and consecrated most,
To match some spots that lurk within this lowering coast.
                    LORD BYRON—*CHILDE HAROLD*

THE plain of Thessaly is cut off from that of Thebes by a chain of mountains which in former times were only to be crossed at the pass of Thermopylae on the north-east coast. To-day both road and railway run further inland, and it was just beyond the point where the latter descends to the plain after crossing the range that one of the more spectacular 'special operations' of the last war was carried out. Here the track which formed the most vulnerable link in the long supply route from central Europe to Rommel's armies in North Africa was carried over numerous ravines on a series of bridges, the most important of which—that crossing the Gorgopotamos—was successfully blown up on the very eve of Alamein by a handful of picked British parachutists assisted by the combined forces of Generals Zervas and Ares.

The career of the latter commander, who was born in the depressing little town of Lamia a few miles to the north, was fantastic in the extreme, but nevertheless affords a useful illustration of a recurrent though regrettable phenomenon in Greek history. The son of a respectable provincial doctor of the name of Velhouiotis, he early displayed that aggressiveness which not uncommonly afflicts intelligent men who are hardly taller than dwarfs and reacted violently against the bourgeois virtues of his home, and as a result appeared in the police-courts of both Lamia and Athens on several occasions, charged with offences ranging from housebreaking to homosexuality. During the Albanian war he was a private in an anti-aircraft battery in Salonika when he joined the Communist Party, in which his advance was rapid, for when the first British officers came into the country after the collapse he was already commanding the only considerable guerrilla force operating in central or southern Greece, having adopted for the purpose the name of Ares in imitation of the practice common among the klepht chieftains during the War of Independence. Brave, educated and completely ruthless, this dapper little sadist soon became, and remained, the most formidable of all the ELAS military commanders, notwithstanding the competition of such men as Mandakas, who combined hardly less bloodthirstiness with far greater military experience. His anglophobia, added to an understandable desire to reserve his energies (together with the arms and ammunition with which H.Q. Cairo so ingenuously and abundantly supplied him) for post-war emergencies, made him extremely reluctant to undertake any operations against the Germans save when by so doing he could provoke reprisals on those of his compatriots who had not enrolled under his personal banner. Instead he applied himself with great success to the business of consolidating his own forces and eliminating those of his rivals. Finally, after the murder of Col Psarros (the leader of a guerrilla band in Aetolia which might well have formed the nucleus of that centre party of which post-war Greece is so sadly in need), whom, despite the fact that he held a safe-conduct signed by the ELAS commander, he literally took for a ride tied to the back of a car, his only surviving rival was General Zervas. This redoubtable figure was able to maintain himself in Epirus and even carry on a campaign against the common enemy until the civil war of 1944 when led by his excessive anglophilism into abandoning, under orders from Cairo, positions without which his whole front became untenable, the discipline of his forces sadly undermined by the totally erroneous news broadcast (one hopes in error) by the B.B.C., he was driven into the sea.

In December 1944, Ares, who at the time of the Liberation had been busy 'cleaning up' the Peloponnese, where he greatly pained some of his more naïve admirers among the British and American war correspondents by grimly maintaining that the number of prisoners which he was alleged to have executed with his own hand had been grossly underestimated, took over the command of the forces which were intended to seize the capital, or so it was said at the time. Subsequently when the extraordinary lack of skill with which that campaign had been handled by ELAS became manifest, this honour was very generally disclaimed. Nevertheless the unusually large massacres of prisoners and hostages and the savage mutilations to which so many of the victims were found to have been subjected encourages the belief that Ares even if he were not in charge was active in the neighbourhood.

When the Varkiza agreement brought the hostilities to an end he refused to recognize its provisions and continued, with a price on his head, to maintain himself and his band in roving independence in the mountainous country along the Albanian and Jugo-Slav borders. For a long time past he had shown signs of what in a more sophisticated Communist circle than the Greek is known as 'leftward deviation', and at no time had he allowed the strict letter of the Marxist law to hamper his personal activities. Unfortunately for the party bosses, his almost legendary fame had gained him enormous prestige with the rank-and-file of ELAS, who, quite untroubled by ideology, rightly saw in him a latter-day incarnation of such popular historic figures as 'le roi des montagnes' and Ali Pasha, and they were loath to excommunicate. Finally he was surrounded by gendarmerie in the Pindus when accompanied by only a few of his remaining followers and after a short action they were all dispatched. After death his head was cut off and exposed on a lamp-post in the main square of Trikkala, where it proved such a popular attraction that it was taken down and pickled for subsequent exhibition in the capital. This intention was actually abandoned through fear of the criticism and misrepresentation to which such a spectacle might give rise in the press of less full-blooded countries. Fortunately for the Party they had at last taken the plunge and excommunicated their old hero two days before his death and were thus spared the difficult task of awarding him a martyr's crown.

The wide Thessalian plain which has suffered the domination of innumerable Ares since the break-up of the Empire has little but its width to commend it. Undulating and, by Greek standards, green, it supports large herds of cattle and horses and nomad Vlachs, but the villages, made up of one-storey cottages lower and more Balkan in appearance than elsewhere, are shabby without being picturesque and the few towns modern without convenience. Lamia, clinging to the slope of a low hill, wears an aspect as unremarkable as its history ; Larissa, once the capital of Achilles himself, has to-day been reduced by earthquakes, invasion and civil war to an appearance of unrelieved depression ; Trikkala alone, by the possession of a Turkish castle and a couple of dilapidated mosques, achieves some faint character of its own. Westward from the last, however, the landscape changes ; the lands lying at the foot of the great wall of the Pindus are under the plough or covered by vineyards and orchards, and the peasants, many of whom retain their traditional costume, wear a less depressed more self-reliant air.

At the end of the long straight road which traverses this enclosed arm of the plain rise the astonishing pinnacles of the Meteora. Normally I am not one in whom the freaks of nature arouse an unqualified enthusiasm :

stalagmites and stalactites, cliffs in the silhouettes of which the eye of faith can descern the profile of Napoleon, caves which the guide-books delight to describe as ' Gothic chancels', leave me not merely unmoved but resentful ; nature has no business, I consider, to go monkeying about in the province of art.   But these extraordinary rocks, rising vertically from a cluster of low grassy hills divided by narrow wooded glens, like the decayed and irregular denture of some gigantic mammoth, would be remarkable even had their extravagance not been lent point by human ingenuity.   Given their inaccessibility it is not surprising that in the disturbed centuries which preceded the final collapse of the Byzantine Empire these eyries should have proved a popular refuge for those wishing to abandon the world for a life of contemplation ;   what is remarkable is that aerial platforms and ledges which might properly have supported a colony of stylites should, in the course of time, and with Heaven alone knows how much labour and patience, have been adorned with no less than twenty-four monasteries, ' A sign betwixt the meadow and the cloud ' more astonishing by far than St. Simeon himself.

Of the original twenty-four only half a dozen remain complete, of which the largest and most impressive is the great Meteoron.   Formerly one arrived at this fastness at the end of a rope attached to a windlass in the monastery, a method of access of which a contemporary guide-book gives a very cosy account.   ' A gentle upward motion then begins, the net twists slowly round and round, the traveller, as the sides of his cage contract, is gently shaken into a ball, and, except for a strange sensation of absolute helplessness, the ascent is not otherwise than agreeable.   On reaching the level of the platform the net is fished in by means of a hooked pole, its inmate, still rolled up in a ball, is tumbled upon the floor, the meshes are detached from the hook, and the traveller is set free.'   To-day a less hardy generation climbs up a stairway cut out of the face of the vertical cliff which rises some two hundred feet from the summit of the hill to topmost ledge on which stands the monastery, eighteen hundred feet above sea-level.

The principal church is a good but not exceptional example of late fourteenth-century architecture with subsequent additions, the exterior adorned with delicate mouldings and details all in a rosy coloured brick. Within are a number of paintings, traditional in style with little to distinguish them from other work of a period when much of the virtue had gone out of Byzantine art.   The *ikonostasis*, by which the monks set great store, is a terrifyingly involved and elaborate affair of carved and gilded wood of local workmanship.   Why is it, one wonders, that of all modes of artistic expression wood-carving should so obviously be the one in which the skilled practitioner finds it hardest to exercise a minimum of restraint ; in which even a genuine creative artist such as Riemanschneider too often slips into passages of pointless virtuosity ? All over Greece one is being constantly called on to admire riotous tangles of birds and vines, snakes and flowers, laboriously conjured into writhing life by the pocket-knives of a devout but unimaginative peasantry, just as ingenious and boring as those fretwork fantasies with the manufacture of which the Swiss are accustomed to beguile the tedium of the long Alpine nights, or those prickly mid-Victorian Gothic chests which were once the pride of many a Scottish baronial hall.

The remaining monastic buildings are dignified, austere stone structures, whitewashed and furnished with wide eaves and long ranges of wooden galleries of which the innumerable supporting rafters and cross-beams form complicated patterns of shadows on the walls and floorboards. One of them must once have housed the library where Curzon failed at the last moment to obtain that large quarto manuscript of the Gospels, illuminated on vellum in the finest style resembling in many respects the Codex Ebnerianus in the Bodleian, in circumstances which, as he narrates them, must surely bring tears to the eye of every bibliomane. Now but a handful of monks remain, and whatever treasures escaped the attention of Curzon's less scrupulous successors were carried off by the Italians in the Occupation, under which the whole of this district suffered particularly heavily. Not only have all the monasteries of the Meteora been pillaged in varying degrees, but the town of Kalabaka itself, lying at the foot of these hills on the main road to Epirus, was in the summer of 1945 just a ramshackle collection of temporary wooden huts standing in a circuit of blackened hearths and shattered chimney-stacks which is all that remains of this considerable provincial centre, the whole place, including four churches of, reportedly, much interest, having been burnt down by the Germans in '43. The early fourteenth-century basilical cathedral, unique of its kind in Greece, still stands, but stripped of its fittings, including a number of exceptionally interesting ikons of the sixteenth-century Cretan school, which vanished when the building was converted by the occupying troops into stables.

The road over the Pindus from Kalabaka is probably the finest piece of engineering in Greece. Completed just before the war by General Metaxas, to whose skill and foresight in military matters not only Greece but all the united nations owe a debt which ideological fashion makes them cravenly loath to acknowledge, it contributed more than any other single material factor to the success of the Albanian war ; without it there would have been no possibility of supplying that remote and savagely contested front. The scenery through which it passes is in the grandest possible manner ; the mountains hereabouts are conceived on an altogether larger scale than the steep but not lofty crags and pinnacles of the Peloponnese and Euboea, and the valleys and passes are of a Turneresque magnificence. Just below the highest point of the road, whence begins the long descent to Jannina, lies the little town of Metzovo, the administrative centre of all this rugged, cloud-wrapped region. First seen across the wide valley a good half hour before one reaches it along the winding route with its innumerable hair-pin bends, a tight huddle of grey roofs adhering grimly to the steep side of the mountain, it has all the air of a typical highland fastness ; it is not until one has arrived in the place that the measure of difference separating it from the majority of Greek mountain villages becomes apparent. The houses are solid two-storey four-square stone buildings, which, with their low-pitched stone-tiled roofs, their well-spaced windows and excellent pro- portions, have a curiously eighteenth-century English look, and it is only such minor details as the shape of the chimneys, the incorporation of a curved return at the point where the door-jambs meet the lintel, and the practice of chamfering the angles of the outside walls to a height of some four or five feet from the ground that give to them anything of an exotic air. This apparent familiarity of the domestic architecture is reinforced by the general aspect of the place, which, with its well-stocked gardens bounded by dry stone walls, large number of trees and general atmosphere of unaccus- tomed tidiness recalls in some measure the small towns of the Mendips or Cotswolds. This lay-out is not peculiar to Metzovo, but common to all the villages in this part of Epirus, where the prevailing air of solidity and well- being (at the moment almost entirely illusory) is in a large measure due to the remarkable combination of enterprise and conservatism which charac- terizes the Epirotes. Formerly a very large proportion of these people were accustomed to seek their fortunes abroad, particularly in the United States, but unlike almost all other Greeks who at length return to their native shores, (the pathetic ' hallo-boys ' whose aggressive friendliness ruins one pleasure in so many Greek villages), they did not sacrifice their ancient traditions to the illusory ideals of transatlantic progress. Instead of burdening the streets of their native village with some imitation Main Street horror, complete with bathrooms that don't work, department store furniture, and coloured photographs of film-stars piously preserved from the Sunday supplements of the Chicago *Tribune*, they put up large stone houses in the traditional style, with solid built-in beds surrounding the fireplace in the principal living- room in the manner of their ancestors, enlivened solely by brilliant home- woven rugs and a needlework picture of the maidens of Suli gaily dancing over the precipice.

Although Metzovo, with its gigantic plane tree in the middle of the little square, its stone-paved streets and abundant gardens, is typical of many a village in Epirus, in respect of its inhabitants it is unique. The Vlachs, to which race these people belong, are nomads, claiming with some degree of probability descent from the Roman colonists of the Danube valley. In former times they were far more numerous than to-day, occupying the larger part of Thrace and Macedonia and establishing in the twelfth century a Bulgaro-Vlach empire in Thessaly which survived in practical independence until the coming of the Turk. Although for the most part herdsmen, horse-breeders and shepherds following their beasts from pasture to pasture and living in temporary encampments of round wattle huts, the existence of urban settlements, of which Metzovo is the most considerable, would seem to afford evidence that, unlike the Gypsies, their nomadism is not natural but acquired. In general they are fairer in complexion and more industrious in their habits than the Greeks, whom they affect to despise, and play a rôle in the national life, more particularly since they are no longer officially regarded as a racial minority absolved from military service but deprived of full citizenship, not dissimilar to that of the Scots in our own land being markedly successful as bailiffs, factors and in industry. In their own communities both men and women make and wear their traditional dress which in Metzovo consists, for the former, of a blue-serge tunic, belted at the waist, long white woollen stockings and a little round, black pill-box cap, and for the latter of a low-waisted red dress bordered with black with three-quarter-length sleeves very wide at the cuffs.

From Metzovo the road descends to the valley of the Arachthos and then, climbing over another, more barren range of mountains, descends to the lake of Jannina by a route on which Curzon had his macabre encounter with an unfortunate traveller strapped to the side of a mule in a small box, whom he assumed to be a dwarf until it was explained that this peculiar mode of travel was occasioned by the fact that the man had just had both his legs cut off by robbers. The distant prospect of Jannina from this road is one of the most singular which Greece affords. This strange mingling of Oriental and Alpine elements, minarets, domes and cypresses crowning the rocky eminence of a small peninsula that juts out into the green waters of a lake which, although it reminded Curzon very forcibly of Genesareth, may well be considered by those whose travels have not been so exclusively near-eastern to be not wholly dissimilar scenically to certain stretches of water in the Salzkammergut, is not to be found in so strong a solution elsewhere. Moreover, closer acquaintance does not, as so often proves the case, fail to sustain the interest the distant prospect has evoked. The town itself,

though it has sadly decayed since the days of Ali Pasha, thanks to the fact that it was only incorporated into Greece in 1912 and to the Pindus which, until the construction of the new road, rendered it inaccessible save by mule or aeroplane, has preserved much of its nineteenth-century character. The older houses, with their lower storeys of stone above which the upper rooms project on consoles, with their wide eaves and grill-protected windows, are in a style which, though common enough in all the European provinces of the old Ottoman Empire and which may well derive from the tradition of domestic architecture current in Byzantium, is here carried to its fullest pitch of development. Three of its sixteen mosques yet remain tolerably intact, as does the minaret of a fourth ; the immensely thick walls of the Kastro are still upstanding, though in places quarried to make air-raid shelters, and such modern development as has taken place is mercifully confined to the outskirts of the town away from the lakeside. Many of the windows of these ' Turkish ' houses are surrounded by mouldings of considerable beauty and variety, and in some of the larger houses the rooms on to which they give have retained their original stucco decorations in a curious rococo style of great delicacy and charm. For a long time I was puzzled by the curiously familiar English look of so many of these façades, which at length I discovered derived from the prevalence of the sash window. This admirable device, which one had always believed to be strictly confined to our own country and Holland, whence traditionally we borrowed it in the seventeenth century, strikes a strangely inappropriate Georgian note, not only in these semi-oriental surroundings, but also in almost every town in Greece which has retained a Turkish quarter. When and how this noble invention reached this part of the world has never, to my knowledge, been satisfactorily explained. It has been suggested that along with cricket and ginger-beer, it is a relic of our rule in the Ionian islands, but as it is to be found as far away from this alleged place of origin as Samos and Salonika, far more frequently indeed than it is in Corfu, and, moreover, many of the buildings so equipped almost certainly antedate our occupation of the

Septinsular Republic, this explanation is not readily acceptable. For my part I incline to the theory that it may have had its origin in the Levant, whence it was introduced into Europe by the Dutch and English merchants from Smyrna. However it got there, it is undoubtedly to the presence of the sash window that the older quarters of Jannina owe their peculiar character. To the courtyard of the one untouched khan it lends an improbably Dickensian, coaching air (that is increased by the presence over the gateway of a rusty metal plaque stamped with the device of the Sun Insurance Company with an eighteenth-century date) and provides a cosy antiquarian frame for the spectacle of the

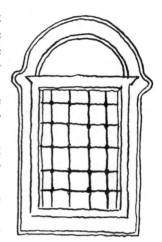

compositors setting by hand in the light of a single oil-lamp to-morrow's edition of the town's principal newspaper.

Although possessing no earlier history, Jannina achieved in medieval times an importance, both cultural and commercial, which it managed to retain almost throughout the period of Turkish rule. In the eighteenth century the merchants of this remote outpost of Hellenism maintained close relations with the principal business houses of such distant centres as Leghorn and Moscow (Napoleon's destruction of the latter caused, we are told, a panic in the financial circles of the town) and its schools were long celebrated for the zeal with which they encouraged Greek studies. The Orthodox faith was here kept vigorous by the not infrequent necessity of combating such original schismatics as Dionysius the Skelosoph, or Dog-Philosopher, whose heretical teachings, which had already cost him the bishopric of Trikkala, finally proved of so anti-social a nature as to involve him

with the secular arm of an alien faith which removed him to Constantinople, having previously flayed him alive and stuffed him with straw. It was, however, at the end of the eighteenth century that the town reached the climax of its prosperity and fame, due very largely to the abilities and personality of Ali Pasha, who at that time managed, by a skilful mixture of intrigue, fraud and homicide, to secure the pashalik. This remarkable character, whose sway extended, at the height of his power, over the whole of continental Greece save for Euboea and Attica, was, with the possible exception of his fellow Albanian, Mehemet Ali, the most considerable figure in the whole of the Sultan's domains at that date. The remote descendant of an Anatolian dervish who had settled in Epirus some two centuries earlier, he rose from extreme poverty to an exalted position and immense wealth, solely as a result of his own unaided efforts. Singularly benign in appearance, with kindly, twinkling blue eyes and a long white beard, exquisitely courteous in manner, foreign visitors to his court, who included among their number Byron, Hobhouse and Cockerell, were hard

put to it, despite the evidence provided by the cornice of freshly severed heads which formed the original and regularly renewed decoration of the principal gateway of his palace, to credit the deplorable tales which circulated of his fantastic cruelty and ruthlessness. (Owing to the equivocal appearance of the numerous youths who were constantly in attendance on their master, curious rumours as to the ambiguous character of his private life were less easily discounted, even by the resolutely unsophisticated Hobhouse.) Not that the old gentleman himself ever made the smallest attempt to reduce the number of the murders, massacres, impalements, flayings, burnings, mutilations, drownings and poisonings with which he was quite correctly credited in the public imagination ; nor, it must be added, did the long tale of these butcheries arouse any very lively indignation among his Greek subjects who, had it not been for his exceptional avarice, were quite prepared to accept him as a capable if eccentric ruler, in exactly the same way that their descendants a century later would gladly have overlooked the all-too-similar characteristics of General Ares had they not been allied to a strong Slavophilism.

When Ali was at the height of his fame the Kastro, which to-day retains within its immense walls only two mosques, some ruinous Turkish baths and one wing of the palace, a yellow-washed building with rather Baroque gables in the usual curiously Dutch style of late Ottoman secular architecture, presented the most fantastic spectacle. In the principal courtyard, the great gates of which were generally ornamented with the crucified remains of at least one malefactor, a crowd of wasp-waisted and magnificently overdressed Skipetars, the brave and ferocious Albanian tribesman on whose loyal support the Pasha's power principally rested, mocked and badgered a throng of unfortunate petitioners desperately waving their various requests attached to the ends of long sticks in a jostling crowd by the entrance to the palace. Beyond this doorway, from which the eager supplicants were firmly held back by the sentries, lay an extraordinary world of kiosks and pavilions, painted saloons with plate-glass windows overlooking the mountains and lake, and women's apartments guarded by negro eunuchs with

naked scimitars, filled with gold-embroidered divans and cages of nightingales provoked to unseasonable song by the green gauze with which they were enshrouded. Against this highly-coloured background moved a procession of inmates no less exotic; Ali's youthful personal attendants, bare-foot with their long golden hair flowing unrestrained to their waists, half-naked dervishes to whom a strong streak of superstition in his character encouraged the Pasha to allow every licence, Greek advisers and Albanian mercenaries, Italian doctors and French artillerymen, and, as often as not, an English " milor " registering interest without approval. Occasionally an extra stir and bustle in the ante-room announced the arrival of some outstanding personage of the court ; Mukhtar, the Pasha's elder son, whose lust was so uncontrollable that he frequently raped women in the public street in broad daylight, or his younger son, the courteous and distinguished-looking Veli, who possessed the largest library of pornography in the whole of the Near East, or his favourite general, the gigantic mulatto, Yusuf Arab, known, not without good reason, as the Blood-drinker. But in the very heart of this gilded warren where the Pasha himself, reclining on a crimson silk divan, puffed his long pipe, dictated masterpieces of sycophantic insincerity to his sovereign on the Bosphorus, counted up his hoarded millions or simply meditated elaborate and enjoyable schemes of revenge for injuries suffered forty years before, perfect peace and tranquillity habitually reigned.

The end of this potentate's extraordinary career, which came in his eighty-second year, was appropriately sanguinary and dramatic. At long last the Porte lost patience with their always insurbordinate and for many years almost totally independent vassal and entrusted a large army to the command of his personal enemies with orders to achieve his final discomfiture. Deserted by most of his allies and almost all his family, the old lion was finally driven into the Kastro, where he still managed to hold out for a considerable period, but which he was finally forced to abandon for the greater security of a pavilion on the small island in the lake, not, however, before he had ordered, and witnessed, the bombardment of his capital from its batteries. The end came when his enemies, having landed by means of a fraud, broke into the room immediately below that in which he had barricaded himself and started firing through the ceiling. A stray shot hit the Pasha in the groin and he soon after expired in great agony, breathing defiance and threats of revenge until the last. After his death the ruined town, which never recovered from the effects of that final vindictive bombardment, sank into a provincial stagnation which has outlasted the rule of the Turk. When Curzon visited the place some ten years later the population had much declined, ruins were everywhere and the great bazaar that had once been among the most celebrated in the whole Levant (although Hobhouse, much to his annoyance, had been unable to have his umbrella covered there), had already dwindled almost to the status of the regional market it is to-day.

Of the surviving monuments of Ali Pasha the most remarkable architecturally is undoubtedly the larger of the two mosques in the Kastro. Here the wide eaves of the central bloc, above which rises a dome supported on an octagonal drum reinforced with angle buttresses, have been extended on all sides on a double arcade of slender pillars to form a species of wide ambulatory, enclosed by a screen of windows that may once have been glazed but are now protected solely by wrought-iron grilles. The whitewashed stone pillars, the green-painted woodwork of the window surrounds, the simple lines of the grilles, the graduated grey-stone tiles of the roof all combine to produce an effect of coolness and light which is ' modern ' in the best sense of that much-abused word. From the top of the graceful minaret, with its needle-thin Turkish-style cap, the view of the town and lake with the great mass of Mount Metzekeli rising seemingly perpendicularly from the water's edge, more than compensates for the not-entirely irrational feeling of insecurity induced by the present condition of the muezzin's perch. Despite

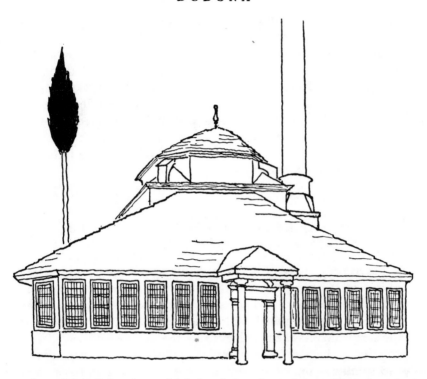

the neglected condition into which its shrines have been allowed to decline, Islám is here, however, architecturally far better represented than Christianity, for the town's principal church is an uninteresting basilical structure, much restored, with a more than usually restless *ikonostasis* of carved wood.

Jannina in the early days of archaeology was frequently thought to be the site of the celebrated shrine of Zeus at Dodona, where the judgment of the oracle was pronounced by the rustling of the leaves in the sacred oak-grove in the divination of which the resident priesthood had developed a high degree of skill.

> Oh ! where, Dodona ! is thine agéd Grove,
> Prophetic Fount, and Oracle divine ?

In fact, this sacred spot, across which both the poet and Hobhouse all unknowingly passed, lies in a secluded valley some six miles to the south of the town and is to-day to be distinguished by the tumbled remains of a considerable theatre and the excavated foundations of a temple of Zeus. The oaks have long since vanished, but the immense mountains surrounding this saucer-shaped valley, together with the general air of remoteness, form a sufficiently impressive setting for a shrine that is traditionally the earliest to be erected by the Achaeans to their ancestral thunder-god after they had crossed the border into the lands of the Pelasgian worshippers of the great mother-Goddess of the Mediterranean world, who was thenceforward, under the name of Hera, to be relegated to a secondary position in the new pantheon.   Beyond the great mountain to the west lies the celebrated district of Suli which held out so long against the repeated assaults of Ali Pasha and of which the inhabitants displayed so remarkable a courage and were distinguished by so proud and romantic a bearing as to have left an indelible impression on the imagination of Byron.

> Oh ! Who is more brave than a dark Suliote,
> In his snowy camese and his shaggy capote ?
> To the wolf and the vulture he leaves his wild flock,
> And descends to the plain like a stream from the rock.

Indeed, the scenery, no less than the inhabitants, of the whole of this region affected in a most powerful manner, as well they might, the impressionable poet in his 'twenties and to-day some acquaintance with the former will still, despite all the calculated exploitation of natural beauties of the more dramatic sort which has been achieved by the picturesque traveller and the film-producer in the past century, serve to render less extravagant and more easily acceptable some of the more highly coloured passages and steel engraved dramas of Childe Harold.   In particular I recall a ravine close to the village of Monodendri, a little to the north of Jannina, which, whether or not Byron ever visited it, produces just that effect of genuine awe which his generation so restlessly and incessantly sought.   Here a small monastery is perched on the very edge of a vertical drop of some eighteen hundred feet opposite an even higher and hardly less precipitous cliff face across which the shadows of the wheeling eagles far below silently and disquietingly slide. The solitary monk who spoke English with a strong German accent, acquired, so he said, while working on the Dar-es-Salaam railway as a youth, claimed for his view a world-wide fame, alleging that travellers had come from Athens, America and even China for the express purpose of inspecting it. I confess I am sufficient of a travel-snob to hope and believe that he had been provoked to falsehood by a commendable pride.

From Jannina to Arta the road follows for much of the way the course of the river Arachthos, here shaded by groves of enormous planes and confined within the steep sides of a narrow gorge, across which it is carried on the outskirts of the latter town by a most remarkable Turkish bridge of nine almost semicircular arches, the construction of which forms the subject of the best known of all modern Greek folk-ballads. According to the story, which in its outline is common to the folklore of many countries, the builder found himself unable to complete the last span of his work, which invariably collapsed the night before the keystone was to be laid in position. Eventually, after repeated disasters, the demon of the bridge, in the form of a raven, informed the frustrated man that his only chance of completing the job lay in his promising to bury alive in the foundations the first living thing that approached along the road. Inevitably the first to come in sight was the builder's wife, whom he regretfully but firmly dealt with as instructed. As the unfortunate lady, in a long and mournful speech which, in an effort to excite her husband's pity, she related as she was being lowered into position, revealed that a similar fate had overtaken both her sisters, who were also married to bridge-builders, one's sympathy is somewhat tempered by the consideration that in that case she might well have had the sense to keep away from her husband's business enterprises until they had been brought to a successful conclusion. However, it is probable enough that were the foundations to be examined they would be found to contain a skeleton of some sort, animal or human, for the primitive custom of sacrificing to the demon of any building under construction, who has generally been regarded in all European countries as particularly avid of blood, lingered on in Greece until very recent times : it is to-day regarded as the height of ill luck should your shadow fall on the foundation stone of an unfinished building, involving almost invariably death within the year.

Apart from the bridge, the one object of interest in Arta is the church of the Hagia Panaghia Paregoritissa, Our Lady of Consolaton, which is one of the most extraordinary of all the existing monuments of Byzantine architecture. A square block considerably larger in scale than the majority of Byzantine churches, three of its façades are pierced by a double row of windows on first and second storey level, which in their disposition and decoration, together with the bands of decorated brickwork which enclose them, recall very forcibly some of the less successful efforts to revive the Venetian Gothic style in the English provinces in the last century, while the fourth is provided with the customary projecting apses. The roof, which from the ground appears flat, supports no less than five high domes and a cupola resting on open arches immediately above the entrance. Internally the arrangements are no less unusual, the central dome, of which the side-arches are not carried over the aisles as vaults, rests on pillars corbelled out from the walls that are pierced to give access to two superimposed galleries. The unusual height, together with such details as three-dimensional sculpture and some ogival arches, has led certain experts to detect in this interior signs of a Gothic influence, derived perhaps from Naples, with which in the thirteenth century the relations of the Despots of Epirus, whose official church this was, were close. The most remarkable features of the whole church, however, which so far as I know have never been described or photographed, are the bands of sculptured angels and animals which border the arches supporting the dome. These forceful and exceptionally animated figures are in a style which has no parallel anywhere else in the Byzantine world, and although at first glance they would appear to be Gothic in feeling, as close an inspection as is possible with field-glasses from floor-level reveals an apparently far closer affinity with Romanesque work in northern Europe than with any thirteenth-century Gothic sculpture in the south. It is to be hoped that they may be properly examined and recorded without undue delay, for the whole fabric of the church, which was already in a sadly ruinous condition, was badly shaken by German demolitions in the close vicinity, and the rooks which are happily nesting in the dome and befouling the faint traces of wall-paintings which yet remain may well prove the harbingers of a complete collapse. The only other distinction enjoyed by Arta is that of having been the birthplace of the courageous and genial General Zervas.

Arta is on the southern confines of modern Epirus, and soon after quitting it the road enters Archarnania, of which the history is as confused and unmemorable as the scenery. On one side lie the almost enclosed waters of the Ambracian gulf, in which in summer the bathing is warmer than most hot baths in post-war England, and on the other range after range of low and barren hills. In those, to me, dark and mysterious centuries which lie between the end of the Macedonian Empire and the rise of the Roman, the whole district formed part of the kingdom of Pyrrhus, King of Epirus, whose teeth, instead of being divided in the normal manner, were formed of two continuous strips of bone (the only concrete fact that I have ever retained from a long course of Latin ' unseens '), but who is perhaps more generally remembered for the expensive character of his victories and his progressive employment of elephants in warfare. Past the dilapidated little port of Amphilochia, deceptively picturesque when seen across the enclosed arm of the gulf on which it stands, the road descends to the wide but not remarkably fertile valley of the Asopus before reaching Agrinion, the most depressing town in Greece. Situated in the midst of a hot and swampy plain that produces finer tobacco even than Macedonia, its architecture is as unpleasant as its climate ; buildings of any antiquity are non-existent and the modern specimens are vulgar without being funny. The inhabitants are notoriously Left Wing in their political sympathies, which, considering their environment, hardly occasions surprise, but in their actions they are unusually moderate. Thus during the period of EAM ascendancy the town was never the scene of those massacres and persecutions which took place elsewhere, and the local authorities established a reputation for responsibility and moderation. Needless to say, this avails them nothing now, and all power is concentrated in the hands of reliably reactionary officials brought in from outside.

A short distance off the main road to the south-west lies the town of Missolonghi, which, though just as unhealthy and malarial as Agrinion, and almost as completely lacking in architectural interest, nevertheless possesses a certain melancholy character of its own that does not wholly derive from literary and historic associations. Here at the western extremity of Greece the land does not so much come to an end as fade away ; amidst these reedy lagoons and mosquito-ridden swamps it is impossible to say with any certainty where exactly the coastline runs. Salt marsh and sandbank and mudflat stretch away in heat-hazy perspective towards the west, where an occasional cottage raised on piles or an isolated patch of reeds lends an improbable, lake-like character to the open sea. Missolonghi, set in the midst of this desolate landscape, would seem to be the last town in the world ; indeed, I have never seen a place that wore a more final air. At first one feels very, very sorry for Byron, but on reflection the subdued and muted character of this setting acquires a certain melancholy appropriateness. Even at midday beneath a blazing sun it has a twilight look, and it seems fitting enough that the final scene of a drama in which the main action had taken place against the architectural backdrop of northern Italy, the stuccoed façades of Regency London, and the awful grandeur of the Pindus should be played out in the unaccented romanticism of this sad coast. For nowhere else possesses quite this atmosphere of absolute finality ; as one watches the sun go down into the sea beyond Cephallonia, it is difficult to believe it will ever rise again and one looks round expectantly for that large crab to scuttle across the sand into the oily waves which, in Wells's story, was the only sign of life that disturbed the placid beauty of the last sunset on the terrestrial globe.

THESSALONIKI is a city of illusions, a series of superimposed panoramas which, as one advances from the sea, slide away into the wings like the scenes in a toy theatre. First seen as one sails up the gulf, with the low and fertile coast of Chalchidike to the right and Olympus hanging like a jagged white cloud far above the horizon to the left, it creates a highly romantic effect ; the sea-front is apparently lined with noble and imposing buildings ; domes and minarets rise above the house-tops ; and the hill behind the town is crowned and ringed with a vast girdle of castellated towers and walls. As one draws nearer, this stimulating mirage dissolves and vanishes ; the noble buildings resolve themselves into modernistic office-blocks, super-cinemas and a neo-Byzantine hotel ; the presence of innumerable caiques moored against it cannot disguise the fact that the water-front is, indubitably, a seaside promenade ; while the massive fortifications have now all sunk beneath the sky-line save for the celebrated White Tower which, though impressive enough in its way, even the most besotted antiquarian would be hard put to it to deny bears a striking resemblance to a crenellated gasometer. It is all, one decides, very like Southsea.

As one fights one's way up any of the side-streets running at right angles to the front against the never-ceasing north wind, the terrible Vardar, ice-cold and razor-sharp in winter, dust-laden and suffocating in summer, nerve-racking at all seasons, one's gloom increases. The buildings on the promenade, for all their hideousness, did at least display a flashy contemporary glitter ; the Via Egnatia, the town's principal thoroughfare, lined with dilapidated art-nouveau flats, department-stores striving pathetically to emulate the brassy glories of the Samaritaine or the Galeries Lafayette, and dingy little hotels as immoral in appearance as they undoubtedly are in purpose, has the sordid air of a third-rate Belgian watering-place on the pretentious scale of a business street in Liverpool.

But this too is an illusion. Continuing up the hill one discovers that

178

these weather-beaten Beaux-Arts façades are but a painted back-drop concealing nothing. Behind them lies a quantity of rusty steel scaffolding, depressing memorial of some long-damped building enthusiasm, a few one-storey shops and a vast open space across which the wind blows a ragged cloud of dust and scraps from the various rubbish heaps which, together with an abandoned air-raid shelter, enliven its expanse. At the further extremity, where the ground begins to rise more steeply, stands a line of low hovels, while closer at hand are visible the clustered domes, weed-grown and faintly steaming, of a Turkish bath, and the over-restored fabric of a small Byzantine church which appears, so much has the ground level risen with the years, to be built in a deep basement. These, save for a few half-finished tenement blocks away to the right, are the only buildings in sight.

Despairingly one plods on, and having traversed this mournful, littered plain, selects at random, with no very sanguine expectations, one of the alley-ways between the hovels, and immediately finds one-self in a different world, a different century. The path ahead, paved with stone-slabs and bisected by an open drain, twists upwards between three- and four-storied timber-  framed houses with wide jutting eaves and projecting solars supported by carved consoles, and little walled gardens with figs and acacias across the tops of which rises an occasional pink-washed cupola. At last, quite suddenly, one comes on the battlemented walls, far more massive and sub-stantial than from the sea one had supposed, extending downwards from the citadel on the summit of the hill in two magnificent sweeps to the quays. Beyond lies an open space, fringed by a few Asia-Minor shacks, on the slopes of which little boys are flying kites and which merges without a break into the dusty, *terre-verte* downs of southern Macedonia.

The clearly defined and seemingly unrelated stratifications of which the town is built up reflect accurately enough its fantastic history and demand a knowledge of the past for their proper interpretation. Thessaloniki was founded by a brother-in-law of Alexander the Great, who named it after his wife, the conqueror's sister. In classical times it enjoyed a considerable, largely commercial, importance and was honoured by the presence, involuntary in the first case, of Cicero and St. Paul, but it only attained to a dominating position in the eastern Mediterranean in the later days of the Empire. It was the Emperor Theodosius (who always retained a curious affection for this rather bleak neighbourhood) who was largely responsible for its early greatness and who by a regrettable lack of self-control was the direct cause of an incident which in its sordid origins and sanguinary consequences forms an admirable curtain-raiser to the subsequent history of the town.

In the year A.D. 390, while the Emperor was away in Milan, the government of the city had been entrusted to a certain Botheric, a distinguished general high in the esteem of his sovereign. At this date Thessaloniki was already in the grip of that passion for chariot-racing of which the evil effects, perhaps less insidious but certainly more spectacular than those attending our own passion for the ' dogs ', were so frequently to be felt in the history of the Eastern Empire, when it so happened that the most popular charioteer of the day, on the very eve of the most important meeting of the year, conceived and attempted to gratify an unnatural passion for a good-looking youth in the general's entourage. Botheric, who was probably a barbarian, reacted promptly and unsportingly, and the idol of the race-track was straightway clapped in gaol. Whereupon the keen Thessalonian public staged a demonstration which, as in this climate demonstrations so frequently do, got out of hand ; with the result, in the absence of an adequate number of troops due to the Italian campaign, that the unfortunate general and several members of his staff were lynched. Theodosius, when he heard the news, was convulsed with rage and at once, despite the protests of his bishops, dispatched orders for an exemplary punishment to be inflicted on the riotous citizens ; a hasty decision, the deplorable outcome of which, vividly described by the historian, he lived bitterly to regret.

" The punishment of a Roman city was blindly committed to the undistinguishing sword of the Barbarians and the hostile preparations were concerted with the dark and perfidious artifice of an illegal conspiracy. The people of Thessalonika were treacherously invited, in the name of their sovereign, to the games in the Circus ; and such was their insatiate avidity for those amusements, that every consideration of fear, or suspicion, was disregarded by the numerous spectators. As soon as the assembly was complete, the soldiers, who had secretly been posted round the Circus, received the signal, not for the races but of a general massacre. The promiscuous

180

carnage continued three hours, without discrimination of strangers or natives, of age or sex, of innocence or guilt ; the most moderate accounts state the number of the slain at seven thousand ; and it is affirmed by some writers that more than fifteen thousand victims were sacrificed to the manes of Botheric."

The period of which this deplorable slaughter marks the beginning, and the sack of the city by the Saracens in 904 the end, is commemorated by numerous monuments ; indeed, it may be doubted whether any city of the Western world, with the exception of Ravenna, has more of importance to show dating from those mysterious but not irretrievably dark centuries. Of these the earliest, save for the remains of the arch of Galerus, an ill-preserved and not absorbingly interesting provincial structure, is the church of St. George. This immense rotunda was originally intended, apparently, for a mausoleum for members of the Imperial family, but was probably converted into a place of Christian worship within a century of its erection. A projecting apse was built on the east and the outer wall was pierced by eight great barrel-vaulted arches giving on to a wide ambulatory that completely encircled the building. This latter feature has long since vanished and the arches are now bricked up, but the vaults are still decorated for their remaining length with contemporary mosaics in the so-called *asaroton* (i.e. unswept) style first developed in the second century B.C. by Sosos of Pergamon which became very popular for vault decoration in the earliest period of Christian art. These all-over patterns of birds and flowers scattered with a studied carelessness over the whole surface have a chintzy charm of their own and serve their immediate decorative purpose adequately enough ; but they cannot compare in interest or importance with the astonishing display in the dome. Here one perceives a ring of saints, spaced out at wider intervals than is customary later, full-faced and vested, each standing in front of the altar rails of a church, the fantastic and elaborate architecture of which fills up the background in golden perspective. Strzygowski detects in this décor a strong Syrian or Oriental influence foreshadowing such great architectural compositions as those in the Great Mosque at Damascus and probably deriving from the scenery in use at the theatre at Antioch (and who are we to contradict Strzygowski ?) ; nevertheless, for me they are tinged with the neo-hellenism of the slightly later mosaics in the orthodox Baptistry at Ravenna. Whatever their origins, these arcades and baldachinos were to have an astonishing progeny ; preserved throughout the Middle Ages in the stylized backdrops and borders of innumerable illuminated manuscripts, with the rediscovery of perspective they expanded and developed with the speed of a housing estate between the wars, reaching their final unsurpassable limits in the theatrical designs of the Bibbiennas. The one undeniably Oriental effect immediately recognizable to the in-expert eye is provided by the glittering gold background (one of the earliest instances of a device that was so richly to be exploited in Byzantine art) which invests the whole composition with an indescribably mysterious and other-worldly atmosphere, very different from that prevailing in the altogether too solidly constructed paradises of the High Renaissance.

One other building in the city dates from the fifth century, the church of Hagia Paraskevi, which, although its decoration can in no way compare with that of St. George, is architecturally of considerably greater interest, for it is the only intact example of a basilica of this date existing in Greece. Well restored in the present century, it preserves in the spandrels of the arcade arches mosaic decorations of baskets of fruit, flowers and birds in which scholars have detected a most interesting Alexandrian influence but which, pretty as they are, the sophisticated student may consider approximate more closely to that style of decoration evolved by the late Lovat Fraser and rendered so popular twenty years ago by Messrs. Heals.

Until 1917 Hagia Paraskevi was completely outshone by the Church of St. Demetrius, that must, until its destruction in that year by the disastrous fire which swept away half the town, have been the most magnificent basilica in Christendom. Founded originally in the fifth century it was rebuilt, in the form in which it or rather its ruin stands to-day, in the seventh ; roofless, but with its high apse almost intact, its calcined pillars with their magnificent capitals held together by rusty iron bands, it still forms a not unworthy shrine for its one great remaining treasure, the eighth-century mosaic panels on the piers of the choir. Of these that representing St. Demetrius between the donor and a bishop, which is, perhaps, the finest, though its companion piece of the donor with his children is scarcely inferior, constitutes the greatest remaining masterpiece of the pictorial art of the pre-iconoclastic era in Greece, or with the possible exception of the finest of the Ravenna mosaics, in the world. In these monumental figures one is quite unable to isolate those Syrian, Sassanian and Hellenistic elements, the relentless tracking down of which is the joy of the *kunstforscher*, so com-plete has been their fusion in the crucible of a great artist. They exist in their own right in exactly the same degree as do the figures on the west door of Chartres or the bronzes of Benin, and their genealogy, though doubtless fascinating, is ultimately of as little importance as theirs. Save for certain of the capitals of the arcade pillars which have survived, in particular those in that style known as ' wind-blown acanthus ', of which no finer examples are to be found even in St. Mark's, there is nothing else remaining of this quality. There do exist, however, some traces of wall-painting in the south arcade which have a certain interest as depicting the sack of a church, possibly the very disaster which overwhelmed the early fifth-century foundation, with the female members of the congregation receiving very rough treatment in the flame-wreathed arcades of the women's gallery and with a spirited rescue party headed by the Emperor himself, mounted and haloed, approaching rapidly from the left, bearing a remarkable, and perhaps not entirely fortuitous, resemblance to Christ entering Jerusalem.

The cathedral of Saint Sophia, the remaining monument of this epoch, is one of the great problem buildings of Christian architecture ; its date, its relationship to its greater namesake in the capital, its importance in the history of the development of the domed basilica, its mosaics, have all been the subject of the fiercest controversy. As far as the mere layman is in a position to judge among the innumerable theories, cast back and forth between the embattled ecclesiologists with all the venom of brickbats, it seems probably that in its present state the building post-dates by some years Santa Sophia at Constantinople ; possibly having been erected shortly after the first great dome of the latter church had collapsed, which would account for the unnecessary and apprehensive thickness of the supporting walls and piers. The total effect, if somewhat marred by the tasteless character of the decoration it received on its reconversion to a Christian church in 1912, is bold and spacious, though a certain clumsiness in the means employed for its achievement is not completely concealed. (The dome springs not from a circle but, owing to the exceptional size of the piers, from a figure approximating rather to a rounded octagon with unequal sides.) The mosaics in the dome which have survived intact not only the long Turkish use of the building as a mosque but also a couple of Italian bombs which in 1941 penetrated a corner of the roof, are placed by some experts as early as the sixth century, by others as late as the eleventh. It would seem most likely, however, that they were put up right at the end of the iconoclastic period in the very late eighth century, though to the casual observer there would appear to be some difference of style between the Ascension in the centre and the row of angels and apostles with which it is ringed. These latter standing between formalized olive trees are of the greatest beauty and interest ; they lack, it is true, the monumental repose of the figures in St. Demetrius, but have acquired a certain lively quality of line which, although far from naturalistic either in effect or intent, modifies without compromising their essentially hieratic character. They are in fact halfway between the St. Demetrius panels and those in the narthex at Daphni. The figure of the Virgin in the apse, behind which it is still possible to trace the golden shadow of the cross which was all that the nonconformist conscience of the iconoclastic age would allow in the way of representational art, though presumably of the same date, seems to retain more of the formal, static quality of the earlier age.

While the dispute as to the correct interpretation of the second commandment was being prosecuted throughout the Empire with an enthusiasm which has never since been equalled, even by the Kensitites or the most elevated of High Anglicans, a new and infinitely more numerous sect, whose views on representational art were characterized by an uncompromising severity to which the most fanatical iconoclasts had scarcely attained, was launched on a career of conquest which carried it from an obscure oasis in the Arabian desert to the walls of the Great City itself. It was not, however, until 904 that the Saracens descended on Salonika ; but their visitation was none the less formidable for being delayed. At this date the city was the second in the Empire and, although not unacquainted with barbarian descents had hitherto usually escaped the worst consequences, thanks to the intervention of its patron St. Demetrius, on one occasion *in propria persona* but subsequently by remote control. On this occasion the saint failed to respond and a very large proportion of his quarter-of-a-million fellow citizens were either slaughtered or sold into slavery. Luckily the Imperial throne was now occupied by the great Macedonian dynasty, and thanks to such energetic rulers as Romanus II and Basil the Bulgar-slayer the Empire was in time restored to its former greatness.

Strangely enough Salonika, compared with other parts of Greece, has little enough to show for a period of renewed artistic expansion which has rightly been called the Macedonian renaissance ; perhaps the after-effects of the Saracen raid were so disastrous and prolonged as to leave insufficient time for complete recovery before the next visitation. (This, which took place in 1125, was provoked by the descent of a Sicilian fleet commanded by the redoubtable Tancred which succeeded in capturing the city after a prolonged siege. These Normans, however, were but tourists who retired after a profitable sack ; the Franks who three-quarters of a century later overthrew the Empire came intending to stay, and as a result of the collapse Salonika found itself elevated to the status of kingdom ruled over by Baldwin of Montferrat.) Whatever the reason for this sterility, the only building of any importance which is now attributed to this period is the church of St. Elias, a domed trefoil which was probably largely rebuilt at a later date, when the paintings in the interior were certainly executed.

The Latin Kingdom of Constantinople was not of long duration. In the middle of the thirteenth century the formidable Theodoros, Despot of Epirus, wrested the city from the incompetent heirs of King Baldwin, making it the capital of his extensive possessions which, scorning half-measures, he firmly raised to the dignity of an Empire. Unfortunately there existed at Nicea a rival claimant to the Imperial dignity, and Theodoros's impulsive assumption of the purple provoked a bitter feud between the Greeks which was successfully envenomed by the differing views on the procession of the Holy Ghost from the Other Persons of the Trinity and on the use of leavened bread in the Sacrament held by the rival ecclesiastics. This was only finally resolved, after Theodoros had suffered a signal defeat at the hands of the Tsar of Bulgaria, by the reabsorption of Salonika into the Byzantine Empire, a connection which remained unbroken until 1423 when the then Emperor sold his rights to the Venetians, who for once in a way got the worst of a deal as they were relieved of their purchase seven years later by the Sultan Murad II in the possession of whose successors the city remained until 1912.

The final flowering of the Byzantine genius which marked the period between the recapture of the capital from the Franks and its ultimate overthrow is characterized by the taste and ingenuity with which the difficulties created by the sharp fall in the artistic standard of living were circumvented and overcome. No longer could the reduced Empire afford to decorate its shrines with gold and precious stones ; fresco must now do duty for mosaic, brick for marble. While there is nothing remaining in Thessaloniki to compare with the series of murals at Mistra, among the numerous examples of contemporary architecture there exists one outstanding building which is quite without rival. The Church of the Holy Apostles, standing in a little untouched square in the old quarter of the town, is an elaborated version of the cross-in-square dating from the early years of the fourteenth century. With additional north and south aisles, a narthex and an exo-narthex, and crowned with no less than five domes rising on exceptionally tall drums, its silhouette is romantic and pleasantly involved, but it is to its texture and surface decoration that it owes its pre-eminence. Never, even among the chimney-stacks of Elizabethan England, can the decorative possibilities of brick have been so lavishly exploited as they are here : eaves, window surrounds, string-courses all display a variety and ingenuity of treatment unparalleled elsewhere. But it is for the decoration of the apses that the bricklayers have reserved the ultimate flights of their skill and fancy ; here the courses ripple and weave, twist and turn into every imaginable geometrical formation in a way that is saved from riotousness by being firmly kept within the architectural bounds of the

185

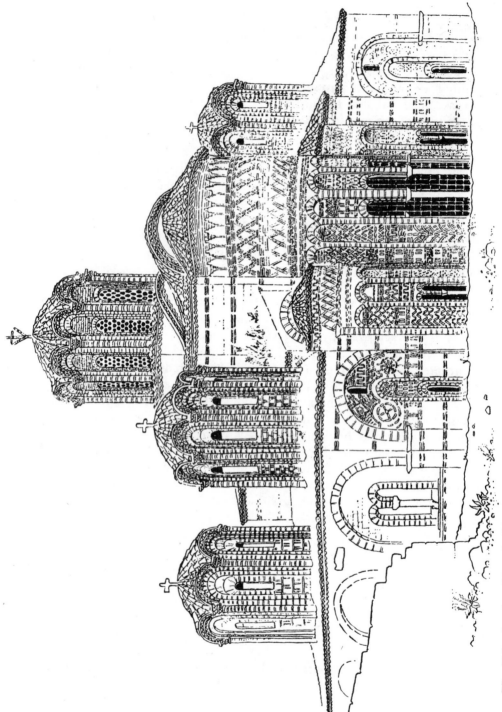

The Holy Apostles, Thessaloniki

blank arcading. As an example of brickwork this east end gains its effect by means exactly the opposite of those employed by the architects of the great Gothic churches that once graced the Hanseatic cities or by Wren in the Kensington Orangery where large surfaces of plain bonding impress by their unbroken regularity and a simple return achieves an unescapable emphasis ; here the bricks are handled and pointed like the *tesserae* of a non-representational monochrome mosaic in an attempt, apparently, to rival on a more extensive scale the surface richness produced by the jeweller or embroiderer. The architect's triumph lies in the fact that in attaining his object he has avoided, admittedly by the narrowest of margins, arousing those feelings of confusion and surfeit which marr one's pleasure in such buildings as the Flamboyant Church St. Pierre at Caen, or the Manoeline churches of Portugal.

After the excitements of the exterior the inside of the church may seem an anticlimax ; nevertheless, the wall-paintings, though less immediately arresting than those at Mistra, have considerable merit. In particular those in the dome, only recently uncovered, which repeat the theme of the dome mosaics in the cathedral, deserve attention, as does, though for slightly different reasons, a panel in the prothesis. This provides a vivid representation of the martyrdom of St. John the Baptist where a sinuous, but rather prudishly clad, Salome is shown dancing before a fascinated Herod with all the carefree assurance of a *ballerina assoluta* while balancing the Baptist's head in its golden charger on top of her own ; a hagiological variation from the usual treatment that lends a unique interest to the familiar scene.

With the coming of the Turks the city did not, as did so many Greek cities, gradually decline into a provincial stagnation. Its geographical position, which rendered it the ideal entrepôt for Balkan-Mediterranean trade, assured its position as the second city of the Empire under the Otto-mans as under the Palaeologoi and gave it in the course of time a popu-lation more fantastically mixed than that of almost any city in the world. The original indigenous population which was probably Illyrian, racially akin to the modern Albanians, had become substantially hellenized at a very early date. To them was added in Byzantine times a very consider-able Slav element with a strong tendency to increase, a certain number of Albanians and Vlachs, and such extraordinary freak minorities as the Yuruk Turcomans whom the Emperors valued highly as mercenaries but considered better removed from a possibly embarrassing proximity to the capital and accordingly planted on the plains to the south of the city. After the fall of Constantinople a strong Turkish ruling class was soon established, and in the fifteenth century the racial pattern was further confused by the arrival of large numbers of Spanish Jews, refugees from the persecutions of Ferdinand and Isabella, who came to join the compact colony of their co-religionists who were already flourishing in the days of St. Paul. In addition the commercial life of the city was soon rendered more exacting by the appearance of the Armenians, while in the present century the place of the majority, though not all, of the Turks has been taken, thanks to the exchange of populations in 1923, by Greek refugees from Asia Minor.

The appearance of the city at the time of its recapture by the Greeks in 1912 was decidedly and charmingly Oriental ; the newcomers, however, soon set about changing all that. The sea-wall, already partially demolished

by the energy and passion for tidiness of the English Consul, Mr. Blunt, was now swept away to form a promenade, and the minarets, the most celebrated both for their number and their beauty in the whole Levant, were pulled down in an extraordinary outburst of vindictive nationalism by a Greek mob whom neither the remonstrances of the prefect and metropolitan nor the large number of fatal casualties they sustained from the crashing masonry could deflect from their purpose until all but two of these elegant though alien structures had fallen to their destructive hysteria. However, the victorious Hellenes themselves sustained a far more serious loss a few months later when their sovereign, the popular and venerable George I, was shot dead by an anarchist while walking in the vicinity of the White Tower.

The history of the last thirty years at Thessaloniki is as gloomy and apocalyptic as those which went before. In the first German war an allied expedition, disregarding the protests of the Germanophil King Constantine, took possession of the town, where it established the headquarters for a campaign which provided more striking instances of muddle, jealousy, procrastination, incompetence and all the other ills which Allied High Commands are heirs to, than any military enterprise since the Crimea ; depressing evidence of the effects of which in the medical sphere are provided by the crowded cemeteries—British, Australian, French and Russian—on the outskirts of the town. More distressing to the inhabitants than the epidemics, however, was the disastrous fire which, caused, so the Greeks maintain, by carelessness on the part of allied troops, in 1917 swept away the whole centre of the town, leaving the dreary waste described above.

Almost the whole of the old Turkish quarter vanished in a night, save for a few streets to the north of St. George, where, incidentally, some years previously in a large pink-washed wooden house, still standing, had been born one of the more remarkable natives of Thessaloniki, Kemal Ataturk.

The influx of refugees after the Asia Minor disaster produced the usual scabby fringe of appalling slums but did in some measure counteract the disastrous effects of the exodus to Athens on the part of all more ambitious members of the community which had been, and still is, one of the less fortunate effects of the reincorporation of the city into the kingdom of Greece. Nevertheless, despite the unalterable neglect with which each successive Greek government, as soon as the charm of novelty had worn off, treated Thessaloniki, the city, and particularly the port, flourished well enough in the years between the wars ; but with the coming of the Germans a fresh period of horror and disaster began which culminated in a planned butchery that lacked even the small shred of justification that clings to the Theodosian massacre and was more extensive in its operation than the Saracen sack. In 1941 the Jewish population of Thessaloniki numbered between sixty and seventy thousand ; when I first visited the city early in 1945 less than twelve hundred remained. Of the rest a few had managed to escape abroad, others had been hidden by Greeks, but the vast majority had been carried away to Poland, where such as survived the foodless journey in cattle trucks perished in the labour camp and the gas-chamber.

During the civil war the town escaped the fate of Athens and was spared any actual fighting, thanks almost entirely to the patience and skill of the British Consul-General, Mr. Rapp, and the restraint and good sense of the local ELAS commander, General Bakirdtzis.

But its present condition is infinitely more melancholy than that of the capital. The wharves and harbour installations of the modern port are, despite the considerable work of clearance and restoration undertaken by the British, shattered and idle. On the dusty plain to the north-west line after line of blitzed and weather-beaten rolling stock, on which the faded but familiar legends, *Cie Internationale des Wagons-lits et Grands Expres Européens*, *Mitropa*, *Chemins de Fer de l'Est*, *P.L.M.*, bear witness to the plunder of a continent, are rusting away on the sidings of what was once one of the most important links on the great trunk line from Calais to Constantinople. Along the roads from the north and west straggling columns of refugees from the bandit-ridden border districts shuffle towards the city in ever-increasing numbers. The suburbs with their dingy walls scrawled with slogans are noisy with night shooting and each morning the gutters give up their dead. Of the desperately needed supplies on the tramp steamer in the harbour half will appear on the black market before ever the cargo reaches the lorry on the quayside, while each week a succession of strikes slows down the already funereal tempo of reconstruction.

The whole life of the city is congealing with fear. The merchants fear the mob, the mob fears the police, the police fear the communists. The Slav minority in the town fear the Greeks, the Greeks fear the Slavs beyond the frontiers, the Jewish remnant fears everyone, and everyone with even the shortest of memories fears the Bulgarians. In this atmosphere a menace lurks in even the most normal of everyday activities ; to go to the cinema on the front is, as likely as not, to be confronted with a Soviet feature smuggled across the frontier to provide funds for the local communists ; to switch on the radio is to be deafened by a stream of rabid Macedonian autonomist propaganda from Belgrade ; and to perform, even involuntarily, either act is to risk trouble with the police. But the overriding fear, common enough to-day the world over, but here stripped naked of all the disguises which are available in happier lands, its bitter taste unsoftened by the comforting sauces of hope or illusion, is the fear of the future.

· · · · ·

The dusty fig-tree cries for help,
Two peasants kill one snake,
While in our rocky heart the gods
Of marble hush and break.

After long ages all our love
Became a barren fever,
Which makes us glow in martyrdom
More beautiful than ever.

· · · · ·

DEMETRIOS CAPETANAKIS—*THE ISLES OF GREECE*

I.   CORFU

A PECULIAR fascination attaches to all towns wherein two or more distinct and alien cultures have flourished side by side but where no synthesis has ever been achieved.   Too often, however, the full improbable flavour of the resulting contrasts is diluted by segregation ; only in the few streets adjoining the ' native quarter' where the minaret overshadows the Empire-builders' pebbledash and half-timbering or where the upcurving eaves of a pagoda project behind the correct façades of the Third Republic can it be savoured in all its intensity.   But in Corfu an architectural *mélange* of the most surprising sort is evenly established in the very heart of the town.   Standing in front of the entrance to the *castello* one is faced across the " Esplanade " (sic), sparsely covered with grass and having in its centre a wrought-iron bandstand that might well have been borrowed from Devonshire Park in Eastbourne, by two handsome terraces erected by the French in imitation of the Rue de Rivoli beneath the arcades of which the Corfiot *jeunesse dorée* sit eating ices.   To the right lies the restrained and familiar façade of the palace of St. Michael and St. George, recalling with its flanking colonnades and general air of sober grandeur the garden front of Buckingham Palace ; immediately behind, in front of a rusticated, high-renaissance gateway, a marble statue of Graf von der Schulenburg in half-armour and a full-bottomed wig commemorates in the most lively Baroque the heroic defence of the town in the seventeenth century, while a little further off to the left the virtues of a later governor, Sir Thomas Maitland, popularly known to his compatriots as the ' Abortion ', are more restrainedly perpetuated by a chaste Ionic temple.

Such diverse structures serve well enough to emphasize the eclectic history of this beautiful island on which the Almighty lavished every gift of climate, landscape and fertility, only to nullify them all by the geographical position He allotted to it.   Lying a couple of miles off an alien shore, commanding the straits that divide the Adriatic and Ionian seas, the stormy fate of Corfu was from the first implicit in its situation.   In classical times the revolt of the Corinthian colony of Corcyra was the immediate, if unlikely, cause of the most disastrous struggle in antiquity during the course of which the island was the scene of the earliest and most ferocious outbreak of class warfare of which we have any record.   Later, after various vicissitudes it passed under the rule of Rome and it was in the principal harbour that Octavius assembled his fleet for the Battle of Actium.   In the Middle Ages, after passing from the Greeks, to the Normans to the Angevins to the Despots of Epirus, the inhabitants finally of their own free will surrendered their territory to the Venetians, accurately surmising that the Serene Republic was the only power sufficiently strong to afford them adequate protection from the Turk. In 1797 by the treaty of Campo Formio it passed, together with the rest of the Venetian possessions, to the French, who lost it to the Turks and Russians, regained it as a result of Tilsit and were finally relieved of it by the English. From 1814 to 1864, as a result of its incorporation, along with the other six Ionian Islands, into the British Empire, Corfu enjoyed a period of relative tranquillity and good government which continued, only slightly modified, after its cession to the Greek crown on the accession of King George I.   During the course of the first German war its sufferings were slight, but very soon afterwards it became the scene of Mussolini's first essay in direct action and of a *cause célèbre* from which the reputation of the infant League of Nations gained little lustre.   In the most recent conflict it was occupied both by the Italians and the Germans and bombed by almost all the belligerents operating in this theatre ; at the time of writing, as a result of the mine disaster in the Corfu channel, it seems likely to prove as fruitful a source of trouble at U.N.O. as it once did at Geneva.

It is not altogether surprising, therefore, that the town of Corfu should have little to show that can be regarded as specifically Greek.   The domestic architecture is predominantly Italian in style, relieved here and there by a façade which is to the discerning Anglo-Saxon eye unmistakably Regency. The principal church is a plain basilical structure with an elaborate coffered ceiling in a provincial version of the seventeenth-century Venetian manner, and adorned with a series of large ikons in which the saints of the orthodox calendar appear in almost Roman travesty.   The palace of St. Michael and St. George and the royal villa of Mon Repos are uncompromisingly and successfully British ; the former very much in the style of Nash, the latter strangely reminiscent of the work of Henry Holland who was almost certainly dead at the time of its erection.   The fortifications are plainly and expectedly Venetian.

Nor has the countryside much in common with the mainland.   Enjoying a heavy winter rainfall, the valleys and fields are notably green and lush, while the mountains themselves have nothing of the Attic barrenness. The trees and shrubs are of familiar kind but of quite exceptional size ; enormous stone pines which seem of a totally different species from the tough and ragged little trees which sparsely dot the hillsides of Greece proper, and giant olives, here left unpruned, whose twisted trunks are pierced with innumerable holes the size of a man's hand through which the daylight penetrates in a macabre, Daliesque fashion.   In the countless sandy coves and inlets the most celebrated of which is Palaeocastrizza on the west coast ; the traditional playground of Nausicaa and her maidens, admirably painted by Edward Lear (the only artist who has successfully captured the peculiar quality of this landscape), the olive-groves and cypresses are not, as is usually the case, separated from the sea by a wide stretch of barren and gritty rock, but come right down to the water's edge.   Over the whole countryside there spreads, once the sun has passed its meridian, an extra-ordinary golden light of a varnished mellowness far removed from the astringent sparkle of Attica that lends it a strange enchanted quality well suited to Prospero's isle, as a recent writer has christened it, but which for me has a Tennysonian rather than a Shakespearean flavour.

> All round the coast the languid air did swoon,
> Breathing like one that hath a weary dream . . .

The inhabitants of this exposed paradise differ both in costume and economic status from the ordinary Greek peasants.   Mainland Greece is a country of smallholders where the very few large estates that formerly existed were all, with two exceptions, broken up by the land reforms of Venizelos, but here the feudal domains of the local nobility in many cases remain intact.

These curious relics cling to the titles with which the Serene Republic was so generous to her colonials in the last days of her power when she had nothing else to offer, with an·insistence which in ordinary times was vaguely comic but which during the Italian occupation became, in some cases, a trifle embarrassing. Staunchly royalist, those who have not departed to cut a dash in the society of the capital (an inconsiderable proportion) continue to inhabit their rambling villas, solid, unpretentious buildings in the north Italian style of the seventeenth century, surrounded by their vines and their olives and exercising their seigneurial rights with an accommodating inefficiency. Their tenants, usually darker and slighter in build than the mainland peasantry, live in picturesque but decaying villages which, thanks to an absence of dust and abundance of vegetation, accord far more closely with the popular conception of the Arcadian ideal than does the bleak Peloponnesian reality. The churches are in most cases themselves unremarkable, but the free-standing campaniles, high slabs of wall, pierced with diminishing rows of pigeon-holes, the angles often filled in with Baroque stone scrolls, lend a curiously exotic character to the

surrounding landscape. The women wear a costume of exceptional charm and richness, of which the Italian origin is not in doubt, for its most distinguishing feature, a wheel-shaped turban of coloured ribbons braided in with the hair, has been exactly set down by Titian in his portrait of a Venetian courtesan. Whatever was once the traditional garb of their menfolk, it has now been generally abandoned, and only the two town bands cut any sartorial dash ; the Royal Ionian, glorious in a uniform of the colours of the ribbon of the C.M.G. and a golden helmet heavily beplumed, and the National, staunchly patriotic in white and blue with helmets of silver.

Of all the inhabitants of Corfu, by far the most influential and infinitely the most popular is, though dead, still visible in the flesh. Unlike the generality of mankind, St. Spiridon, although during his lifetime a not inactive bishop who attended the Council of Nicaea, has undertaken his longest journeys and displayed the greater energy in the course of his post-mortal career. At the time of the fall of Constantinople his embalmed corpse, which had long been venerated in that city, had recently been acquired by a certain Calochoretti who, with a repaying prescience, had invested his entire fortune in holy relics. Having successfully escaped from the doomed city, this pious speculator made his way across Thessaly and Albania bearing his holy capital, which included in addition to St. Spiridon the mortal remains of St. Theodora, the wife of Theophilus the Iconoclast, in a country cart concealed beneath a load of hay, arriving finally at Corfu. Once established in the town, his investment proved highly profitable, the resident saint, Arsenius, soon showing himself quite incapable of any prolonged or effective response to the com-

petition of the newcomers, and on his death the old man bequeathed a saint apiece to his two sons. St. Spiridon, who almost from the first declared far the larger dividend, was the portion of the elder, on whose death he passed into the family of Bulgaris, who still retain his person and enjoy his revenues. To-day he lies richly and liturgically clad in an ornate silver coffin in his own church where the more important and influential visitors may inspect him on request; the common people must restrain themselves in patience until his name-day, when robed and mitred he passes in procession through the town seated on the episcopal throne, followed by all the officials and dignitaries of the island. Of his countless miracles, unflagging watchfulness for the island's interests, and prompt attention to the humblest of his supplicants, Mr. Durrell has recently given us a charming and exhaustive account, to which I will only add the most recent proof he has afforded of his protective power. During the last war a large proportion of the townspeople showed themselves when the sirens sounded understandably reluctant to seek the safety of the air-raid shelters thoughtfully provided by the municipality, preferring to entrust themselves to the tried protection of St. Spiridon. One night, in the course of the worst raid which the town had suffered, when the church was as usual packed to its utmost capacity, fire-watchers were horrified to observe a bomb of enormous size whistling indeflectably down upon that elaborately decorated but far from solidly constructed building. At the very last second, when all hope appeared to have vanished, the missile, for no obvious reason, exploded with a terrifying, baffled roar but twenty feet above the roof itself, injuring none and causing but superficial damage. Whatever decline in the saint's popularity may have taken place in the sceptical period between the wars, this awe-inspiring demonstration of his personal intervention has effectively arrested it for many years to come.

Hardly less exalted if more animated visitors have from time to time taken up their residence on the island, ranging from Richard Cœur-de-Lion, who passed some months here on his ill-starred journey back from the Holy Land, to the Empress Elisabeth of Austria, who, rating its charms even higher than those of Ventnor, where she had previously been accustomed to pass much of the summer, built herself a villa some distance from the town. Later her place and her villa were taken by the ex-Kaiser, who redecorated the latter in a style in which tradition and modernity are nicely blended, for in the principal rooms the ceilings are both adorned and illuminated by numerous stucco *putti* blowing what appear to be iridescent bubbles, but what are in fact electric-light bulbs. Another contemporary visitor from the Teutonic north was Herr Böcklin, the Führer's favourite master, who here found the inspiration for his masterpiece, the celebrated ' Toteninsel '.

Nevertheless, despite, or perhaps because of, the attraction which Corfu exerts for the Nordic temperament, its beauties may appear to those with some acquaintance with Greece proper to be of too rich and cloying a quality, infused, though to an infinitely greater degree, with that self-same balmy prettiness which renders *die wunderschöne Insel Wight* so attractive to the Teuton traveller. Beautiful beyond compare, it is yet a beauty that lacks all power to sustain.

> To hear the dewy echoes calling
> From cave to cave thro' the thick-twined vine—
> To watch the emerald-coloured water falling
> Thro' many a wov'n acanthus-wreath divine !
> Only to hear and see the far-off sparkling brine,
> Only to hear were sweet, stretc'd out beneath the pine.

Undoubtedly ; nevertheless, after a few days in Corfu one has, one realizes, after all, a Puritan streak.

2. CRETE

Crete, to a greater extent, perhaps, than any other place in the world, certainly any place of similar size, possesses a power strangely to stir the imagination, even of those who have never been there, which the mere sound of the long flat monosyllable of its name is sufficient to quicken. In a large measure this is due undoubtedly to the knowledge of the vast tracts of time through which this island has played a rôle in history—to the realization that as many years before the birth of Christ as have passed since His death a complex civilization had here already passed the climax of its achievement and had entered on a long period of immensely sophisticated decline : but even if the Minoan culture were still as dimly apprehended as it was before the coming of Sir Arthur Evans, it would yet be impossible to treat of Crete as just another Mediterranean island, remarkable only for its greater size.

The scenery and the inhabitants, although the mists from the legendary past may serve to magnify their scale, would always even when seen with the naked, factual eye appear unrelated and unique. The landscape of the northern coast, as it appears from the sea, immediately strikes a fabulous, unlikely note. The narrow coastal plain, separated from the shore by long sandy beaches and fringed with great clumps of feathery reeds, is backed by a low range of hills behind which rises a range of considerable mountains ; if this were all, the scene though beautiful would not be unparalleled, but way behind these summits a further range hangs snowcapped in the blue as far above the intermediate chain of heights as these are above the foreground hills. This triple barrier of three superimposed silhouettes of which the upper edges are clearly defined while the bases tend to lose their firmness of outline in a flat haze that forms the background for the sharp summits of the range immediately below, has much of the quality of a Chinese water-colour of the best period and produces a hardly-to-be defined impression of artifice and unreality.

The figures which pass before this heroic backdrop seem, fortunately enough, to be all just slightly larger than life and to display a theatrical air without which they would assuredly be overwhelmed by the immensity of their surroundings. Physically, the Cretans differ considerably from the Greeks of the mainland, being in general of taller stature (although it should be remembered that the average Greek is not nearly so diminutive as the Anglo-Saxon imagination too often pictures him) and swarthier in complexion, both of which traits may perhaps derive from a strong Berber strain in the Arab corsairs, who almost extinguished the original inhabitants of the island in the ninth and tenth centuries. Their peculiarity, in which they take immense pride, is further marked by their carriage and their eyes ; the former is characterized by a dignified swagger that comes in part, doubtless,

from their habit of always wearing high-polished boots, quite regardless of whether or not they are likely even to see a horse, and the latter are extravagantly black and piercing, jettier and more brilliant by far than the oily blackness as of a Kalamata olive, which distinguishes the eyes of the Asia Minor Greek. These physical distinctions are further emphasized by the traditional costume, which is here far more generally worn by the men than it is on the mainland. The baggy Turkish breeches with the extraordinary pouch in the seat, traditionally designed to catch the infant Mahomet who on his second coming will be born of man but which is utilized in the meantime, anyhow by Christian wearers, to carry anything from a Primus stove to half a dozen hand grenades ; the immense cummerbund whose countless folds serve more than a purely decorative purpose as they afford an admirable and much-needed protection to the liver and kidneys in a climate where the temperature is subject to violent changes in the course of a few hours ; and the small black turban with a pendant, satanic fringe level with the eyebrows—all combine to produce an effect of elegant ferocity which is still further enhanced by the immense moustaches lovingly cultivated by all those of an age to do so.

Although in classical and modern times Crete never again attained the unrivalled position it had enjoyed in the Minoan period, its history was sufficiently remarkable and unlike that of the rest of the Greek world to ensure its continued peculiarity. Colonized by the Dorians, it played an inconspicuous rôle during the most glorious periods of Hellenic history, and in the earliest years of the Christian epoch was only distinguished by the widespread reputation for untrustworthiness achieved by the inhabitants ; a reputation so firmly established that St. Paul himself did not hesitate to

198

accept it, and by so doing give it a world-wide currency. As part of the Byzantine Empire it acquired, owing to its geographical position, a new importance that rendered it the pivot on which the whole naval strategy of the Empire turned, and its capture by the Arabs in the eighth century ushered in one of the most miserable periods in the history of the eastern Mediterranean. When a term was finally set to this alien domination by the victory of Nicephoros Phokas and Byzantine rule was re-established, the character of the island had suffered considerable change and differences had been established which are still apparent. Owing to the Arab practice of liquidating the male population, either by the sword or in the galleys, and stocking their harems with the female, the inhabitants had acquired a distinctly duskier tinge, and it is not perhaps too fanciful to see a further result of this prolonged occupation in the architecture of many of the villages which, with their square, flat-topped houses and drumless, whitewashed domes, exhibit to this day a strangely African look. With the decline of the Byzantine power the island passed to the Venetians, whose mild rule not only served to preserve the native culture from the Turkish blight for more than a century longer than any part of the Greek mainland but to establish a connection with western Europe during a vital period in the continent's history which bore unexpected fruit in the art of Crete itself and, in one notable instance, of Europe. During the last period of the Empire the influence of the Cretan school of ikon-painters had spread all over the Greek world, gradually replacing that of the earlier Macedonian school. With the coming of the Venetians the island artists were brought into direct contact with the Italian Renaissance, with the result that not only is the characteristic formalism of Orthodox art much relaxed and a new, scientific vision of reality superimposed, by no means invariably successfully, on the old hieratic Byzantine conception, but whole compositions and motifs are freely borrowed from the West. The traffic, of course, was not entirely one way, and in the person of El Greco, Crete nobly repaid with compound interest what she had, perhaps rather unwisely, borrowed. So much, however, has recently been written about the importance of the Byzantine element in that painter's work that it may not perhaps be out of place here to point out that the art with which Theotocopuli was acquainted in his native land was already markedly hybrid and that the late Robert Byron's portrait of the young traveller in Venice, on whose rigidly non-realistic, Orthodox vision Renaissance naturalism had an undoubtedly stimulating but in the long run superficial effect, needs some modification. As an example of how far the Venetian influence had already affected the Cretan painters, let me cite an adoration of the Magi by a contemporary of Greco in the possession of M. Kaliga in Athens in which the whole group in the foreground is, in composition though not in colour, an almost exact copy of a painting of the same subject by Bassano in a private collection in this country.

The western European inoculation which the inhabitants of Crete received during the Venetian period served to maintain their native vigour and spirit at a higher pitch than that of the other Greeks during the long years when they were all subject to the Porte. The result was that there was no time in those centuries when the Cretans could have been said to have been acquiescent subjects of the Sultan, and the years after the libera-tion of the mainland when Crete still remained within the Ottoman Empire were marked by an almost continuous series of revolts and up-risings which, although they invari-ably failed of their main objective, did secure for the island a certain cautious respect from their overlords and incidentally provided the earliest lessons in leadership and statecraft for the great Venizelos. When at last, in the early years of the present century, victory was achieved and  Crete was reunited to the rest of Greece, the islanders almost at once began to have second thoughts. The warm embraces with which they were received by their fellow countrymen were soon discovered to have masked the most shameless pocket-picking, and the wealth of an island which was self-supporting to a degree unattained by any other portion of Greece was rapidly reduced by the depredations of successive governments, who made little or no return in the way of social services. It is not therefore altogether surprising that old men are still to be encountered who look back as to a golden age to the last days of Ottoman rule, when the professional story-tellers were to be heard every evening in the cafés of Candia and Canea recounting their traditional sagas to an audience of grave Turks with lacquered moustaches and little sachets of musk tucked beneath their arm-pits, and the rhythm of an ancient way of life had not yet been disturbed by the shoddy modernity of Athens and the Piraeus. Nor is it surprising that among the younger men there are many, particularly those who as guerrillas co-operated with our liaison officers during the occupation, who advocate autonomy for an island the inhabitants of which have for years maintained an undeviating liberalism equally unacceptable to the extreme monarchists and the Marxian democrats who alternately flourish so vigorously on the mainland.

Fascinating and occasionally impressive as are the incidents and monuments of recent Cretan history, they must inevitably tend to appear parochial and insubstantial when compared to the achievements of the race that flourished here at the very dawn of European history. Dorians, Arab corsairs, Venetian adventurers, German parachutists have all come and gone, leaving nothing to mark their passage but an occasional entrenchment and a faint smell of blood, but in half a dozen places there are visible extensive remains of a people which, while remaining in many ways mysterious, are clearly seen to have attained a degree of material civilization unsurpassed until the present century, although they vanished from the historic scene more than a millennium before the Birth of Christ. Of these Minoan sites the best known and most easily accessible is that of Knossos, which would appear to have been the capital of a marine empire embracing all the Aegean, and lying a mile or two outside the bombed and shabby modern town of Heraklion. The so-called palace of Minos, though infinitely less moving than Mycenae, is undoubtedly of even greater interest. The extent of the remains, their excellent preservation and the highly ingenious reconstructions of Sir Arthur Evans all shed a clear, unromantic light upon the ancient Minoans very different from that shifting twilight through which loom the indeterminate but occasionally familiar features of the Myceneans. But this hard, clinical illumination is curiously arbitrary and incidental in its operation, with the result that while certain aspects of the characters on which it falls are as brilliantly lit and easily studied as those of a person opposite one in the Tube, others are left completely in the dark. Whereas the inhabitants of Mycenae are like the figures in some faded and weatherstained fresco, their outlines shadowy and indistinct but their general form still ascertainable, the builders of Knossos may be compared to fragmentary statues of which certain limbs and the torsos are perfectly preserved but of which other parts, including the heads, are completely missing.

It is at once obvious that as architects the Minoans were inspired by quite different ideals from those pursued by the builders of classical Greece. For one thing they were staunch believers in the ‘ open plan ’ (that is to say that their buildings were conceived from the inside out, and the external elevation was only of secondary importance) and are thus to be classed with the architects of the Middle Ages, the Chinese, Sir Edwin Lutyens and the leaders of the Modern Movement as opposed to Ictinus, Palladio, or Sir William Chambers. In this enormous warren of a palace

The water-front at Canea

comfort and convenience were of primary importance to which external appearance was entirely subordinate and defence did not, apparently, even have to be considered. Bathrooms, lavatories, small private apartments and pleasant loggias alternate around a great central court, vast ceremonial halls are conspicuous by their absence and even the throne-room is on a reduced intimate scale. But if the Minoan ruling class were indifferent to display, they were certainly luxurious : the decorations, fittings and plumbing all indicate that here flourished no unworthy passion for austerity for its own sake, and that the knowledge and material resources were readily available for a standard of living that was exceptional even in our own distant days of prosperity. Of the purely aesthetic character of the Minoan achievement it is far harder to form any just estimate. The mere tract of time during which this art developed, flourished and declined, over two millennia, renders all generalization dangerous, and while it is tempting to draw parallels between various of its phases and those readily detectable in the art of more recent times, the scanty and fragmentary nature of the examples which have come down to us make any such efforts woefully inconclusive. Like that of the Egyptians, it would appear to have been strongly decorative in character but informed, as that of the Egyptians never was, by a recurrent vein of naturalism that was at once its principal source of strength and of weakness. When still controlled by a traditional respect for form and composition, as we see it in the so-called Kamares ware of the Middle Minoan III period, this naturalism achieves effects of a delicacy and charm unmatched outside the Far East, but later the restraint is weakened and in the Palace style the flower stems and octopuses, which were among the most popular decorative motifs, begin to twist and writhe with an almost *art-nouveau* abandon. In the final stage, immediately before the collapse, this passion for the crowded, naturalistic marshalling of marine objects has passed completely beyond control and many of these vases covered with star-fish and shells, octopods and squids, would seem excessive even on a table at Pruniers. Curiously enough, it is the nature of this decline which links this art most clearly with that of the West, where a tendency towards exaggerated sinuosity of line occurs again and again just at those moments when a particular style has become exhausted and overblown, and these writhing tentacles have much in common with the window tracery of late Flamboyant Gothic, the final spasms of Rococo plasterwork and the attenuated water-lilies of Walter Crane.

The palace itself in its present state dates from a period when the decline had already set in but was happily not far advanced and must have stood in much the same relation stylistically to the earlier building which it replaced, as did Nash's Buckingham Palace to Inigo Jones's Queen's House at Greenwich. Allowing for the fact that the frescoes as they appear to-day are largely the work of a talented French water-colourist, the general effect created by the surviving decorations is one of immense sophistication and a carefully cultivated taste. The human figures which appear from time to time, doing the most extraordinary things with bulls or watching ballet-dancing in an olive grove, are quite unlike any others that appear in ancient art. Quite devoid of that power to trouble the emotions with a suggestion of a mysterious inner life with which in varying degrees the statues on the west portal at Chartres, the earliest Chinese figure paintings or the mosaics at Hosios Loukas are endowed, they are at the same time entirely untouched by that ferocious animality that characterizes the stone carvings of the Incas or so many negro masks. These people, one feels, were a race of happy little extroverts unshadowed by that inhibiting preoccupation with the future life which so troubled the contemporary Egyptians and quite unconcerned with the intellectual problems which engaged the fascinated attention of the classical Greeks. The curious dualism which characterizes their acceptance and interpretation of the visible world, which finds expression on the one hand in naturalistic renderings of fish or crocuses, and on the other in the elaborately stylized convention used for the representation of rocks (which are shown, as it were, split open and polished, their internal veining displayed in as great detail as it would have appeared on a highly finished marble slab), finds an echo in twentieth-century Paris in the work of such artists as Dufy and the early Miro and is saved from triviality by just that same dynamic element, though here controlled and rendered docile by an accepted tradition, which sustains Picasso and which may well be symbolized in both cases by the frequently recurring image of the bull.

Quite suddenly, almost overnight, this whole complex world vanishes, the bulls and the ballet-dancers, the water-closets and the double-headed axes. In some apocalyptic convulsion of which vague rumours survive in the legends of the Minotaur and the correspondence of the Egyptian Foreign Office, the thalassocracy of Minos is overwhelmed, its unwalled cities cast down and its palaces consumed with fire. But its accumulated knowledge and experience was not wholly lost, the tombs of Mycenae and the frescoes of Tiryns acknowledge the tradition of Knossos, and the naturalism which first found expression on the pottery of Kamares is transmitted by Cretan refugees to the Ionian settlers in Asia Minor and by them left as a legacy to classical Greece. The very suddenness of the disaster which brought to an end this first European civilization, together with that earlier, perhaps volcanic, catastrophe which occurred at the end of the Middle

Minoan period, seems to be in keeping with the extraordinary character and landscape of this island and to have established a tradition. The tempo of history one feels can never be the same in Crete as elsewhere, and the triumphs and disasters that occur on its shores will always have a cataclysmic quality whether they be occasioned by vast tidal waves thrown up by some submarine convulsion, the unheralded descent of seaborne barbarians, or a German army-corps dropping from a cloudless sky.

3. THE AEGEAN ISLANDS

The Cyclades, seen from the sea or the air, have none of that dream-like quality with which one is accustomed, doubtless unjustifiably, to invest the Isles of Greece and which does in strong measure attach to Corfu. Barren, concrete and unyielding, their uncompromising silhouettes unsoftened by mists or even, so clear is the air, by distance, they provide visible proof that grimness is not necessarily always grey nor solely an attribute of northern climes. The hard blue sea, the brilliant white of the few scattered buildings, the reddish earth (so inextricably mingled with the grey rocks as

to produce from a distance a curious purplish tint that has nothing in it of crimson), make up a scene that is none the less austere for being highly coloured. Samos, however, is nicely traditional ; avoiding on the one hand the lushness of Corfu and on the other the Cycladic harshness, it approximates far more closely to the traditional conception than any of the islands I have seen. Sufficiently restricted in size to render it impossible ever to forget one is on an island, close enough to its neighbours and the mainland to preclude any uncomfortable feeling of remoteness, amply provided with wooded creeks and long beaches,

it would seem to fulfil the most exigent island-fancier's every demand.

In ancient times Samos was chiefly celebrated for its great temple of
Hera and its wine ; to-day the former is reduced to a few pillars, among the
earliest known examples of the Ionic order, situated at one end of a magnificent beach facing the coast of Asia Minor and the Dodecanese that was once
the waterfront of the capital of the island, but the latter, a sickly sweet
vintage, is still produced and marketed in large quantities. (There is also
a dry Samian wine which is excellent but hard to come by as the islanders
very rightly export extremely little.) In the most flourishing period of its
independence, before it was sucked into the world empire of the Athenians,
it was ruled by the tyrant Polycrates, who enjoyed a proverbial good
fortune in all his undertakings, of which the most remarkable, a great underground aqueduct piercing the mountain immediately behind the city, still
remains. Needless to say, in a world controlled by jealous and touchy
Olympians, his good luck finally deserted him and he was murdered by his
host when on a friendly visit to the governor of the neighbouring mainland
city of Pergamon. The subsequent history of the island does not differ
greatly from that of the rest of the Archipelago ; raided by the same corsairs,
contested by the usual improbable collection of Frankish adventurers, it
succumbed to the universal foe. In one respect only was it in later times
unique ; during most of the nineteenth century, while remaining nominally
subject to the Porte, it in fact enjoyed an almost complete independence
under its own Hereditary Prince. The rule of this, the dimmest, surely, of all

obscure potentates, continued in theory, despite innumerable insurrections, several of them engineered by the ever-resourceful M. Sophoulis, until the time of the first German war.

The principal town, Vathi, is situated on the opposite side of the island to the ancient Samos, at the head of a bay that narrows almost to the dimensions of a creek. The houses are for the most part in the 'Turkish style' with wide eaves, projecting upper storeys and those curious little wooden pilasters or newel posts at the corners of the façade, ranged in tiers up the lower slopes of the mountain behind and separated one from another by frequent small gardens and bracketed by cypresses. Much of the charm of the place lies in the miniature scale on which it is conceived ; leaning from a first-floor window on the minute quay it would appear possible without undue exertion to shake hands with a friend aboard one of the small caïques tied up below. The churches in the town itself are not remarkable, but on the surrounding heights, and indeed throughout the island, are a number of monasteries neither very old nor in the accepted sense important, but which with their abundance of painted domes, their colour-washed walls and invariably inaccessible situation, lend a pleasingly theatrical, almost Russian ballet, air to a landscape in which the various elements, the mountains, valleys, cliffs and sea are already so compressed, and as it were out of perspective, as to achieve a sophisticated yet primitive quality more often to be found in the stage sets of Goncharova or the back-grounds of an ikon than in nature. Though these buildings are in general most effective from a distance and few of them conceal any architectural or

decorative treasures, their gardens are frequently charming, and in some of the churches are to be discovered modern folk-carvings in which an ancient tradition is infused with an unusual and quite unselfconscious vitality.

The island of Chios, away to the north-west, differs from Samos in almost every respect. Large in size, with a long history of commercial importance, celebrated in ancient times as the birth-place of Homer and in modern times as the scene of an appalling massacre that inspired Delacroix and delivered an effective jab to the well-cushioned con-science of Christendom, it quite lacks

the remote and unexpected quality of its
smaller neighbour. The port itself makes
no very favourable impression ; along the
quayside stretches a line of drab, 1900
buildings, cafés, offices and stores, many of
them in an unattractive yellow brick
meticulously pointed ; and only the skeletons of the big sea-going caïques in the
shipyards and the row of windmills along
the water's edge give character to the
prospect. Immediately behind this depressing façade the scene, though more
animated and less Western, is scarcely
more rewarding : a not very impressive
mosque, a bazaar that is confused without
being picturesque and a plane-shaded

market-place chiefly filled with the wares of the local potters, flat dishes
usually marred by meaningless decorations in chalky white and high-necked
amphorae that have a mean look after the splendid big-bellied pots of Crete,
and that is all. At the south end of the town, however, the scene is completely different. Here the dingy shopping streets gradually lose themselves
between the high walls and shady lanes of the campus, the most remarkable
residential suburb of which perhaps any town can boast. If one steps aside
through any of the ornamental but crumbling gateways which impose an
ineffective barrier of rusty wrought iron between the urban squalor of the
street and the discernable greenery beyond, one enters an Eden-like region
of terraced but neglected gardens, long perspectives of olives and thick groves
of lemon stretching away up the gentle slope until they merge imperceptibly
into the open mountainside. Technically one is trespassing, for these
gardens, or rather this park for no visible boundaries divide one property
from another, are the private paradise of the long-established and immensely
wealthy Chiot ship-owning community, but none will question one's presence,

for these shuttered stone-built mansions that loom up
here and there through the green shade are almost all
empty and deserted, as silent and abandoned as the
shipyards in the harbour, and their owners a thousand
miles away in the air-conditioned comfort of the Dor-
chester or the rhododendron-shrouded cosiness of some
half-timbered Surrey mansion, far beyond the reach of
the compelling fragrance of the lemon blossom which is

here so strong as to be discernible, so it is said, when the wind is offshore, five or six miles out to sea.

Apart from shipping, the former prosperity of Chios was based on the cultivation of the mastic. This small and unimpressive-looking shrub produces a resin of manifold value ; an essential component of all the higher grade varnishes, the foundation of a peculiarly powerful series of *schnapps*, it also provided the earliest form of chewing-gum. Curiously enough, it was this last property which proved originally the most profitable, for the ladies of the Sultan's harem were insatiable in their demands for a delicacy which no other spot in the world save Chios (and here only the southern part of the island) could produce ; and in order to safeguard the supply when the general massacre of 1821 was ordered the mastica villages were specifically

exempted. To-day, various *ersatz* products such as cellulose have diminished its commercial importance, and many of the most profitable markets, such as Czecho-Slovakia, are closed ; the Seraglio is long since empty and Messrs. Wrigley satisfy a taste which is no longer specialized ; and as a drink mastica has to compete in the home market with all the varieties of *ouzo* and *arak*, while abroad its peculiar qualities are not those most readily appreciated by Western palates. With most of its merchant fleet at the bottom of the sea and the owners supporting themselves in considerable luxury on the insurance money in London, caïque-building held up for lack of timber, and the mastic trade crippled, life in Chios is stagnant indeed.

Though the present is gloomy and the past unusually distant, the island possesses one monument of supreme importance. Four hours' away, just below the summit of the mountain which rises behind the town, stands what is left, after the violent earthquake in the 'eighties of the last century, of the great monastery of Nea Moni. The church has been much restored and in its present condition with whitewashed walls and buttresses exhibits a somewhat Russian look ; the only features of architectural interest visible externally being the horseshoe-shaped Anatolian-style apses. But within are preserved a series of mosaics which, though sadly damaged and abominably ill lit, are no whit inferior to those at Daphni and Hosios Loukas.

In style these pictures are midway between the other two great eleventh-century series ; not so harsh as the latter yet less sophisticated than the majority of the former, they are in colour more sombre than either. Curiously enough, although the artist (or artists) is distinguished by a line more flexible and less rugged than that of his contemporary in Phocis, which yet involves no sacrifice of power, and the general effect of austerity and restraint is untempered by the over-refinement of Daphni, of the three Nea Moni has received by far the least attention. Indeed, a certain amount of vagueness as to the correct attribution of these splendid panels still persists among the *cognoscenti*, for whereas Professor Talbot Rice regards them as typical products of provincial monasticism in direct contrast to the metropolitan style as displayed at Daphni, Mr. Arnott Hamilton states roundly that they are the work of artists specially imported from Constantinople.

Although the most celebrated, the mosaics are not the only artistic treasures of the monastery. On emerging from the church we were accosted by the abbot, who had obviously been awaiting us with some impatience. Having ascertained what our long inspection of the mosaics had led him to suspect, that we were interested in the fine arts, he announced with modest pride, stroking his long but ragged beard with a filthy hand (he was the thin, scarecrow type of abbot as opposed to the plump and glossy variety), that he himself was a painter and one not without a certain reputation in Orthodox circles. Having accepted with pleasure the expected invitation to view his works, we were led through his bedroom, where he had recently been frying some minute fish on a charcoal fire, to his studio, where was displayed a small but choice collection of the most hideous ikons I have ever seen. In the production of *bondieuseries* our host, it was obvious at a glance, was a supreme master ; not the chromolithographers of Maynooth nor the plaster-tinters of Lisieux or Lourdes could provoke quite this degree of nausea or achieve quite so high a standard of oozy sentimentality. (The heights of bad taste that the good abbot might have reached had the cult of the Sacred Heart been encouraged in the Orthodox church remain unimaginable.) After we had feasted our eyes on these works for the length of time prescribed by politeness and I had expressed my quite genuine admiration of his technique, for to have obtained with oil paints on a plain board a surface texture that would have been difficult to rival working in golden syrup on American cloth represents no mean feat of craftsmanship, he brought forward what he described as his only secular picture. Eager to see what this immensely specialized talent would contrive when religious inspiration was lacking, on turning round I was unable to suppress a gasp of the most genuine astonishment, for the canvas held out for my inspection was a straight-

forward and perfectly competent self-portrait painted with a rather dry brush in the loose modified Impressionist technique much in vogue in St. Ives round about 1920 and still regarded as modern on the walls of the Royal Academy. My first reaction was that the old gentleman was romancing and that this was the work of some determined English female traveller on the look-out for 'good types', but further questioning only elicited the firm statement that this was the only remaining example of what the artist described as 'my other style'. If, indeed, he was speaking the truth, and it was difficult to see what purpose was served by falsehood as he quite obviously regarded this work as very small beer compared to his religious masterpieces, the Abbot of Nea Moni remains the most extraordinary example of the stylistic schizophrene that I have ever encountered.

In sailing from Chios to Mytilene one passes the mouth of a gulf at the head of which lies the city of Smyrna, a town that was once the most important Greek centre in the whole Levant, Giaour Ismir, but which to-day is but the decaying provincial capital of a formerly fertile region reduced in twenty years to a barren jackal-infested wilderness. Nevertheless, as the spiritual home of the Anglo-Levantines, the most influential and for the English traveller perhaps the most dangerous of all the various Greek minorities, it still exercises a certain influence on the life and fortunes of modern Greece. Descended from the English merchants of the Levant Company, and all bearing aggressively Saxon names, these people present a most fascinating study in the conflicting effects of heredity and environment. At first sight their essential Englishness is overwhelmingly apparent ; their pipes seldom if ever leave their mouths, their Harris-tweed jackets are split up to the shoulder-blades, all their ties are club, while the likeness of their homes, sticky with shiny chintz and plastered with Cecil Aldins, is not to-day to be found elsewhere outside the pages of *Punch*. Yet should the conversation take a business turn it is not long before the lupine Levantine skeleton is discernible beneath the old Marlburian sheepskin ; a sudden elevation of the eyebrows involuntarily expressing not surprise but negation, a vaguely circular gesture lightly sketched by a firmly gripped pipe-stem, and a tell-tale crack appears in the beautifully modelled Metroland mask. Completely bilingual and clinging firmly to their British nationality, the Anglo-Levantines are undoubtedly useful not only to various commercial firms but also to H.M.G. in the rôles of Consuls and Vice-Consuls and, in time of war, of liaison officers. Unfortunately they labour under the considerable disadvantage of being detested by the Greeks, in whose eyes their assumption of the old school-tie in season and out is but a threadbare disguise which, when adopted by those in whose veins there flows no English blood of later vintage than the eighteenth century, is by implication an insult to the Greek nation.

Mytilene is second in size to Crete among the Greek islands but far further removed in the scale of natural beauty. Not that it lacks attraction, but rather that its quality has a slightly tarnished, Riviera flavour and, where nature has rested content with her easier, slicker triumphs, man has achieved prodigies of laborious ugliness. The capital is one of the most self-consciously hideous small towns it has ever been my lot to visit, and whereas the deliberate intention may possibly have been outdistanced in England or northern France, the effect, in the absence of the merciful blurring of less-favoured climes, is unsurpassed. Save for the ruins of the castle, now sheltering, as is usual in these latitudes, the local brothel population, no traces of antiquity remain, nevertheless the principal monument of the town, the cathedral, though modern, is certainly not deficient in architectural interest. A large four-square building in a dingy reddish stone that one might assume, on first catching sight of its writhing silhouette, to be the work of some provincial Austrian architect of the 'eighties who had at some time acquired a nodding acquaintance with the works of Norman Shaw, closer inspection will prove such a judgment superficial. The extraordinary quality of the detail, that seems rather to have been squeezed out of a toothpaste tube than hewn in stone, the elephantine proportions, the arbitrary but undeniably original employment of classical motifs, all lead me to classify it as what I can only suppose, being quite unacquainted with the Turkish mainland, to be a variety of very late Asia Minor Baroque. While no single building in the town can approach the cathedral in exotic excitement, the general villa style prevailing in the residential quarters has points of almost equal interest. Those ornamental bargeboards, for instance, where on earth did they spring from ? Are they the vestigial appendices to which the fretted latticework of Moslem lands has here been reduced, or have they reached these shores from Belsize Park via Smyrna and the Anglo-

Levantines? Most extraordinary of all is the multiplicity of gables, planted with a gay disregard for style or utility above every sort of façade ranging from Second Empire Renaissance to provincial Othonian. In many cases it is, indeed, obvious that they are the work of architects who had in fact never seen a gable save in elevations, for on turning a corner one quite frequently discovers that the aspiring Gothic silhouette which has dominated the skyline from immediately ahead proves to be simply a triangular section of brick wall rising from the parapet, and quite unattached to the sloping roof behind, enclosing an elaborately shuttered but dummy window.

Mercifully it is only the town of Mytilene which fulfils the rôle of museum of stylistic monstrosities; outside its walls one is not called on to inspect further examples of the Siamese twins and two-headed chickens of architecture. And indeed the journey from the coast to the extraordinary village of Agiasso produces much of absorbing and legitimate architectural interest. The houses along the coastal belt are, at first sight, admittedly extravagant in design, but their oddity is not in the least wayward but the result of an intelligent response to an overwhelming functional need. Throughout the coastal districts of the Mediterranean it was formerly the custom, which indeed prevailed even in our country in less settled times, to build the lower storeys of a house in stone as a measure of defence, allowing as few windows or other openings as was feasible. Here, where the pressure of corsair raids was probably more sustained and intense than anywhere else, the response proved correspondingly drastic. As a result the typical isolated dwelling-place anywhere within easy reach of the sea consists of two or three living-rooms of lath and plaster projecting on carved wooden consoles from the summit of a square stone tower. The effect, though undeniably bizarre, in fact represents the perfectly rational local solution to exactly the same problem that in Scotland confronted the builders of the Border towers.

On leaving the coastal plain the road passes above what at first sight appears to be an immense lake, but which is in fact an enclosed arm of the sea with an entrance so narrow as to be completely undetectable a quarter of a mile offshore, yet so large and deep as to have afforded during the war before last anchorage to the entire Mediterranean fleet. Here and there on its surface are discernible small circular patches of bubbles from which there ascend faint plumes of steam; these mark the points where a number of hot springs, prized since Roman times for their medicinal value, burst through the sea-bed. Shortly after leaving this inland shore the road mounts, and entering a narrow valley soon passes a wayside *taverna* where one can study a phenomenon which, at any rate for me, far surpasses in interest any commonplace geological freak. The external walls of this building, which in all other respects differs but little from half a hundred similar places of refreshment in Greece, with the usual half-dozen tables, immense shadowing planes and clear fresh-water spring, here gurgling up from the bottom of a little rock-bordered pond, have been frescoed by the celebrated Theophilos, one of those untutored primitives who remained laughing-stocks during their nineteenth-century lifetimes, but to whose works is now attached a considerable, and admittedly occasionally exaggerated, importance.

The son of a Greek porter born in Smyrna at a date when memories of the struggle for independence were still fresh this single-minded and engaging character remained throughout his long life intensely conscious of his nationality. Not only did he invariably dress in the full klephtic costume, *fustanella, tzarouchia* and long white stockings, but Greek history, both classical and modern, was ever the main inspiration of his art and provided the subject matter of the vast majority of his paintings. Quitting Asia Minor in early youth, he first pursued his calling on Mytilene and later, after various periods of fighting with the Greek guerrillas in the continual border warfare with both Turks and Bulgarians which took place on the Macedonian frontier during the years immediately prior to the Balkan wars, transferred to the mainland and worked principally at Volo in Thessaly. Unlike the Douanier and most modern primitives, he was not merely a ' peintre de Dimanche ' who looked to some prosaic but more profitable regular employment for his main support, but found a sufficient local demand for inn-signs, portraits and murals to be able to devote himself wholly to his art. As a result his paintings are more fluent and assured than those of Rousseau (whose creative gifts were, however, considerably greater), and quite lack that quality of perfectly sincere but occasionally pompous self-importance. Moreover, he displays a sense of place which the customs officer was entirely without ; his landscape backgrounds are recognizably and peculiarly Greek for all their arbitrary perspective and Byzantine disregard of scale in a way that Rousseau's are not specifically French. This is, I am assured by those who know the district, particularly the case with his views of the country round Smyrna, which were painted from memory in later life and occupy much the same position in his *œuvre* as do the Mexican fantasies in that of Rousseau.

Theophilos was peculiarly lucky in the place and time of his birth, for it is probable that there existed no other country in western Europe of sufficiently unsophisticated taste during the last half-century to have afforded an artist of his type a humble but sufficient livelihood, but nevertheless he might have been even more fortunate had he flourished a little earlier still ; his work would, one fancies, have gained an additional strength had he been the contemporary of that great Greek primitive, Zographos, the illustrator of Makryannis' history of the War of Independence, and subject to the discipline imposed by the then still-flourishing tradition of ikon painting. Had he been born thirty years later, on the other hand, in the unlikely event of his having been able to maintain his artistic and financial independence in the face of the competition of cheap chromo-lithographs and coloured supplements in imported magazines, he would undoubtedly have been overtaken at an earlier and more impressionable stage of his development by the fate which in fact befell him during his last years. For in the late 'twenties Theophilos was ' discovered ' by some cultivated ' Paris ' Greeks who bought his pictures, lauded his talents in the left-bank reviews, and finally provided him with paints, canvases and an assured income in return for his whole output. The result, naturally enough, was a large number of paintings not wholly without value but in which the naïve qualities have been deliberately exaggerated and the spontaneity replaced by a somewhat mechanical charm. Like most simple artists, he had no false shame about borrowing wholesale from the work of others and a great many of his compositions, particularly those dealing with the War of Independence, are highly individual copies of post-cards, illustrations, and those dreary Academic canvases commissioned by Otho from prominent Bavarian artists to glorify the national struggle. In the case of the frescoes on this *taverna* I was able straightway to identify one of the scenes, that of Ali Pasha being rowed across the Lake of Butrinto, as a personal transcription of a lithograph from Dupré's *Voyage à Athènes* published in Paris in 1825. His technique, about which he was always highly secretive, remains somewhat mysterious. His colours, limited in range but perfectly adequate to his artistic purpose, were hand-ground and nothing out of the ordinary, but the medium with which he worked them is not obvious. Apart from his frescoes most of his painting was done on unprimed canvases which were never apparently stretched, but although many of them have long been kept rolled up or folded, there is no evidence that the paint, which admittedly was applied very thin, has ever cracked or flaked.

Continuing along the road which runs past the *taverna* of Theophilos one comes eventually, after crossing a pass, in sight of the pilgrimage village of Agiasso, crowning the summit of a rounded hill. Immediately on entering the place one is aware of an extraordinary, enclosed atmosphere as of a stronghold of some remote and peculiar people. The houses, which are without exception old, line narrow, twisting streets across which stretch thick trellises of vines, lending to one's progress the character of promenade through the corridors of some strange green underground. The principal

church, celebrated throughout the Islands for the number and sanctity of
its ikons, is a large basilica with an exceptionally broad nave up which some
pious peasant woman in enormous baggy Turkish trousers is invariably
progressing on hands and knees, prostrating herself full-length on the stones
every other yard.   The ikons, which range in style from one or two quite
good examples of the sixteenth-century Cretan school to numerous glossy
productions similar to those on which the reputation of the artistic abbot
of Chios was based, include several interesting specimens of genuine folk art,
notably one of Elijah being fed by the ravens which, with its curious angu-
larities and its strangely metallic figures, might well have come out of

the studio of M. Leger.   Outside, the
church is surrounded on three sides
by a range of elegant cloisters glazed
with wide sash windows. Just beyond
the principal entrance lies the small
open place which does duty for the
market-square, but which, despite the
fact that here the vines do not form
a continuous ceiling and the daylight
is allowed to penetrate in patches, is
yet so shuttered and enclosed as to
retain the air of a principal reception
room in some enormous warren of a
house rather than of an ordinary
village *platia*. Even the *taverna* on
the corner is markedly out of the
ordinary ; a high one-storey building,
of which three of the walls are in

effect but glass screens, so large a space is occupied by the enormous sash
windows, it has the appearance of an eighteenth-century orangery inter-
communicating so freely with the street as to make it almost impossible to
decide where the one begins and the other ends.

The inhabitants of this amazing ant-heap are as remarkable as their
town.   The men are all clad in the traditional island costume, baggy dark
blue Turkish breeches encircled at the waist by a wide black cummerbund,
a sleeveless braided waistcoat and a round fur cap, but despite this con-
formity of dress they have a strangely alien look.   As elsewhere, they tend
to cluster all day long in groups in the *platia* which here, however, quite
lacks the normal animation of a Greek village crowd, and the usual high-
pitched buzz of chatter audible several streets away is replaced by a low and

slightly sinister swell of humming and muttering. It is said that this apparent surliness is quite in keeping with the local character, for the village has a bad reputation all over the island, which, combined with the local dialect, spoken nowhere else and quite incomprehensible a few miles away, has encouraged the belief that the Agiassotes are a race apart, descended perhaps from some aboriginal people who, before the coming of the Ionians, lorded it over the whole island but were driven in the course of the centuries back into the central mountains where this village represents their last stronghold.

Elsewhere the attitude of the Agiassotes might not strike the casual visitor as noticeably abnormal. But in Greece what would in other countries appear as an expected and understandable distaste for becoming involved with strangers strikes an unfamiliar and surprising note. For the national reaction to foreigners is endearing but logical ; whereas the average villager in our own country is astounded that anyone having the leisure to do so should trouble to visit his particular neighbourhood and straightway supposes that an interest in the local sights has been assumed to cover some dark and not too easily to be comprehended plan of exploitation, the Greek assumes as a matter of course that his own village is generally acknowledged to be one which it is worth an infinity of trouble and expense to visit. Hitherto the majority of visitors, apart from those that have come gun in hand, have been middle-class Anglo-Saxon intellectuals intent on culture and oblivious of discomfort. It seems unlikely that in future the bulk of such travellers as Greece is likely to attract will be drawn from this company ; in the place of the rural deans, female water-colourists, budding archaelogists and the like, the country will receive a flow of hard-headed economists, tough business men in search of contracts and international experts zealous for world, and particularly American, security. Their advent will undoubtedly be welcomed for the high-powered executive or big business tycoon of Anglo-Saxon origin of whom the average Greek could not get the better within twenty-four hours of their first meeting has not yet been born. But it is possible that once the joy of care-free exploitation has passed the Greeks may come to regret the passing of less profitable, but possibly more appreciative, travellers. For the Greek is always a realist and, while to neglect any possibility of making a profit would appear to him to be imbecile, he has never fallen victim to the illusion that happiness can be calculated in terms of financial advantage. Whether or not the inhabitants of Hellas are likely to shed a tear for the sentimental and financially unrewarding company of the old-fashioned philhellenes, one at least of them is making no attempt to repress a sigh for a country which world events seem all too likely to put out of bounds for an indefinite period.

INDEX

INDEX